Seeing Like a Commons

Seeing Like a Commons

Eighty Years of Intentional Community Building and Commons Stewardship in Celo, North Carolina

Joshua Lockyer

LEXINGTON BOOKS
Lanham • Boulder • New York • London

Published by Lexington Books
An imprint of The Rowman & Littlefield Publishing Group, Inc.
4501 Forbes Boulevard, Suite 200, Lanham, Maryland 20706
www.rowman.com

6 Tinworth Street, London SE11 5AL, United Kingdom

British Library Cataloguing in Publication Information Available

Library of Congress Cataloging-in-Publication Data

Names: Lockyer, Joshua, author.
Title: Seeing like a commons : eighty years of intentional community building and commons stewardship in Celo, North Carolina / Joshua Lockyer.
Description: Lanham : Lexington Books, [2021] | Includes bibliographical references and index. | Summary: "In Seeing Like a Commons, Joshua Lockyer traces the development of one of the United States's oldest intentional communities from its founding in 1937 to the present. Lockyer examines how community members have developed flexible sets of cooperative processes for the stewardship of the land and other resources"— Provided by publisher.
Identifiers: LCCN 2021010231 (print) | LCCN 2021010232 (ebook) | ISBN 9781498592888 (cloth) | ISBN 9781498592895 (epub)
Subjects: LCSH: Celo Community—History. | Collective settlements—North Carolina—History. | Cooperative societies—North Carolina—History. | Utopias—North Carolina—History.
Classification: LCC HX656.C45 L63 2021 (print) | LCC HX656.C45 (ebook) | DDC 307.7709756/873—dc23
LC record available at https://lccn.loc.gov/2021010231
LC ebook record available at https://lccn.loc.gov/2021010232

♾™ The paper used in this publication meets the minimum requirements of American National Standard for Information Sciences—Permanence of Paper for Printed Library Materials, ANSI/NISO Z39.48-1992.

Contents

Preface and Acknowledgments

I started writing this book in 2019, but its roots go much deeper than that. In the winter of 2000–2001, I was in the middle of my second year in the graduate school in ecological and environmental anthropology at the University of Georgia and I was struggling to settle on a topic for my doctoral research. That winter, I visited a lifelong family friend named Bruce Wachter who lives in the South Toe Valley in the Appalachian Mountains of western North Carolina. Bruce had been part of my family's life since before I was born when he and my dad worked together as independent home builders in my native southern Arizona. They built passive solar homes and also co-owned a drill rig with which they drilled water wells for the homes they built in the Sonoran Desert. Both of these things probably contributed to my environmental consciousness as I grew older. In any case, by the time I was applying to graduate school in the late 1990s, Bruce had moved to western North Carolina and he traveled south to accompany me on my visit to the University of Georgia just before I decided to enroll there in fall 1999. That trip significantly shaped the course of my life.

A year and a half into graduate school, as I pondered the possibilities for doctoral research topics, I decided to pay Bruce a visit and seek his advice. During my conversation with him that winter, I laid out the intellectual context that surrounded my search for a dissertation topic. On my mind was a vague critique of Western, capitalist colonialism and a recognition that the roots of many of the social and environmental problems in the world stemmed from the ongoing processes through which this model colonizes the world. I wanted to turn the ethnographic gaze on groups of people working to solve some of the problems in a holistic way, but I didn't want to just study the politics of protest nor did I want to focus on reformist projects endorsed by state and capital such as large-scale conservation of human rights initiatives. My basic, relatively unformed idea was: "If we are going to do something about the growing litany of social and environmental crises, we need a new cultural paradigm; who is creating that?" Bruce said, "Well, there's this 'community' down the road that I think you might be interested in." Bruce outlined some of the basics of Celo Community for me: it was founded in the 1930s, several dozen households owned and managed 1,200 acres of land together, their governance process was grounded in Quaker principles, and they supported each other in trying to live simply and worked together to cooperatively steward the land in an environmentally sensitive manner. I was intrigued.

Every winter, the community members helped to organize a series of events known locally as "Cabin Fever University." Bruce and I consulted the list of upcoming events in the mimeographed calendar the community distributed. One event that fit the schedule of my short visit involved gathering at the Celo Community Center and watching a video about advertising and patterns of overconsumption in American culture followed by a group discussion. Our participation in that discussion intrigued me further. Here was a group of people, many of them refugees from middle-class suburbs, all bound together by a commitment to owning land cooperatively and living simply, who spent their Friday evening talking about what they could do to avoid falling into the trap of commodity fetishism created by advertising and thereby also avoid contributing to the attendant social alienation and environmental destruction.

That first visit to Celo Community helped to clarify the intellectual trajectory I was on—a trajectory that stretched back to my childhood. As a kid in southern Arizona, I had watched the Sonoran Desert bioregion around me being eaten up by suburban development. This included the destruction of places I had played with my friends, been enthralled by wildlife, and encountered petroglyphs, pottery, and arrowheads left behind by previous inhabitants of the area. As I got older, I became aware of ongoing debates about grand plans to conserve the Sonoran Desert, to balance growth with preservation of wildlife habitat. There were also concerns in the news about whether there was enough available water to support all the new golf courses and swimming pools that accompanied Tucson's rapid growth, even after having spent billions of dollars to build a canal to divert the Colorado River 300 miles uphill to water the desert.

As a teenager, I bounced my growing awareness of these issues off of my vague but growing awareness that there were other ways of perceiving the world and going about our business in it. There were those petroglyphs, pottery sherds, and arrowheads I had come across as a kid marking past human inhabitation of the land I knew as home. How had those people made their way in this place and what happened to them? When I was young, my family took many trips throughout the American Southwest and northern Mexico during which I caught glimpses of indigenous, non-Western lifeways where people seemed to go about life in a different manner. I also started to understand that these groups were still being impinged upon by what seemed like inexorable forces of colonization, modernization, and globalization. It appeared that locally appropriate methods of inhabitation, ways often constructed through long processes of collaborative trial and error, were rapidly being replaced by new systems that were inherently unsustainable and driven by relentless needs to privatize and commoditize resources that were increasingly conceived in the abstract.

My first class on my first day of college at the University of Arizona was Introduction to Anthropology. While I did not commit to an anthropology major for another year or two, I knew then that anthropology could help me make sense of some of this stuff. As I learned about indigenous cultures, colonialism, modernization, development, and world systems theory, my forays into different cultural territory continued. As an undergraduate, I accompanied a group of Mescalero and Chiricahua Apache folks for a week as they retraced their past in the southwestern United States and northern Mexico, sharing folklore, rituals, and traditional desert foods along the way. My family continued our trips to Sonora, Mexico, where we were developing a relationship with a small, agrarian ejido community where people lived simply and relatively happily despite vague and ominous forces bearing down on them from across the horizon, not least of which involved the break up and privatization of ejido lands and the impact of a new free trade agreement.

Back on campus, my anthropology courses made it clear to me that the same imperial system that was gobbling up and commoditizing the Sonoran Desert around my boyhood home had likely affected the Apache folks I traveled with and the Mexican agrarians I spent time with, and was deeply impacting other ecosystems and cultural communities around the world in often tragic, unjust ways. I was making connections I hadn't made before. My undergraduate honors thesis on water perception and management over time and across cultures in southern Arizona also made it clear that complete answers to social and environmental problems were not be found in a simple, blanket romanticization of indigenous, non-Western cultures; overconsumption of scarce water resources had also contributed significantly to the collapse of Hohokam society during precolonial times and to new adaptations as Hohokam descendant communities dispersed and decentralized.

As I moved on to graduate school, I equipped myself with more theoretical tools. James Scott's work in *Seeing Like a State* (1998) outlined how the grand designs of state and capital, grounded in high-modernist authoritarian rationality enacted from the top down have (re)made the world and its local communities so that they are more legible, simplified, and easily commodified. This was accomplished in part by enclosing the commons, foreclosing local knowledge and cooperative practice, and causing great social and ecological damage. Scott's insight was that the world has been remade in a way that erases the diversity, cooperative associations, and place-specific knowledge that make the world resilient. Similar work by Arturo Escobar (1995, 2008) complemented this critique and highlighted that more just, sustainable, and resilient paths forward will require local scale, cooperative ventures that see and engage across difference and constructed binaries (including the human-nature binary). And Elinor Ostrom (1990), along with a whole group of scholars inspired by her work, highlighted the wide variety of cooperative organizations working to successfully steward local environmental resources in more just manners.

Projecting the above work forward, David Graeber (2004) suggests that scholar-activists can work with those designing such ventures to help realize just and sustainable future possibilities. Similarly, Gibson-Graham (2006, 2014) call on ethnographers to engage with "diverse economic practices" to help bring into being an economic future that is more in line with the well-being of people and the planet. In doing so, they show how we can illustrate that economics does not just include things like capital, labor, and markets which are presented as inexorable and all-encompassing, but also things like trust, care, sharing, reciprocity, cooperation, love, equity, solidarity, stewardship, spiritual connection, and environmental and social justice. They challenge social scientists to engage with such work. In their words, "For ethnographers today, no task is more important than to make small facts speak to large concerns, to make the ethical acts ethnography describes into a performative ontology of economy and the threads of hope that emerge into stories of everyday revolution" (Gibson-Graham 2014: S147). As an emerging scholar activist concerned about the state of the world and with the roots of the crises in my own cultural backyard, this seemed like the kind of work I wanted to do.

All this led back to the question I had in mind when I first visited Bruce and Celo Community in western North Carolina in winter of 2000–2001: Who is doing something about this; who is building the alternative? If so many of the social and environmental problems in the world can be traced back to the very cultural system that had shaped my own view of the world, who is doing something to change it, to create a different approach to seeing and being in the world? I wanted to know who was creating a different way of living within the belly of the beast. Celo Community seemed to provide an inkling of that and, starting in the summer of 2001, I set out on a long process of trying to gain a deeper understanding of their cooperative endeavor. This book is one outcome of that adventure.

In the years since my feet first landed on the ground in Celo, I've spent many years working with a broad array of cultural, environmental, and social justice activists all cultivating different ways of being in their own communities. One outcome of this work is a book I coedited with James R. Veteto in which a diverse group of contributors shined our lights on initiatives in bioregionalism, permaculture, and ecovillages. In the introduction to that book, we stated that all the contributors "share a belief that in the current global context of increasingly negative news about interrelated social and environmental conditions, it is time to put forward work that is solution-focused rather than problem-oriented" (Lockyer and Veteto 2013: 2). My continued work in this vein including, most prominently, collaborating with the members of Dancing Rabbit Ecovillage in Missouri, USA, has led to some of the most fulfilling, and hopefully impactful, accomplishments in my career thus far.

However, throughout all of this, I maintained a distinct interest in and connection to Celo Community. Across the decades and generations, the members of this particular community have created something unique but also something that can offer rough models and lessons to others seeking more cooperative ways of living together and living with the land. When I first visited Celo, I immediately began conceptualizing the community in terms of the commons, but it is only over the last several years that I've had the opportunity to revisit the community and dedicate myself to more fully elucidating how Celo's members have taught themselves to "see like a commons." It is with gratitude to all members of the community past and present that I offer this book as my modest contribution to a much larger search for resilient and regenerative ways of being human on this planet.

AIMS OF THE BOOK

The principal focus of this book is on the resilient institutions and processes Celo's members have created for managing the commons resources they share. The book demonstrates how a growing group of people have, over the last eighty years, deliberately built a cooperative community around the stewardship their 1,200 acres of commonly owned land in the southern Appalachian Mountains of western North Carolina using processes of egalitarian governance and place making. At a fundamental level, this book is about cooperation, collaboration, and the development of mutual trust and goodwill not only among the members of Celo Community, but also with a much broader community of like-minded neighbors that has grown up around them. This work highlights a cultural heritage of cooperation and communalism often overshadowed by our national cultural emphasis on competitive individualism and market relations. It suggests that reinventing the local commons is one productive avenue for the cultural changes that are necessary to save our global commons; learning to "see like a commons" at a local level can, when accompanied by an awareness of global interconnectedness and structural inequalities, enables people and communities to become better stewards and citizens of our global commons.

While one other book has been published on Celo Community (see Hicks 2001), the analysis in that book was based on data collected in the 1970s and 1980s, it did not interpret the community within the context of the environmental challenges that became more apparent beginning at the end of the twentieth century, and it did not present a clear understanding of the community as a commons. This book brings the story of the community up to the present, situates the community as a viable commons response to problems of social alienation and environmental degradation, and challenges some of the conclusions about the community as a failed utopia made in that previous book.

This book traces the community's development from its founding in 1937 to the present day. It shows how the members of the community have developed sets of rules and processes for sharing commonly owned land and making decisions about the management of land and other common resources. Based on long-term ethnographic familiarity, it examines how the community is dealing with contemporary issues such as balancing ecologically sound land management priorities with an increasing community population, an aging community membership, and the incorporation of new community members from younger generations.

Celo Community is one of thousands of intentional communities that have existed in North America since the establishment of the first European colonies on the continent (see Miller 2015 and Pitzer 1997 for overviews). Such communities have been formed in pursuit of a wide variety of visions for improving human society, but beginning in the 1990s a large number of intentional communities began focusing on themes of cooperative, simple living, and ecological sustainability (see Litfin 2014, Lockyer 2007, Lockyer and Veteto 2013, Sanford 2017). Celo Community is a unique forerunner to these latter communities and, as I have documented elsewhere (see Lockyer 2009), some of these more recent intentional communities have used the model institutions created by Celo as foundations for their own endeavors. This monograph seeks to explore how the rules, processes, and institutions crafted by Celo might be applicable beyond the realm of intentional communities as both scholars and citizens seek commons solutions to social and environmental problems.

Celo's founding in 1937 by Arthur Morgan came at a time when large-scale, industrial production and land management was ascendant in the United States and when more local-scale, community-based economies were being pushed aside. Celo's founder is an embodiment of these diverging trajectories in American culture; he was both a philosopher of the importance of the small community (see Morgan 1942) and the first chairman of the Tennessee Valley Authority, one of the United States' first major industrial-scale development initiatives. While much has been written about Morgan's work as head of the TVA and president of Antioch College (see Kahoe 1977, Purcell 2014, Talbert 1987), very little has been written about this experiment in small community development that he helped initiate at Celo.

This book aims to make modest contributions to three areas of scholarship and practice: commons and commoning, communal studies, and utopian studies. Studies of the commons are increasingly accompanied by a growing body of work on practices of commoning put forth by commons practitioners and scholar-activists. Collectively, these works ask: How do people organize themselves cooperatively to successfully steward resources beyond the realms of the market and the state? Garrett Hardin's 1968 "Tragedy of the Commons" essay articulated the idea that state-based institutions or individualized private property are the only means of stewarding natural resources and that community-based stewardship endeavors are bound to fail. The work of Elinor Ostrom and her colleagues was a watershed in demonstrating that alternative models for working together to successfully steward resources do exist. This book expands our understanding of the commons by highlighting community-based institutions that have proven resilient over eighty years in American society and by describing a working commons in the context of a long extant intentional community. As such, it contributes to current work that describes and theorizes active processes of "commoning" whereby diverse groups of individuals are joining together to actively create commons as alternatives to environmentally destructive and socially alienating arrangements governed by the state and organized around the market (see Bollier and Helfrich 2012 and 2015b).

The primary structure of the book is derived from the eight design principles identified in the work of Nobel Prize–winning political economist Elinor Ostrom for the successful functioning of common property institutions (see Ostrom 2010). Each of these design principles is the subject of one chapter in the second part of the book wherein I describe in detail how Celo Community has manifested each principle, how they have dealt with challenges, how they have adjusted their arrangements over time to changing circumstances, and how these arrangements are sometimes still vague and still evolving. Each of these descriptions is preceded by one or more ethnographic vignettes that aim to provide a solid grounding for, and examples of, the more abstract discussions that follow.

Second, the book situates Celo within the long tradition of American utopian community building which, as communal studies scholars such as Pitzer and Miller illustrate, began with the founding of the first colonies in North America. Despite being one of the longest-lasting American utopian communities, little has been written about Celo. While situating the community in American communal history, this project demonstrates how people in Celo and, to a lesser extent in this book, other contemporary utopian communities are using models of communalism and processes of commoning to address prominent socio-environmental concerns. As such, the book presents a call for greater theoretical and practical engagement with American communal societies as active experiments in commoning.

Finally, the book follows the work of utopian studies scholars in emphasizing that processes of utopian striving for a better (and, in this case, more cooperative and environmentally focused) society are, while potentially perilous, both necessary and firmly within the traditions and ideals of American culture. As such, the story of Celo is an antidote to widely accepted conclusions that cooperative utopian endeavors are bound to follow paths to disaster characterized by state-sponsored communism or Jonestown communalism. Emerging from the contexts of the Great Depression, the back-to-the-land movement, and growing socio-environmental concerns of the late twentieth century, Celo's institutions are living manifestations of processes of utopian striving for participatory democracy and environmental sensitivity that, while perhaps not completely replicable, can provide models for a more equitable, cooperative, and regenerative future. Emerging from a long and ongoing process of learning to "see like a commons," Celo Community is a concrete manifestation of intentional commons community building that represents hope for a more equitable and sustainable future.

OVERVIEW OF THE BOOK

This work is divided into three parts. Part I provides an introduction to the overarching theoretical framework that structures my analysis and presents the reader with a history and contemporary overview of Celo Community. Part II is an ethnographic description of the community viewed through the lens of Ostrom's eight commons design principles. The final part of the book offers conclusions and implications in a broader context focusing specifically on what learning to "see like a commons" entails, especially in a world riven by divisions, differences, and deep structural inequalities.

In chapter 1, I offer overviews of relevant ideas and literature from the fields of commons studies, communal studies, and utopian studies. At the risk of reification, I attempt to loosely define the commons, intentional communities, and processes of transformative utopian striving. Preceding, and serving as a background for this discussion, are overviews of James Scott's critique of state projects of legibility and simplification that so often precluded local commons arrangements along with a nod to historian Steven Stoll's (2017) proposal for a "Commons Communities Act" for the Appalachian region. These two approaches to organizing human life in the world, one of them top down and the other distinctly bottom up, represent an inherent tension in the concept of utopia and processes of utopian striving, a tension that underlies and remains unresolved throughout this work.

Chapter 2 provides a portrait of Arthur Morgan, the self-made educator, college president, philosopher of community, and flood control engineer who played the key role in founding Celo Community and setting in motion this experiment in commoning that continues to this day, almost fifty years after his passing. Morgan's dual roles as first chairman of the Tennessee Valley Authority under Franklin Delano Roosevelt and, at the same time, principal founder of Celo Community encapsulates the tension between hegemonic, state-based utopian designs for industrial development and bottom-up, democratic utopian designs for commoning highlighted in the first chapter.

The history, current structure, and make-up of Celo Community are presented in chapters 3 and 4. Chapter 3 shows how, following a rough start under Morgan's leadership in the early years, a group of people came together to do the nitty-gritty work of building the community and its commons institutions based on a common Quaker background. Through influxes of conscientious objectors to World War II and, later, back-to-the-landers, community members experimented with and established basic governing institutions and processes for the community that still function today. Finally, it discusses how community members have sought to find balance between community building and land stewardship among other contentious issues. Chapter 4 offers an overview of the community and its members as it exists at the time of this writing, recognizing that the community is a dynamic, complex phenomenon that can't be fully captured in this format. Here, I recognize that Celo has distinctly porous boundaries and describe some of the community's links to broader communities in the South Toe Valley, both local and in-migrant in nature. I end this chapter by challenging a previous representation of the community as a utopian failure.

Part II of the book is divided into nine chapters, one for each of the eight commons design principles followed by a discussion of some of the other factors my analysis suggests have contributed to Celo's resilience and longevity. Chapter 5 describes Celo's common land and other resources and the processes through which one becomes a member of the community and a co-steward of the community's commons. The ways in which Celo's members developed governance processes and institutions appropriate to local social and ecological contexts and the costs and benefits of participating in those processes and institutions are the subjects of chapter 6. In chapter 7, I describe the ongoing process of participating in adaptive governance procedures in the community. This chapter highlights the flexible process of consensus decision-making that the community has cultivated. Chapter 8 explains how the community monitors (or sometimes doesn't monitor) the status of the commons and the internal and external users of those commons. Chapters 9 and 10 outline the processes Celo's members have developed for dealing with conflicts and violations of community rules and governance procedures.

Chapters 11 and 12 allow me to begin expanding the view of the commons out beyond Celo Community. One of Ostrom's commons design principles indicates that, as long as the world is dominated by the power of states, every commons needs some sort of official state recognition to effectively function over the long term. Chapter 11 elucidates how Celo has achieved this in part by forcing official legal vessels such as nonprofit incorporation to meet their particular needs. In chapter 11, I focus on how multiple "nested layers" of governance characterize Celo. Here, a telescopic view is presented demonstrating how decision- and policy-making in Celo Community extends from the individual and household through subcommittees to the community as a whole and beyond that to various local and state agencies whose policies and decisions impinge on the community. The final chapter in part II of the book draws on other studies of intentional communities and on my own long-term analysis of Celo Community to suggest some other factors beyond the commons design principles that have helped make Celo one of the longest-lived and most stable intentional communities in the United States over the last eighty years.

Part III of the book, consisting of only one chapter, offers some broader implications of my description and analysis of Celo Community. It characterizes Celo as an attempt to recreate the forms of practical, place-based skills, and intelligence that are so often foreclosed by projects of legibility and simplification that characterize state- and capitalist-based development projects. In this context, I explore the implications of learning to see like a commons as a form of bottom-up transformative utopianism that has to navigate perilous waters of difference, division, and bridge-building in order to reach for more just, inclusive, and regenerative forms of commoning. I conclude by suggesting that scholars have key roles to play as critical allies to such commoning endeavors in a world facing multiple social and environmental crises.

ACKNOWLEDGMENTS

As suggested above, this book was a long time in the making. There are so many who provided inspiration and assistance along the way. I hope to acknowledge most of them here and that those whom I fail to mention by name recognize that any omissions are unintentional.

My first and biggest thanks go to all the members of Celo Community including, especially, those who subjected themselves to interviews with me over the years or who put up with my presence as a participant observer and dealt with my endless and inane questions. I don't suspect it is easy to constantly have an outside observer in your midst and I am grateful to those who welcomed me into the community as so much more than that. I learned many lessons about how to be a good person and about what is important in life from my time in the community and, for that, there will never be thanks enough. I would also like to express my gratitude to those who came to presentations and participated in open discussion forums about the book in 2019. My gratefulness extends to all community members past and present who contributed their energy and enthusiasm to this truly unique experiment in commoning.

A number of current and former community members agreed, perhaps without fully understanding what they were getting into, to review the bulk of the manuscript once I thought I had it in a workable state. These include Joyce Johnson, Bob McGahey, Dotty Morgan, and Clark Tibbits, who collectively share almost two century's worth of experience in the community. A much newer community member, Matt Riley, offered a complementary perspective from someone who sees the community with fresh eyes. Matt challenged me to take on difficult subjects including topics such as white privilege and racial diversity. I hope I have done justice to the feedback and suggestions you all provided based on your deep knowledge and personal experience. Any shortcomings are, of course, my own.

Jon Andelson, Don Pitzer, and one anonymous reviewer provided essential feedback and perspectives based on their expertise in anthropology, history, and communal studies. Jon and Don both took time out from their busy schedules on very short notice to answer questions and make valuable suggestions during the course of long phone conversations. As above, any remaining errors, misjudgments, and failings remain my own.

Dear friends inside and outside Celo Community provided gracious hospitality during my many sojourns in the community over the years. In recent years, these folks included Bruce Wachter and Paulina Etzold, Ron Abraham, and Jim, Benny, and Jeanne Veteto. Peggy and Clark Tibbits gifted me a full month stay in their home during my first period of fieldwork in the community without ever having met me. That month was crucial in starting me on the path to this book. In an outstanding manifestation of the generosity, Ron Abraham and Donna O'Toole accepted me into their home for the better part of six months during the latter periods of my graduate research. I still tell stories about Donna's coconut cream pie. I miss her!

I would like to extend specific thanks to multiple people who helped me navigate different sets of archives in Celo Community and beyond. In Celo,

Nancy Raskin, Joyce Johnson, and Marnie Walters spent time showing me around, dusting off files, and helping me locate those specific meeting minutes I was looking for. Scott Sanders at the Olive Kettering Library at Antioch College in Yellow Springs, Ohio, had relevant files from the Antiochiana Archives and Special Collections waiting for me when I arrived. Marilyn Thielman and Casey Harison at the Center for Communal Studies at the University of Southern Indiana did the same. This book would be much diminished without their help.

Some passages in this book are adapted from my 2007 dissertation "Sustainability and Utopianism: An Ethnography of Cultural Critique in Contemporary Intentional Communities," which I completed in the course of earning my doctorate in anthropology from the University of Georgia. I would like to recognize the faculty who helped guide me through that process—especially the chair of my committee, Pete Brosius—and former fellow students who accompanied me on the journey and provided encouragement when I needed it.

Essential funding and time for this project were made available to me by a number of parties. The Office of Academic Affairs and Dr. David Ward in the Department of Behavioral Sciences at Arkansas Tech University made possible a yearlong sabbatical in 2019 during which I had the chance to return to Celo Community, visit relevant archives, and travel widely to discuss my ideas and analysis. The Center for Communal Studies at the University of Southern Indiana awarded me a small travel grant that enabled me to visit their collections in search of relevant documentation of Celo's early years.

The Communal Studies Association, the Society for Applied Anthropology, the Appalachian Studies Association, and the Rooted in the Mountains symposium at Western Carolina University provided forums for me to present preliminary work on the book manuscript. Each of these helped me refine my analyses and descriptions.

My colleagues in the Department of Behavioral Sciences at Arkansas Tech University, as always, provide a supportive and collegial environment for scholarly work even as we all face the challenges of "doing more with less."

And last, but certainly far, far from least, my wife, Dr. Emily Beahm, and our dogs Myles and Twinkie not only put up with me while I wrangled with this manuscript over the course of several years but also nurtured me, reassured me when I got lost in doubt, and lifted me up when I needed it. I couldn't have done this without you!

Part I

INTRODUCTION AND HISTORY

Introduction

Intentional Community, Commons, and Utopia

In his groundbreaking book *Seeing Like a State*, James Scott provides an "account of the logic behind the failure of some of the great utopian social engineering schemes of the twentieth century" (1998: 4). He recounts how, across a multiplicity of state-making and industrial development endeavors of the twentieth century, a regime of "legibility and simplicity" was laid across the global landscape.[1] In places and states as diverse in sociocultural, political-economic, and geographic traits as Soviet Russia, Tanzania, Brazil, and the United States (see also Scott 2006 for the latter), high-modernist, industrial-scale enterprises backed by authoritarian state power transformed and simplified complex sociocultural and natural realities in efforts to "improve the human condition." While Scott acknowledges that many of these endeavors were distinctly well intended, he points to the undeniably disastrous results of many of them for local communities and ecosystems and to the ways in which these projects undermined "the indispensable role of practical knowledge, informal processes, and improvisation in the face of unpredictability" that characterized the local communities upon whose backs modern states were built (1998: 6). Scott's account shows how complex and diverse forms of socio-environmental organization were erased to allow for the more efficient functioning of the state and the more profitable commod-itization of natural resources.

Two things that were often lost in this process of high-modernist order-ing of the world were forms of cooperative knowledge and practice that had been adopted and adapted by specific communities in specific places over long periods of time along with the forms of communal land tenure in which these forms of knowledge and practice had often been cultivated. While Scott's account is clearly a story of growing dominance of state, industry, and capitalist rationality, it is, on the flipside, an account of the erasure and delegitimization of the commons. As the world was rationalized and made legible by state agents, it was also transformed and commodified. In this process, communities have been restructured, complex socio-ecosystems have been transformed into "natural resources," and the nuanced ways that communities conceived of, adapted to, and oftentimes cooperatively used ecosystems for subsistence have been swept aside. While Scott does not directly invoke the language of the commons, the processes of state-based utopian social engineering that he describes entailed enclosure of the local commons.

The present work is an account of a small-scale "utopian" project, an intentional community called Celo Community, Inc. that has, over the last eighty plus years, worked in the opposite direction, toward the rebuilding of a local commons from within the context of state and capitalist colonization. Beginning in 1937, in a southern Appalachian valley, a small cooperative community began experimenting with patterns of commoning, setting in motion a process of (re)learning to "see like a commons" that continues to this day. That the impetus, although not the long-term supervision, for this project was provided by one of the people that Scott specifically identifies as a "most thoroughgoing exponent of high modernism" (2006: 21) illustrates that potentialities for rebuilding the commons lie even within the milieu of modern, state-based, industrial civilization.

COMMONS AND COMMONING

At the end of his sweeping account of the enclosure of Appalachian mountain commons *Ramp Hollow* (2017), historian Steven Stoll presents "The Commons Communities Act" as his proposed solution to the ongoing social dispossession and environmental destruction that has been, and is still being, visited on Appalachian mountain communities. The act reads in part:

Section 1. The United States shall create a series of commons communities, each designed to include a specified number of households within the larger landscape that will be managed by them, the residents. This landscape will provide the ecological base for hunting and gathering, cattle grazing, timber harvesting, vegetable gardening and farming. The ecological base will be owned as a conservation easement or land trust under the authority of the states and/or counties where each community resides.

Section 2. Commons communities would be organized according to the design principles developed by the economist Elinor Ostrom, who was awarded the Nobel Prize in Economic Sciences in 2009 for her work on the economic governance of common resources. Each community shall include well-defined boundaries and members. Each will devise rules for appropriation suitable to the environment, along with sanctions and penalties for those who violate the rules and take too much or otherwise abuse the resource. Each must establish a means of conflict resolution and governance. In the event that residents need to sue the community or other residents, they would use the county, state, or federal courts. (Stoll 2017: 272–273)

While Stoll's imagined bill was speculative, one of my main arguments in this book is that a working model for such a commons community has been present and under cultivation in the southern Appalachians for over eighty years. Celo Community Inc.'s collectively stewarded 1,200 acres is organized as a cooperative land trust and provides an ecological base for the partial subsistence and economic activities of its resident members and households. While the community was not explicitly designed according to Ostrom's "design principles," it does appear to manifest and function by them. Celo Community has distinctly defined boundaries and membership. Community members have designed rules and sanctions for using the land along with governance procedures for changing the rules, and conflict resolution mechanisms for solving disputes. It has even managed to gain some state recognition for its institutions despite their novelty. Going against the grain of a fairly thoroughly high-modernist society, Celo's members are beginning to (re)learn how to "see like a commons."

Elinor Ostrom's life work can be conceptualized as a response to an influential essay authored by Garrett Hardin and published in *Science* in 1968 (see Wall 2017). When Hardin published "The Tragedy of the Commons," he did so based on legitimate concerns about human overexploitation of the planet's environmental capacity as a result of individualist, "rational" calculations of costs and benefits. In the late 1960s, the West was waking up to real and significant environmental problems. Garret Hardin was one of the messengers attempting to shine a light on this situation, but his rendering of the nature and cause of the problems was grounded in an ethnocentric view that misconstrued human nature. In attempting to articulate the situation, and in the process confusing open access commons with collectively managed commons, he inspired a large, interdisciplinary body of research on the commons and, ultimately, a whole series of social movements actively engaged in remaking the commons through deliberate acts of cooperative commoning.

Recognizing that Hardin's parable of rational herdsmen inevitably overexploiting their pasture falsely ascribed short-term, individualist, utilitarian thinking to all humans, Elinor Ostrom set out to understand how groups of people around the world have long cooperated to successfully conserve and sustainably steward what she called common-pool resources through the use of common property regimes. Growing from an interdisciplinary workshop at the University of Indiana, Ostrom's work has flowered into a large body of transdisciplinary scholarship that directly challenges the assumptions that underlay Hardin's work and the conclusions and proposed courses of action that stemmed from it. This literature is too large to review here, but representative samples can be found in a number of volumes that Ostrom herself wrote, edited, or coedited (see Dolšak and Ostrom 2003, Hess and Ostrom 2011, Ostrom 1990, Ostrom et al. 2002, Ostrom, Gardner, and Walker 1994, and Ostrom and Ostrom 2014 among many others). It also continues to bear fruit in a number of interdisciplinary journals such as *The International Journal of the Commons*. As Stoll acknowledges, the significance of Ostrom's work on the commons is such that she was awarded the Nobel Prize for Economic Sciences in 2009, the first woman to be so recognized in this category.

One of the outcomes of Ostrom's meta-analysis of commons case studies was her distillation of eight "design principles" that characterize successfully functioning commons arrangements (Ostrom 2010; see also Cox, Arnold, and Tomás 2010). These principles, now expanded to eleven with the splitting of three of the original principles into two subprinciples each, outline the general characteristics of commons institutions that have sustained themselves over time. They include general statements about the need to clearly identify the boundaries of the resource and the users of it. The principles state that the users of the resource should be able to participate in making the rules that govern resource use, that the rules be appropriate to local social and environmental contexts, and that the rewards of participating in processes of contextual rule-making, enforcement, and conflict resolution be commensurate with the costs. Resource users must be able to participate in the monitoring of the resource and uses of it and conflict resolution mechanisms and graduated sanctions should be in place to deal with transgressions of the rules. Finally, Ostrom's design principles indicate that any commons system must be nested within larger systems of governance and resource use at larger scales and that the state must acknowledge and recognize the legitimacy of the local commons systems to some degree. These design principles function in this work as a heuristic grounding for my analysis of Celo Community and will be outlined in greater detail in the chapters that follow.

Ostrom's analysis of the commons, including her design principles for the commons, can be applied to the understanding of any of a vast diversity of different types of commons situations. We might identify indigenous commons that existed prior to and outside of European colonization and the establishment of Western, state-based governance. In many cases, such commons still exist in the margins where the reach of state and associated capital-based projects of authoritarian high modernism have not fully penetrated. Following periods of European colonization and expropriation of native lands, colonial settlers on the frontiers of state expansion often operated in a commons context until the state could more firmly lay down its grids of legibility and simplification. This was true of much of the Appalachian region in the United States well into the twentieth century where predominantly Euro-American settlers obtained many of their needs through use of a vast "de facto" commons landscape (Newfont 2012, see also Stoll 2017). Throughout the history of the United States, a large number of intentional communities have been based around shared ownership, use, and stewardship of physical property and financial resources (see below). Commons need not be physical or local in nature. In recent years, things as diverse as the atmosphere and the high seas (Vogler 2012), human and other biological genomes (Contreras 2014), global stocks of agricultural biodiversity (Halewood, Noriega, and Louafi 2013), and information and knowledge sharing projects such as Wikipedia and open source software (see contributions to Frischmann, Madison, and Strandburg 2014) have all been conceptualized as commons. In this work, my focus is on a group of people attempting to recreate a land-based commons in a context in which a grid of private property was already laid across a landscape colonized by state and capital. It is within such contexts that many contemporary, bottom-up acts of commoning take place.

A concise, widely accepted definition of what constitutes a commons is elusive in the scholarly literature. As suggested above, the commons includes both a resource and the ways it is managed collectively by some group of users. Both the resource (the common property) and the institutions used to manage the resource (the common property regime) are subject to analysis and, combined, are taken to constitute the commons. Originally, the commons was used to refer specifically to situations of natural resource management, but the conceptual realm of the commons and of commons analysis has expanded to include, among other things, digital, cultural, and political commons. The widespread use of the commons framework to analyze these diverse realms has resulted in what Vaccaro and Beltran (2019) characterize as "conceptual blurriness." In this blurred context, confusion exists regarding whether the resource in question is common pool, public, or open access and, consequently, how to conceive of the ways in which it is managed. It is not my intention here to resolve the conceptual blurriness that surrounds the commons nor the intellectual tensions that accompany it. Indeed, while my focus in the book is on a fairly classic commons situation involving a defined group of people collectively managing a shared "natural resource" (in this case, a piece of land), I make the case that the members of Celo Community also share stewardship of other types of resources that are not necessarily physical in character.

In working through the content of the book, and especially in communicating with the members of the commons community I am writing about, I found that a broad definition from the commons activist literature works to most concisely and productively convey my general meaning when I speak of the commons. This definition encompasses those things referenced above (defined resources, a group of users, institutions for managing collective resource use) and expands them into more abstract territory that often surrounds community-based commons. According to Bollier,

A commons is:

- A social system for the long-term stewardship of resources that preserves shared values and community identity.
- A self-organized system by which communities manage resources (both depletable and replenishable) with minimal or no reliance on the Market or State.
- The wealth that we inherit or create together and must pass on, undiminished or enhanced, to our children. Our collective wealth includes the gifts of nature, civic infrastructure, cultural works and traditions and knowledge.
- A sector of the economy (and life!) that generates value in ways that are often taken for granted—and often jeopardized by the Market/State (2014: 175).

While we might quibble about how precise or appropriate this definition is, I believe it captures the general essence of the commons as manifested in Celo Community. In any case, since this book is more about an active process of commoning emergent within civil society than it is about precise conceptual definitions, and since Bollier's definition resonated well with those about whom I write, I find it an appropriate framework upon which to build this account.

Finally, it is worth emphasizing that a commons is not simply a resource; it is a situation in which a defined community of people *actively* manages a resource or set of resources according to a shared set of rules and norms. As such, there is no commons without acts of commoning. The importance of recognizing the active dimension of the commons (i.e., commoning) is explicitly noted in both scholarly and activist commons literature. As Bollier and Helfrich state, "[t]he drama of *commoning* is an active, living process—a verb rather than a noun . . . the commons . . . is fundamentally an *experiential practice* that cannot be understood through theory alone" (2015a: 3, emphasis in the original; see also Bollier 2014). While Ostrom herself did not use the term "commoning," this understanding of the commons as an active process is commensurate with her descriptions and analysis of the phenomenon. This active, experiential frame for understanding the commons is also essential for understanding the process of community building described in this book.

Inspired to a significant degree by Ostrom's work, and in many cases drawing directly on Ostrom's insights and design principles, broad and diverse coalitions of neo-commoners have taken up the task of creating and rebuilding the commons around the world. In the introduction to one edited volume that provides an overview and sampling of these movements, Bollier and Helfrich describe the driving force of these movements:

> It has become increasingly clear that we are poised between an old world that no longer works and a new one struggling to be born. Surrounded by an archaic order of centralized hierarchies on the one hand and predatory markets on the other, presided over by a state committed to planet-destroying economic growth, people around the world are searching for alternatives. . . . People want to emancipate themselves from governance systems that do not allow them meaningful voice and responsibility. (2012: xi)

Bollier and Helfrich go on to describe how the commons initiatives described in *The Wealth of the Commons* constitute a shift in perception, a transformative vision with the potential to empower more just, sustainable, and resilient worlds:

> The commons provides us with the ability to name and then help constitute a new order. We need a new language that does not insidiously replicate the misleading fictions of the old order. . . . We need a new discourse and new social practices that assert a new grand narrative, a different constellation of operating principles and a more effective order of governance. Seeking a discourse of this sort is not a fanciful whim. . . . Words actually shape the world. By using a new language, the language of the commons, we immediately begin to create a new culture. We can assert a new order of resource stewardship, right livelihood, social priorities and collective enterprise. (2012: xiv)

The contributions to *The Wealth of the Commons: A World Beyond Market & State* describe diverse initiatives for thinking, doing, being, and seeing like a commons taking place all around the world. They include initiatives as diverse as community gardens, transition towns, Brazilian landless workers groups, coastal fisheries, forest management, open source software, and international atmospheric governance. All of these commoning movements challenge conclusions drawn from Hardin's original argument that sustainable stewardship of resources can only be accomplished through mechanisms of top-down state management or capitalist-based, individualized, private property regimes. The current work is an attempt to describe in great depth one such initiative, one that well predates current discussions of commons, using Ostrom's commons design principles as a guide and analytic framework. I use the design principles to help us understand how a particular group of people has begun to emerge from the utopian rationality of state and capital to see like a commons anew.

This review of commons theory and practice allows us to circle back to James Scott's work in *Seeing Like a State* and consider how "seeing like a commons" is different from projects of legibility and simplification that support and enable the state and capital to rule more efficiently. First, it is important to note that Scott ascribes the same characteristics to capitalism as he does to the state: "Large-scale capitalism is just as much an agency of homogenization, uniformity, grids, and heroic simplification as the state is, with the key difference being that, for capitalists, simplification must pay" (1998: 8). For Scott, as the state retreats from its responsibilities for protecting social welfare, capital increasingly fills the vacuum and takes up the tasks of large-scale utopian social engineering. Others have argued even further that the state has largely functioned to pave the way for capitalist expansion into commons territory (see Ioris 2014). As Scott makes clear, state/capital development projects are built on a combination of four "pernicious elements." Each of these elements, taken on its own, may well be used for good; it is when they are deployed in combination that they become problematic and serve to displace and expropriate local commons.

The first pernicious element is the administrative ordering of society and nature whereby complex sociocultural and ecological realities are simplified and rendered more legible to state and capital agents who wish to more effectively bring them under their dominion. The second element is a high-modernist ideology whereby state and capital act with overwhelming self-confidence in the ability of scientific and technological progress to master nature and society and provide for human needs. These first two elements are combined into what Scott refers to as "high-modernist designs" which the state then implements using the third pernicious element, authoritarian power. Fourth, and relatedly, the implementation of authoritarian high-modernist designs is dependent upon the existence of a recumbent civil society that lacks the capacity or institutional opportunity to take action and resist the efforts of state and capital actors to implement their plans. In summary, seeing like a state entails a view that claims omniscience and that simplifies the world and conceptualizes it progressing across a linear trajectory of technological improvement. Seeing like a state also claims an omnipotent capacity to implement plans to move that progression forward and an ability to ignore or discount minimal democratic resistance to the implementation of these designs.

How is "seeing like a commons" different? First, it is important to note that the commons is not necessarily the inverse of the state; commons do not necessarily reject the value of science and technology, nor do they avoid any attempts to use science and technology to help design new relationships with nature or among human beings. However, there are some important differences. For one, commons systems are based on subtle and nuanced understandings of local sociocultural and ecological systems and the dynamic interactions among them. They are thus more open to change and more able to respond and adapt to changes and intricacies in local conditions. Second, the commons are more open to inspirations for design that come from outside Western epistemologies that center science, technology, and linear progress. Such inspirations might include diverse, non-Western, and indigenous epistemologies and may also center more local, affective knowledge derived from in-depth sensory engagement with place. Third, commons are, by definition, more egalitarian, participatory systems built from the ground up rather than implemented from the top down. Finally, it is important to note that while the commons could be read as a rejection of state power, it must be acknowledged that, at least as things currently stand, commons are dependent on the state for recognition and support. In summary, seeing like a commons is, compared to seeing like a state, more attuned to local variation, more democratic, and draws on more diverse sources for its vision, resulting in more adaptable and resilient methods for perceiving the world and organizing collective action within it.

As suggested above, state/capital systems and commons systems are not diametrically opposed. Indeed, in today's state-dominated world, the immediate challenge is to carve out ways for the commons to coexist with and thrive in the context of state and capital dominance while also slowly altering or displacing it. As Scott makes clear, state power can be used for good and, in any case, won't be going away any time soon. The question is how to carve out roles for the commons in the context of the state. This is, to a significant degree, a question of scale. The large scale of the state and industrial capitalism requires simplifications, and these simplifications become divorced from the local ecological and sociocultural realities. Commoning allows functionality and adaptation at a scale more aligned with these local realities. A state that can recognize and delegate power to the commons so local realities can be addressed with greater nuance can become more resilient. On the other hand, and as per Scott, we must beware that local realities can often be unequal, unsustainable, and unjust; local commons must be balanced by a larger-scale, more global awareness and by an emphasis on issues of equity across various terrains of difference. So again, how can the state/capital and the commons be brought into balance; how can these issues of scale be reconciled?

In my analysis, I would like to draw specific attention to the deployment of the commons, or perhaps more appropriately to "acts of commoning," by Celo Community as a design practice in the process of building an intentional community. In doing so, I will draw on Ostrom's theory of "design principles" for effectively functioning commons. Such commons arrangements have served as important ontological beacons helping us to navigate between the two hegemonic poles of capitalism, based on individual private ownership of resources and property governed by market forces, and state-based socialism, based on top-down management of resources and property governed by state forces. Both of these paradigms have had devastating effects on people and the planet during recent centuries even as they have sometimes also improved human welfare, at least for some. The commons represents an alternative path that bisects and helps expand the linear continuum connecting the state and private property by allowing for small group management of resources that would otherwise only be held individually or managed in a simplified, top-down fashion.

Reflecting on the development of her theory of commons design principles shortly before her death, Ostrom stated, "At times I think that I should have called them something else because people confused that term with the idea that we are trying to design something from the beginning. However, I was really undertaking a study of robustness of systems that already existed" (Ostrom 2012: 77). Using these principles as a lens for viewing the organization of intentional communities such as Celo, I argue that these groups are, from the beginning, engaging in forms of design implicitly oriented around the commons. While the members of Celo Community did not explicitly work with Ostrom's principles in mind—indeed she had not even been born when the community was founded—they have, in the process of creating their commons, ended up paying deliberate attention to the characteristics, institutions, and processes outlined by her principles. Like other commons, the existence of these things predated their enunciation by Ostrom and others.

As suggested above by Bollier and Helfrich, and as I will elaborate on below, people engaged in acts of commoning such as those characteristic of Celo are attempting to prefigure a more just, resilient, and sustainable future by, as a beginning, starting to displace the frames of individualism, high-modernist simplification, and short-term, utilitarian maximization that have colonized our minds. When viewed through the expansive lens of "ontological design" proposed by Escobar (2017), small-scale, utopian commoning experiments such as Celo Community may help us, as Escobar suggests, recover future-imagining possibilities that have been largely foreclosed in the global, colonial sweep of industrial modernity perpetuated by state and capital agents. In places such as Celo, we can get a glimpse of groups of people using commons design to "play a constructive role in transforming entrenched ways of being and doing toward philosophies of well-being that finally equip humans to live in mutually enhancing ways with each other and the Earth" (Escobar 2017: xi). In intentional communities like Celo, people are learning to see and be like a commons.

INTENTIONAL COMMUNITIES:
DESIGN FOR THE COMMONS

One goal of this work is to bring literatures and conceptualizations regarding the commons and communal studies into conversation with each other. As stated above, I use Ostrom's commons design principles as a heuristic guide for analyzing Celo Community as an intentional community. At the same time, I offer an ethnographic case study of Celo Community as an example of people engaged in persistent processes of commoning. With a few exceptions (see Baden 1998 and Gibson and Koontz 1998), explorations of intentional communities (the subject matter of communal studies) have rarely been considered in light of commons theory and vice versa. In what follows, I make the case that intentional communities, by definition, constitute commons wherein people, by design, deliberately engage in acts of commoning as a method for building alternative social models.

It will be useful to start with some conceptual definitions. As with the study of the commons, the field of communal studies is interdisciplinary in nature. The Communal Studies Association, the oldest organization in the field, started in 1975 around the same time that the study of the commons was taking shape, defines its mission as follows:

- To encourage and facilitate the preservation, restoration, and public interpretation of America's historic communal sites.
- To provide a forum for the study of intentional communities, past and present.
- To communicate to the general public the successful ideas from, and lessons learned by, communal societies (Communal Studies Association 2020).

Within the community of communal studies scholars there is some debate or "conceptual blurriness" regarding what kinds of human groups should and should not be included in the field (Miller 2019). Putting aside the specifics of that debate, there is general agreement that we seek a greater understanding of communal societies or, to use a term in more common circulation among the members of the communities we study in contemporary society, intentional communities.

The most widely accepted scholarly definition of intentional community, formulated by Miller (2010), states that intentional communities are defined by four general characteristics:

- The group in question must be gathered on the basis of some kind of purpose or vision, and see itself as set apart from mainstream society to some degree.

- The group in question must live together on property that has some kind of clear physical commonality to it.
- The group must have some kind of financial or material sharing, some kind of economic commonality.
- The group must have a membership of at least five adults, not all of whom are related by blood or marriage, who have chosen voluntarily to join in common cause (Miller 2010: 6–7).

I would like to draw attention to two distinct but interrelated characteristics embedded in and implied by this definition. The first is that intentional communities are, by their very nature, concerned with developing alternative models for human social existence in the world and in the context of specific state-based societies. According to Brown,

> The intentional community is one that is purposely and voluntarily founded to achieve a specific goal for a specific group of people bent on solving a specific set of cultural and social problems. . . . Intentional communities represent a kind of "voting with the feet"—a call to action that is personal and communal. . . . The members of these communities often see themselves at odds with or needing to withdraw from the larger society; however, that withdrawal occurs within the context of the larger society. The intentional community is a phenomenon of the nation-state and an important object of study, because it allows us to observe how human beings living in large, heterogeneous societies use community to cope with the exigencies of life. (2002a: 5–6)

The intentionality of intentional communities suggests that the members of any such community share, to a large degree, an understanding of the goals, purposes, values, and vision underlying their endeavor. That this is not always the case can have significant implications regarding the viability and durability of any given intentional community, especially regarding its relative success in stewarding its collective resources. Nonetheless, intentional communities are defined by their attempt to enact visions of social alternatives that are almost always organized around forms of sharing and cooperation.

The purposes driving the establishment of intentional communities and the goals they set out to achieve are diverse and have changed over time. A full explication of this diversity has been the subject of numerous volumes (see Metcalf 2004, Miller 2015 and 2019, and Pitzer 1997a among others), and I will present only a small sampling here. During the colonial period, a number of groups, perhaps most notably the Shakers, came to North America seeking the freedom to practice their religions free from the persecution they experienced in places like England, Germany, and France. The growth in the number of Shaker communities and converts in the early 1800s presaged the establishment of a variety of "utopian socialist" communities in the decades following American independence, New Harmony, Oneida, and Brook Farm, prominently among them. These communities sought to enact alternatives to the social and political ideologies, patterns of organization, and inequalities that accompanied the early industrialization of American society. A similar period of intentional community building marked the Gilded Age at the turn of the twentieth century, a period during which anarchist and socialist communities such as Kaweah Cooperative Commonwealth and Llano del Rio in California responded to labor conflict and urbanization by attempting to build more egalitarian models of society in rural areas. Perhaps the most widely known period of intentional community building took place in the late 1960s and 1970s as American youth rejected emergent consumerism and American militarism and moved back to the land or sought more communal lifestyles in the cities in support of peace and social justice. Beginning in the mid-1990s, another wave of intentional community building appeared in the United States in the form of ecovillages and cohousing communities whose members seek to establish more ecologically sustainable lifestyles that simultaneously address the environmental justice implications of mass consumerism and the experienced social alienation that characterizes life in mainstream, consumerist society.

A second characteristic of intentional communities is that they are almost always based on some foundation of economic commons. There is, to quote Miller again, a group of people who "live together on property that has some kind of clear commonality to it." That group of people is engaged in some kind of "economic commonality" that involves financial or other material forms of sharing along a continuum of more or less intense communalism. As Baden (1998) notes, these kinds of communitarian arrangements raise exactly the types of issues regarding costs and benefits, monitoring, sanctions, free riding, and potential defections that often come to the fore in the commons literature. Miller's definition does not speak directly to the existence of specific kinds of rules, norms, or institutions that the members of intentional communities use to collectively manage their common property and other economic resources. However, communal sharing of land, materials, and other things are almost always central to intentional community-building endeavors and to scholarly analyses of intentional communities of various sorts.

Again, a brief and selective review of some examples will serve to illustrate this general point. Many Protestant Christian intentional communities have drawn inspiration from chapters 2 and 4 in the Book of Acts where statements such as "all who believed were together and had all things in common" and "no one claimed private ownership of any possessions, but everything they owned was held in common" justify or even command the practice of economic communalism. While such communalism may have derived from spiritual inspiration, it was also often an economic necessity for those pushing against the grain to develop social alternatives. According to Brewer, this was true for the early Shakers. "Constantly struggling to provide subsistence, the early Shakers informally practiced communal sharing of goods and services, more out of necessity than religious conviction" (1997: 40). The Amana Colonies in Iowa similarly adopted the practice of common property out of combination of economic necessity and religious conviction (Andelson 1997). Drawing inspiration from the Shakers, but seeking to establish a secular, scientific intentional community at New Harmony in Indiana, Robert Owen used economic communalism as an organizational principle in part to counter the "evil" of "private, or individual property" (Pitzer 1997b: 89). Later socialist communities such as those that appeared in California around the turn of the twentieth century recognized that to be effective, "the economy becomes the religion, and the creed becomes ownership by the community of the means of production" (Hine 1997: 419). Later intentional communities such as many of the hippie communes of the 1960s and 1970s and, ecovillages more recently, adopted economic communalism out of a combination of explicit rejection of dominant economic arrangements and as a strategy for pooling resources to build the desired alternatives to mainstream sociocultural, political, and economic patterns.

In all of these cases, there is a connection between the practice of economic communalism and the deliberate attempt to experiment with and manifest an envisioned alternative to mainstream society. Similarly, failures at creating a shared vision or shortcomings in designing effective sharing mechanisms frequently contributed to the demise of such communities. Analyses of intentional communities often point to a lack of shared understanding of values and vision among the members as one of the main reasons that such communal endeavors do not last. Pitzer's (1997b) analysis of Robert Owen's New Harmony, referenced above, is a typical case in point; the community's open-door policy whereby new members were accepted into the community without any systematic attempt to ensure they shared in some common vision was a significant contributor to the community's short life and early demise. One of the few studies to have viewed intentional communities through the lens of the commons points to the degree to which internal institutions created by community members function to ensure coincidence of values and vision among community members as one of the main factors affecting the ability of such communities to effectively steward their common property (Gibson and Koontz 1998). In the chapters to come, I argue that Celo Community's relative longevity and success is due to their ability to create a set of flexible commons institutions that effectively facilitate both the sharing of a common vision and the effective stewardship of common resources.

One of the most forceful statements regarding the centrality of economic communalism to the intentional community-building phenomenon can be found in Pitzer's theory of developmental communalism (see Pitzer 1989, 1997c, and 2008). According to this theory, the builders of intentional communities often choose economic communalism as one among a number of organizational strategies available to them because it offers them the security, solidarity, and opportunity needed to experiment with the development of alternative social models. However, the model of economic communalism adopted by such groups must be open to adjustment and fine-tuning as new circumstances and opportunities, both internal and external to the group, arise and are encountered. Those groups that insist on adhering to a particular model of economic communalism will, according to the theory, almost inevitably stagnate and die as conditions around and within the community change and dictate adjustment and adaptation. Ironically, those groups that do adjust may ultimately find economic communalism to be no longer useful to the pursuit of their broader transformational goals and choose to terminate the use of economic communalism as a means to their ends. The descriptions of the communal societies in Pitzer's *America's Communal Utopias* (1997a), coming as they do in a volume dedicated to applying the theory of developmental communalism to an understanding of America's communal history, attest to the analytical power of Pitzer's insight.

Pitzer's theory of developmental communalism points directly to processes of commoning as essential, if sometimes ephemeral, strategies employed by the builders of intentional communities in their pursuit of alternative social models. At the same time, it augments Ostrom's commons design principles by suggesting that the rules for managing the commons need to not only be appropriate to local social and ecological conditions; they must also be flexible enough to adjust to those conditions as they change. As I will argue in the chapters that follow, this flexibility in the design and deployment of commons institutions is one among many factors that has contributed to the longevity and relative success of Celo as a commons community.

Pitzer's theory, in its suggestion that economic communalism "is a generic social mechanism available to all peoples, movements, and governments in all ages" (2008: 17) also points us back to one of the conditions that is essential to resistance against the spread and dominance of authoritarian, high-modernist projects associated with state and capital. As Scott suggests, the widespread implementation of authoritarian, high-modernist designs is, in part, dependent on a recumbent civil society that lacks the power and opportunity to resist the dominance of the agents of state and capital. Where such power and opportunity is available to the people, small-scale utopian striving may be deployed to resist the large-scale utopian designs implemented by powerful actors by, in many cases, enacting the commons.[2] That such power and opportunity has been relatively widely available in the United States of America is one reason why intentional communities have flourished there in relatively large numbers. However, a closer look reveals that the opportunity to deploy economic communalism in pursuit of more democratic utopias has not, in fact, been equally available to all groups of people at all times. Indeed such opportunity was only made available in what became the United States of America through the genocide of Native Americans and expropriation of their lands and has, to this day, been much less accessible to different groups depending on shifting terrains of race, class, and gender among other things. Indeed, a broad majority of America's most prominent experiments in intentional community building have been spearheaded by middle- to upper-class white males. While I will return to this inequality of access in several places below, especially in terms of how it shaped the founding of Celo Community and whether and how the patterns of commoning developed by Celo's members might be applicable in other contexts, this is a subject that is deserving of broader treatment than is provided in this account.

COMMUNITIES, COMMONS, AND UTOPIANISM

I don't think utopia is a possibility. I don't think it's the goal. . . . We're in process and utopia implies an end. And to me, that's a pitfall, to think that we're going to get to an end. Then it can become the "end justifies the means." The means are the end, if you want to get really simplistic about it. (Interview with author in Celo Community, November 9, 2004)

In the literature on intentional communities, some variant of the term "utopia" is often used to frame the analysis and discussion. The specific connotations carried by the term depend to a significant degree on who is applying it and what their perspective is. In some cases, the term carries a derisive or dismissive tone and references a naïveté or hopeless romanticism taken to be characteristic of intentional community-building endeavors and, often, of the commons more generally. The advocates of this point of view tend to believe that small-scale utopian projects are at best distractions, and that change can only be achieved by more pragmatic methods. Or, they find a threat in the ways intentional communitarians speak truth to power and thus use the utopian epithet to delegitimize them. In other cases, and especially in more recent theoretical explorations of intentional community building, the term carries more positive connotations denoting the emancipatory and transformative potential embodied in intentional communities' attempts to enact a vision of a better life. The differential use of this term points to broader "conceptual blurriness" and intellectual tensions surrounding the idea of utopia and the ways in which possibilities for the future are imagined far beyond the realm of intentional communities. Since these tensions are intertwined with my subject matter, and since my analysis of Celo turns, in part, on a previous ethnographer's conclusion that the community constitutes a failed utopia, this is a subject that must be taken up here. My conclusions, embodied in the quotation above from one of my ethnographic interviews with members of Celo Community, point to the power of *utopianism* as a potentially emancipatory, transformative *process*, one that has the power to counteract the hegemonic, large-scale utopias of authoritarian, high-modernist projects described by Scott, especially when manifested in the commoning endeavors of intentional communitarians. In this sense, *utopia* is not possible and is not the goal; however, the process of envisioning something better and collectively working toward it is essential.

The word "utopia" was coined by Sir Thomas More as the title to his 1516 critique of theocratic hegemony and oppression in England. Utopia encapsulates the desire for an ideal society, the impossibility of realizing it, and the tension thus generated. The word's Greek roots, *eu*, *ou*, and *topia* mean, respectively, "good," "no," and "place." Most conclude that Thomas More's creation of the term "utopia" was a deliberate conflation of these three meanings (see Sargent 2010). The concept of utopia thus represents a fundamental characteristic of the human condition, especially in a world dominated by agents of state and capital—the tension between the real and the ideal and the inability to completely transcend that tension. Sargent (1994) highlights three common, often intertwined, formats in which utopias appear: literary utopias, utopian social theories, and utopian social practice. While intentional communities are typically classified in the latter category, they are often informed by literary utopias and utopian social theory. As will be clear in the next chapter, such was clearly the case with Celo Community.

As Sargent (2006) points out, one person's utopia is another's dystopia. If a vision for any individual intentional community might constitute someone's idea of a better life, so equally do larger projects of state-based communism, the Islamic caliphate, and global, neoliberal capitalism. In any one of these cases, one group of people may think they are doing God's work in implementing the vision while others may experience the implications and outcomes of implementing the vision as completely dystopian and oppressive. Sargent recognizes the danger in utopianism and problematizes the typical conflation of utopia with blueprints for perfection. The danger of utopia is greatly exacerbated depending on the degrees to which the advocates of any one utopian vision have the power to insist on imposing their blueprint for perfection on unwilling others in a widespread fashion; this is also a question of scale. "[T]he problem with utopia arises when it becomes a system of beliefs rather than what it is in almost all cases, a critique of the actual through the imagining of a better alternative" (Sargent 2006: 12). At the same time, Sargent recognizes that envisioning a better life is a fundamental human condition as well as an essential, and perhaps the only effective, means of resisting totalizing utopian visions. "[I]f we lose hope, we lose our humanity. But there are both inclusive and exclusive utopias, and the differences between the types provide one of the main reasons for utopia being both necessary and potentially dangerous" (2006: 12). If Scott's state-based utopian social engineering projects are large-scale manifestations of the latter, most intentional communities represent small-scale attempts to walk this tightrope—not always successfully—between the essential and the potentially dangerous. This is a theme I will return to in the conclusion where I consider the potential broader applicability of Celo's models.

While most people who live in intentional communities today are averse to the use of the terms "utopia," "utopian," or "utopianism" to describe their endeavors, these terms have long been used by outside analysts of such communities. Marx and Engels admired their "utopian socialist" contemporaries and intentional community founders such as Robert Owen and Charles Fourier for their overall visions of more egalitarian societies and their correct diagnosis of the problems facing the Western world. However, they viewed intentional community building in a negative light, as but a distraction from the class revolution that was on the horizon of history's evolutionary trajectory (Engels 1892). Later observers such as Charles Nordhoff and Arthur Bestor, in his famous *Backwoods Utopias* (1950), came to similar conclusions; while they granted that some of these communities may have created viable social systems, they noted that many of them did not last very long and believed that they were at best offshoots from the main currents of history.

Scholars in the second half of the twentieth century began to view intentional communities as natural laboratories to which social scientists could turn for scientific research on cooperation, commitment, and social interaction (Infield 1955, Kanter 1972, Zablocki 1980). In this regard, Kanter was explicit. "In addition to providing a historical and sociological perspective on the contemporary commune movement, the study of utopian communities in America can also contribute to the understanding of social life in general. Communal orders represent major social experiments in which new or radical theories of human behavior, motivation and interpersonal relations are put to the test. Social science has rarely had 'laboratories' of the scale and scope of utopian communities" (Kanter 1972: viii). However, Kanter counted only those intentional communities that lasted at least twenty-five years as successful and, perhaps partly as a result, held that the utopian communities of the 1960s and 1970s were of diminishing significance compared with those of past periods which, in any case, failed to become models for the rest of society.

Contemporary theoretical treatments seek to gain a greater understanding of the processes of utopian striving by recognizing the dynamism and agency of intentional communities, their ability to have long-lasting effects beyond their utopian and communal phases, and the degree to which intentional communities are networked with each other and other social movements (Brown 2002a; Pitzer 1989, 1997a; Sargent 2006; Sargisson 2007 and 2012; Schehr 1997; Lockyer 2007 and 2009). Work in this vein holds that intentional communities have been dismissed as "free-floating bits of cultural ephemera," not given consideration as sociocultural phenomena whose "complex interconnections can be studied systematically and traced over time" (Boyer 1997: ix–x). It notes that intentional communities can no longer be seen as isolated from national and global political-economic systems as they could even a century ago; rather they are engaged in a dialectic with such forces, influencing them and being constrained by them at the same time (Janzen 1981, Bennett 1974, Brown 2002b, Pitzer 2013).

The work of sociologist Robert Schehr (1997) seeks to instigate a more widespread recognition of the agency of utopian communities and their members, citing them as perhaps "the penultimate social movement." Echoing Sargent's belief in the necessity of utopianism, Schehr's ultimate conclusion is that social theorists, especially those concerned with ameliorating contemporary problems, must embrace the utopianism of contemporary intentional communities for its transformative and emancipatory potential, rather than deriding it because it does not fit within their theoretical boxes.

> While ICs [intentional communities] have traditionally been ignored in the classical social movement literature, largely for their "utopian" constitution, it is precisely this utopian component that I argue is crucial to a successful social movement. Simultaneously granting the persistence of resistance within civil society, and recognition of a utopian vision for the future, make ICs the ideal social movement entity. . . a culture without a utopian vision would be dead because it would have no vision for the future. (Schehr 1997: 174).

Thus, for Schehr, in contrast to many previous theorists of intentional communities and like Pitzer, intentional communities must be examined not in terms of whether they succeed in creating utopias, but rather in terms of the process of striving for their utopian visions.

Susan Brown's (2002b) theorization of intentional communities as forms of cultural critique similar to those framed by Marcus and Fischer (1986) in their attempts to rethink the anthropological enterprise provides an interesting perspective that helps us focus in specifically on intentional communities as part of emerging commons movements that were described above. Drawing on Marcus and Fischer, Brown's work suggests that intentional communities share with anthropology a critical orientation to the predominant culture of industrial capitalism and a utopian effort to demonstrate that alternatives to taken-for-granted, hegemonic sociocultural and political-economic forms are possible. In other words, intentional communities, like much of anthropology, are engaged in forms of epistemological critique and cross-cultural juxtaposition. However, the cultural critiques of intentional communities differ from those of anthropology because they are enacted through lived practice—and often through the rebuilding of the commons—rather than through intellectual theorization and distanced analysis of cultural difference. For Brown, this *enactment* of utopian cultural critique, this lived embodiment of learning to share and to act cooperatively as stewards, gives intentional communities great power.

If the builders of intentional communities have, for centuries, been engaged in an ongoing process of challenging dominant powers and hegemonic models for society by attempting to create emancipatory alternatives within that dominant context, Linebaugh (2008) suggests that commons and commoners have taken a similar course. Again and again, commoners have asserted their rights and sought to retain or enact alternative social forms. Again and again, they have been dismissed as irrational and, more recently, derided as anti-Western by the powers that benefit from the enclosure of the commons.

> Full discussion of the commons is hampered by two abbreviated categories of thought that have become spasmodic intellectual tics. One goes back to the 1790s and arose against the romantic movement; the other developed against the communist movement of the twentieth century. The first scorned utopia and the second denounced totalitarianism; one became the condescending term for all that is foolish, the other the pompous designation for all that is hideous. Yet under the circumstances of actually existing commons, they were irrelevant. Still the attitudes conveniently colonized the mind and shut off debate where it needed to begin. (Linebaugh 2008: 273)

Intentional communitarians attempt to engage, as neo-commoners, in new manifestations of quite old forms of sharing and cooperation. Many of them, especially those in the context of highly "developed" Western societies in the heart of global capitalism, do so not only in pursuit of a more satisfying way to live but also out of the recognition that new ways of living are needed if we are to have a more just, sustainable, and resilient world. In the process of taking greater responsibility for themselves, they aim to allow others greater opportunities to achieve the rights of life and liberty that enclosure of the commons so often forecloses. In doing so, they begin the process of decolonizing not only their individual minds but the collective mind. In learning to see and be like a commons, they create an entry point for opening up the debate again.

NOTES

1. In Scott's subsequent work, it is clear that these patterns of state-imposed legibility and simplicity, or at least their roots, can be traced further afield and deeper into the past. See *The Art of Not Being Governed* (2009) and *Against the Grain* (2017).

2. Ironically, the American politico-cultural emphasis on freedom and *individual* choice is another reason that communalism and intentional communities have existed in relatively large numbers in the United States.

Chapter 1

Arthur Morgan, Utopianism, and the Founding of Celo Community

If intentional communities, acts of commoning, and Stoll's proposal for commons communities in Appalachia, as discussed in the previous chapter, seem hopelessly and unpragmatically "utopian" in today's neoliberal capitalist world, Celo Community's eighty plus years of existence belies this characterization. The community is one of many practical, utopian community-building endeavors initiated by Arthur Morgan in the mid-twentieth century. It provides an example of how cooperative social structures and community-based common resource stewardship remain feasible in today's world. An understanding of Celo as an intentional, commoning community must begin with a brief discussion of its founder Arthur Morgan, a man who one recent biographer (Purcell 2014) characterized as a pragmatic social reformer driven by a sometimes contradictory utopian vision.

ARTHUR MORGAN: UTOPIAN, CULTURAL CRITIC, AND SMALL COMMUNITY ADVOCATE

In 1940, having just reached the end of his appointment by FDR as first director of the Tennessee Valley Authority (TVA), one of the United States' first full, industrial-scale modernization projects, Arthur Morgan wrote:

> Today, as in the ancient past, the small community is the home, the refuge, the seed bed, of some of the finest qualities of civilization. But just as the precious values of the ancient community were submerged and largely destroyed by empire and feudalism, so the present-day community with its invaluable cultural tradition is being dissolved, diluted, and submerged by modern technology, commercialism, mass production, propaganda, and centralized government.

Should that process not be checked, a great cultural tradition may be largely lost. (Morgan 1942: 10)

Morgan was not simply romanticizing premodern communities nor simply critiquing what he thought had gone wrong with the TVA for, even as his term as director of the TVA was winding down amidst significant acrimony, he was the driving force behind the establishment of one of the longest-lasting intentional communities in the United States, a place where the cooperative small community was and continues to be a site of deliberate sociocultural design and experimentation.

A few years after Morgan penned that statement, a group composed largely of Quaker conscientious objectors to World War II began organizing themselves communally on a 1,200-acre parcel of land in the southern Appalachian Mountains that Morgan had helped secure for this experiment. The Celo Community Constitution that they eventually adopted, a document that governs the community to this day, reflects the influence of Arthur Morgan's belief in the importance of the small community and early community members' explicit intention to create a functioning commons.

The aim of Celo Community is to provide an opportunity for its members to enjoy a life that includes personal expression, neighborly friendship and cooperation, and appreciative care of the natural environment. No person is excluded from membership because of national or racial origin, religious belief [, disability, sexual orientation, or gender identity[1]].

We encourage personal enterprise among members by making land and money available when needed for suitable productive use. Regarding ownership of land as a trust, we do not sell it, but assign it for short or long periods at as low an assessment as feasible to those who give promise of improving it while living harmoniously with their neighbors. From our revolving fund we occasionally lend money at low cost to a member for the purpose of improving his property.

In the relation of the Community to its members the legal is an instrument of the moral. The relation is not an external one between a soulless corporation and independent individuals. It is the internal relation between one person of a friendly neighborhood group and all other persons including himself. Thus a member consulting in a Community meeting on a course of action is both a private user and (in consensus with others) a public controller of land. A community member through participating in Community government tends to develop a stable and considerate character along with responsible personal expression. (Celo Community 2018a)

Arthur Morgan (1878–1975) is an intriguing historical figure. Raised in a small family of humble means in rural Minnesota, he became a well-known and admired flood control engineer, educator, writer, and philosopher. In his adult life, his circle of associates, colleagues, and admirers included such well-known figures as Orville Wright, President Franklin Delano Roosevelt and his wife Eleanor, and prominent Quaker Clarence Pickett who served for many years as executive secretary of the American Friends Service Committee, a Quaker-based humanitarian relief agency. If Morgan's most recent biographer Aaron D. Purcell believes that Morgan is one of the most prominent and least well-known American public figures of the early to mid-twentieth century, Morgan's role in founding one of the longest-lasting American intentional communities is even less well known. Indeed, Purcell's 2014 biography of Morgan, despite its strong emphasis on Morgan's utopianism and his community-building endeavors, devotes only a few paragraphs to Morgan's involvement in founding Celo.

Throughout his adult life, Morgan was an advocate of life in small communities, believing that the intimate social interactions characteristic of small community contexts led to the development of moral character and a sense of responsibility on the individual level, and to progress and efficiency on the social level. Morgan held that, along with the family, small communities were the fundamental unit of sociocultural evolution, the key to human progress and the foundation of democratic life. He believed that small communities were being undermined by modern, urban, industrial culture and he included programs aimed at the reinvigoration of small community life in many of his major projects in the areas of flood control engineering, education, and consulting.

Morgan's biographers (Kahoe 1977, Purcell 2014, Talbert 1987) emphasize several primary forces that influenced his vision: the morality, perfectionism, and love for nature of his religiously devout mother; his father's religious agnosticism and pursuit of scientific inquiry; the Progressive movement of the late nineteenth and early twentieth centuries; and the utopian writings of Edward Bellamy, including most prominently his 1888 utopian novel *Looking Backward*. These forces, combined with Morgan's own self-cultivated capacity for critical thinking, resulted in his characteristically idealistic and sometimes conflicted approach to all of the various projects he was involved in over the course of his life.

According to Purcell (2014), Edward Bellamy's 1888 utopian novel *Looking Backward* had a major influence on Morgan and other Progressives of the era. This novel painted a picture of a future society where the social problems associated with industrialism, urbanization, and growing economic inequality in the late 1800s had been successfully addressed. Central to Bellamy's vision was the formation of a centralized industrial army that would ensure all human needs were met and enable the transition from a competitive, hierarchical society to a more cooperative communal one where class conflict had fallen away. Bellamy's designs for the future also included a widespread eugenics program whereby society would be improved by preventing the most "unfit" individuals from reproducing. While Morgan appears to have embraced Bellamy's eugenics (more on this below), he ultimately soured on the potential of centralized, state-based programs for bringing about change, choosing instead to put his faith in the ability of individuals situated in small communities to improve themselves and society. In the final analysis, Morgan's views on utopianism and social change, especially as they relate to Bellamy's writing, were grounded in a quite privileged view that focused on class and individual potential and largely ignored issues of structural racial inequality. It was a view, made possible by Morgan's own relative white privilege, that emphasized the potential for individual improvement and significantly sidelined the need for broader changes to address structural violence and oppression.

Morgan's identification with and involvement in the Progressive movement is worth considering here, especially with regard to his views on race and eugenics. Support for eugenics was among the tenets of the Progressive movement in the decades around the turn of the twentieth century and Morgan was often a vociferous advocate for eugenics. He included eugenics prominently in the moral code he proposed for Antioch College students and faculty in the 1920s when he served as president of the institution and he retained his belief in the importance of eugenics long after such views had been abandoned by most others in the wake of the Holocaust (Purcell 2014). On the other hand, and especially later in his life, he worked extensively with communities and people of color for greater justice and empowerment. Examples of his work along these lines are numerous. In the 1950s, he began a decades-long association with a man from South India who stayed in Morgan's home for many months and to whom Morgan lent great moral and financial support for his efforts to build a community-based educational institution in his home village for the empowerment of people from lower castes in India. In 1963, he joined members of the African American community in Yellow Springs, Ohio, to lead a public demonstration in protest of a local barber's refusal to cut African Americans' hair (see Purcell 2014, which includes a picture of Morgan leading the protest alongside an unidentified African American gentleman).

Morgan's most prominent biographer suggests that Morgan's views as a Progressive were both atypical for Progressives and sometimes contradictory. "He favored Americanizing the immigrants, not restricting their arrival on American shores, but at the same time he feared a decline in the hereditary quality of the next generation. Morgan's elitist attitudes toward race and heredity contradicted his belief that, through hard work and moral actions, anyone could improve themselves" (Purcell 2014: 41). This author has never come across any explicit mentions of race or eugenics as part of Morgan's plans for Celo Community nor is there any mention of nor implicit reference to it anywhere in community documents or meeting minutes. On the contrary, it is clear that the community took deliberate steps to promote racial justice and integration, including hosting African American students at the summer camp that was started by community members on community land in the early 1950s (a practice that continues to this day) well before court cases and legislative action forced integration across the country. Beyond that, it is clear that the low expenses associated with living in the community has facilitated the ability of a number of community members, especially those with a Quaker background, to engage in ongoing racial justice work across the region and nation as well as around the world.

Nonetheless, it is clear that Morgan's concept of community was shaped by his relatively privileged racial background and by the elite class status he had gained through his life's work. It was also grounded to some degree in a Progressive milieu characterized by beliefs about race that, while quite widespread at the time, are quite problematic in hindsight. The people who joined the intentional community that Morgan founded, Quakers most prominently among them, brought quite progressive (with a small "p") views on race, equality, and justice. Despite this, the community has remained mostly (though not entirely) racially homogenous to this day. This fact is worth acknowledging and merits further examination, especially in terms of the applicability of the models developed by community members to broader patterns and processes of commoning. This is a theme I will return to in the final chapter, but it is worthy of broader treatment than I provide here.

The overall goal of Morgan's life's work was to improve society, to use critical thinking, systematic design, and moral guidance to make the world a better place. These characteristics were common to other Progressives of his generation (Purcell 2014, Talbert 1987). At times Morgan could be paternalistic; he believed that he knew right from wrong and he demanded total devotion from his subordinates. On the other hand, his advocacy of the small community was often vague and he had a tendency, in some of his work, to step away and let projects he started run their own course, a pattern that was certainly true for Celo Community. Morgan's utopianism was grounded in the belief that society could be made better if people were willing to wholeheartedly experiment with alternatives to taken-for-granted cultural beliefs and social institutions. Morgan did not emphasize social perfection as an end, but rather critical thinking and experiments as the means of striving for social improvement. He believed that the small community as a social institution had a pivotal role to play in this utopian striving for betterment.

Morgan's utopianism and his belief in the importance of small community life are evident in almost all of the projects he undertook. In his work as an engineer and bureaucrat on the Miami Conservancy District and the Tennessee Valley Authority, the betterment of local society and the establishment of small model communities were always at the forefront of his plans. He created community settings for the laborers on his flood control projects believing that he could simultaneously improve their characters and thus improve society while creating more efficient work forces. The same is true with regards to his presidency of Antioch College where he created one of the first successful work-study programs, an approach to education that combined the development of practical skills with the expanded horizons and critical thinking fostered by a liberal arts focus. At Antioch, he sought to create community on campus by promoting local industries, participatory government, and interaction among students and teachers both inside and outside the classroom. However, his focus on the small community and his utopian desire for the betterment of society is most evident in his writings on community and in the founding of several initiatives focused on the small community including, most prominently here, Celo Community and Community Service, Inc. (now the Arthur Morgan Institute for Community Solutions).

Morgan's understanding of human community is based on his reading of literature in history, anthropology, and rural sociology and upon his own observations as an engineer, educator, and bureaucrat. Morgan's essentialist conceptualization of community grows from an idealized picture of "the ancient village." In 1942, he wrote that "where vestiges of primitive life remain in out-of-the-way parts of the earth we find men living in true communities" (Morgan 1942: 38). He believed that during the development of the human species, local population groups,

> usually in the form of villages, have been the nearly universal settings of human life. Probably more than 99% of all men who have lived have been villagers. Men have been so deeply identified with this way of living that few societies have long survived its disintegration and disappearance. Man is a small community animal. (Morgan 1957a: 12)

To support this view, Morgan quoted George Peter Murdock's work on the Human Relations Area Files at Yale University.

> The community and the nuclear family are the only social groups that are genuinely universal. . . . Nowhere on earth do people live regularly in isolated families. Everywhere territorial propinquity, supported by diverse other bonds, unites at least a few neighboring families into a larger social group all of whose members maintain face-to-face relationships with one another. (Murdock 1949: 79–80, cited in Morgan 1957a: 20)

Morgan believed that the small community was the fundamental unit of human cultural evolution and the "foundation of democratic life" (Morgan 1942).

For the preservation and transmission of the fundamentals of civilization, vigorous, wholesome community life is imperative. Unless many people live and work in the intimate relationships of community life, there never can emerge a truly unified nation, or a community of mankind. If I do not love my neighbor whom I know, how can I love the human race, which is but an abstraction? If I have not learned to work with a few people, how can I be effective with many? (Morgan 1942: 19)

Morgan also believed that the small community, and with it individual freedom and democracy, was under threat from modern, industrial society.

In an industrial society, where the intimate and refining influences of small communities are rapidly disappearing and where great, centralized, impersonal organizations are in control, [we] may lose many of the values of the old community and may retain its worst features, that of servitude and suppression of individuality.

On the other hand, modern "free initiative" such as has prevailed in England and America, through great concentration of economic power has robbed the average man of much of his freedom, but has failed to retain a sense of mutual regard and responsibility. This form of irresponsible power is not the best defense against the evils of totalitarianism.

The problem of community, as of all society, is to save and to enlarge the priceless values of freedom, while yet developing qualities of mutual regard, mutual help, mutual responsibility and common effort for common ends. That is the problem of democracy. (Morgan 1942: 280–281)

Morgan referred to community in two different senses: as a quality of social life and as a name for local population groups. He defined community in terms of personal interactions, mutual interests, mutual responsibility, and common, coordinated action.

A community is an association of individuals and families that, out of inclination, habit, custom and mutual interest, act in concert as a unit in meeting their common needs. (Morgan 1942: 20)

A community [exists] through direct personal acquaintance and relationships, in a spirit of fellowship. Its members are people who to a considerable extent have cast their lots together, who share problems and prospects, who have a sense of mutual responsibility and who actually plan and work together for common ends. There must be mutual understanding, respect and confidence. There must be mutual aid—willingness to help in need, not as charity, but simply as the normal mode of community life. There must be a feeling on the part of each individual that he is responsible for the community welfare. There needs to be a common background of experience, a community of memory and association and a common foreground of aims, hopes and anticipations. There must be a considerable degree of unity of standards and purposes. (Morgan 1942: 22–23)

A superficial reading of Morgan's work might lead to the impression that he believed one either lived in community or one lived without it. His view, however, was more complex than this.

Whatever romantic notions about community Morgan may have held, he made an effort to consider some of the complexities of social life in his writings. He understood that some valuable aspects of the small community do exist in large metropolitan areas and even in large corporations. He also recognized that the development of urban, industrial society freed people from the banalities and prejudices of life in small communities. Small community was not the ultimate manifestation of a good life and metropolitan life was not necessarily in direct contrast to the small community. For Morgan, community was not just an abstract ideal, but rather was connected to all aspects of social life. In his book *The Small Community* (1942), he examined community as an evolutionary, cultural, and historical phenomenon and considered its significance in relation to human health, recreation, religion, and to larger political and economic units.

Morgan's discussion of the small community in relation to political economies of scale includes a lengthy discussion of what, in more recent decades, we might call bioregionalism (Carr 2004, Lockyer and Veteto 2013, Sale 2000). Morgan's discussion along these lines grows from his belief that modern industrial economies were destroying small communities. His narrative encapsulates this critique and emphasizes the idea that more self-reliant communities will be characterized by better cultural life and higher standards of living.

Economic development in America has been partly arbitrary and accidental. There are vast potentialities for efficient local production for local use which have not been realized. A nation-wide development of local and community regionalism might greatly enrich our national life, add variety and indigenousness to our culture and industry, greatly raise the standard of living, and furnish more interesting careers for young people. As in any pioneering, the achievement of this will be a long, difficult job, though a great contribution to American culture.

Always such regional self-sufficiency should be approached realistically and not sentimentally. It should go only so far as the economics and the social values of the situation justify. But that is much further than the public yet realizes. There is no wealth created and no over-all good served simply by shipping goods back and forth, when they can as well be produced locally, with increased variety and income for local people. Many a small community could economically supply more of its own food, services, and supplies. (Morgan 1942: 76)

This discussion suggests that Morgan was thinking about sustainability long before the concept became prominent or the subsequent sustainability discourse arose. It also demonstrates that he understood that the solution to the problems he perceived was not to simply create small communities in isolation. Rather it was to find ways to incorporate the intimate associations, the mutual responsibility and regard, and the common endeavors of small communities into the larger fabric of life in a rapidly developing world. His was essentially a utopian vision of a more ideal society, a cultural critique cast against the trends of modern American life as understood from Morgan's particularly privileged position.

Even as he developed and refined his vision of the importance of the small community, Morgan designed and directed some of the largest industrial-scale projects of the early twentieth century: the Miami Conservancy District (MCD) and the Tennessee Valley Authority (TVA). Even in these top-down initiatives of technocratic state planning, Morgan incorporated his bioregional perspective and his belief in the significance of the small community at fundamental levels. In designing flood control projects, Morgan, like John Wesley Powell before him, recognized that it was geographical watershed characteristics rather than current political jurisdictions that should form the basis for his engineering plans. But his focus was not only on engineering; in both the MCD and the TVA, he devoted significant attention to the planning and implementation of cooperative associations as well as small communities where laborers on the projects and local residents could form intimate, relatively self-sufficient, and largely self-governed small communities. The town of Norris, Tennessee, which Morgan designed as part of his TVA duties and where he lived for some time, is a lasting legacy of this approach even if he was unable to convince Roosevelt and the other TVA directors to build similar towns elsewhere in the TVA region. His establishment at the same time of the Tennessee Valley Associated Cooperatives, an organization that would "promote, organize, establish, manage, finance, coordinate, and assist in the development of cooperative enterprises in the Tennessee Valley" including "cooperative ventures for mills, dairies, and producers of handicrafts" along with a cannery, is another manifestation of Morgan's "early TVA vision for preserving the region's folkways through building small but intertwined communities" (Purcell 2014: 162–163).

When President Franklin Delano Roosevelt selected Arthur Morgan as first director of the Tennessee Valley Authority, one of Roosevelt's signature New Deal Programs, Morgan saw it as a unique opportunity to combine his passions for flood control engineering and social engineering and to scale them both up. As Scott (2006) has noted, the Great Depression opened up unique opportunities for top-down government programs designed to remake society through scientific planning and technological progress. Scott describes the TVA as "the most ambitious attempt in American history to improve the general welfare of millions of people on the basis of plans laid by a vast regional public authority and directed by a technical intelligentsia" (2006: 18). Under the directorship of Morgan and his codirectors David Lilienthal and H. A. Morgan (no relation), the TVA "was *the* original, comprehensive, integrated development scheme," one designed to

> build dams (thereby preventing floods and promoting navigation), generate cheap electricity, encourage industry, start cooperatives, train workers, build schools and clinics, conserve topsoil, replant denuded forests, teach modern agriculture, personal hygiene and sanitation, improve diet, and, in general transform a static, underdeveloped subsistence society into a dynamic, growing, productive society. (Scott 2006: 20)

This form of authoritarian, high-modernist initiative aligned well with Morgan's Progressive outlook; it provided an opportunity to overlay a comprehensive plan on a society he believed was in need of progress and improvement.

The fact that Arthur Morgan took the lead in the founding of Celo Community at the same time, the mid- to late 1930s, that he was acting as first director of the Tennessee Valley Authority is an embodiment of the contradictions that often characterized Morgan's life. On the one hand, the comprehensiveness of Morgan's vision for what the TVA could do is characteristic of Scott's high modernists; the project was not just about flood control and power production, it was also about top-down social engineering on a quite broad scale. It was a project that would, like other authoritarian high-modernist projects, use scientific expertise to justify its reordering of local society and its working around of existing local political structures. It would largely wipe the slate clean, creating a new social order that discounted local experience, knowledge, and practice with a plan created by experts and designed down to the last detail.

On the other hand, Morgan's vision for Celo Community, an endeavor for which he facilitated the purchase of 1,200 acres and provided a rough initial plan during his TVA tenure, was much more open ended and experimental. A description of the Celo project, prepared by Morgan about the time of its establishment attests to this:

> There is no effort to seek agreement beforehand on any theory of social organization. People are not desired who would come primarily as proselytes of any particular way of reforming society and who would plan to force their views on the community. . . . They can work out gradually such types of cooperative undertakings and other social organization as seem suitable. (Morgan 1939: 8)

A letter Morgan wrote to a man hired to serve as community "manager" while the initial organization of the community was worked out further supports the idea that Morgan did not intend for Celo to proceed according to some predetermined plan of his own making. In the letter, Morgan specifically notes that he and the other directors of the project would be open to and welcoming of critique and suggestions from those most directly involved in developing the community:

> Disagreement in details, and sometimes in quite important matters, is one of the natural conditions of working together. Where there is mutual confidence and respect, the working out of those differences is one of the ways by which we can avoid serious errors. The directors of the project will have to rely on you a great deal, and will want your candid opinions. An attitude of deference is not wanted and is not helpful. You should feel entirely free to criticize the policies and methods of the Board and its members as they should feel in criticizing any part of your administration. (cited in Ohle 1957: 28–29)

Morgan further stated that he aimed for the community to take over complete control of community finances, property titles, and decision-making from the original board, composed of himself, William H. Regnery, and Clarence Pickett, once a stable nucleus of community members had been established. Thus, at the same time that Morgan was implementing one of the most rigorously planned, modern, industrial-scale projects ever undertaken, he was also setting in motion a small-scale, open-ended experiment in intentional community building, a community that would "establish a tradition of open critical inquiry in all fields without exception" and that "may have entire control over its destiny" (Morgan 1939: 7–8).

Whether it be achieved through top-down state planning or bottom-up grassroots experiment, Morgan believed that the most fundamental task that confronted humans in modern industrialized societies was the reincorporation of small community life. He believed that there are three ways to approach revitalizing communities and bringing about social betterment. One is violent revolution, an approach that was incongruent with his pacifist stances. A second is gradual reform of existing communities, an approach that characterized his work in Yellow Springs, Ohio, and that formed part of the philosophy he brought to the TVA. The third approach, which he advocated most vigorously in the creation of Celo Community, his creation of the nonprofit Community Service, Inc., and his participation in founding the Fellowship of Intentional Communities in the 1940s (later the Fellowship for Intentional Community and now the Foundation for Intentional Communities), is the creation of "intentional communities" where new and better patterns are experimented with (Morgan 1957a: 139–144).

As an early supporter of the development of an organized network of intentional communities, Morgan decried the fact that "it has been popular to smile at 'utopian' or planned communities as freakish and futile efforts of erratic cults" (1957a: 139). He believed that intentional communities had been unnecessarily dismissed by the general population and that the historical contributions of intentional communities to the unique achievements of American society had been obscured by an obsessive focus on progress through industrial expansion. He noted that while many intentional communities of the past had failed to achieve their stated goals, an even greater number of start-up businesses also failed during their early stages. Noting the many examples of historic and contemporary intentional communities in the United States and outlining some of their contributions to social progress, Morgan believed that the revitalization of small community life could be fostered through the promulgation of intentional communities and the promotion of networking among them.

To promote small community revitalization and the establishment of intentional communities, Morgan established Community Service, Inc. In his book *The Community of the Future*, Morgan reflected on the work of this organization:

> Since the establishment of Community Service, Inc., about 15 years ago, we have contended that the face-to-face community is a fundamental and necessary unit of society; that, along with the family, it has been and continues to be the chief medium for transmitting the basic cultural inheritance. . . . Because the part which it has played and probably must continue to play in our common life has been much overlooked, we have persistently drawn attention to its importance. (Morgan 1957a: 3)

Community Service served as an information clearinghouse and networking center for research on the role of the small community and for the promotion of community development and intentional community projects. Through the involvement of one of Arthur Morgan's granddaughters and her family,

Community Service continued to promote the idea that the small community has grown even more significant in the context of global environmental crises. In the early twenty-first century, the main thrust of their efforts was to promote small, self-reliant communities as solutions to the problems that society will face with the depletion of world oil reserves and what they believed was the coming collapse of the oil economy. Its mission statement at the time stated that "Community Service is dedicated to the development, growth and enhancement of small local communities. We envision a country where the population is distributed in small communities that are sustainable, diverse and culturally sophisticated" (Community Service, Inc. 2007).

More recently, Community Service has been reorganized as the Arthur Morgan Institute for Community Solutions (AMICS). The current mission statement maintains a focus on communities: "The Arthur Morgan Institute for Community Solutions seeks to educate people around the world about ways to make their communities more resilient, vital, and capable of withstanding dramatic shifts due to climate and economic disruptions" (AMICS 2019). The organization maintains strong roots in its original community in small town Yellow Springs, Ohio, working with a variety of community partners and using a recently purchased farm property as a demonstration site for experimenting with environmentally, economically, psychologically, and socially regenerative practices.

Arthur Morgan's life and work have been the subject of numerous publications (Kahoe 1977; Leuba 1971; Talbert 1987; Purcell 1997, 2000, 2001, 2002, 2003, 2014). Many of these works focus on Morgan's idealistic promotion and development of small community models in a variety of contexts. At least one historian labeled Arthur Morgan a utopian in the title of his book about him (Talbert 1987), noting his similarities with other historical utopians, writers, and founders of intentional communities: Robert Owen, Charles Fourier, Count de Saint Simon, and Edward Bellamy. Purcell, in his more recent biography of Morgan, recognizes the important influence of utopian thought on Arthur Morgan's philosophy, but questions whether or not it is appropriate to refer to him as a utopian, preferring instead to use the term "visionary." However, Celo Community, perhaps Morgan's most significant intentional community-building endeavor, is only discussed as an afterthought in four paragraphs at the end of Purcell's biography and receives very little mention in any of the other works about Morgan. Only Hicks devoted significant effort to the analysis of Arthur Morgan's role in the founding of Celo Community (Hicks 2001). Although Morgan did not live in Celo, and while his influence on the community was mostly indirect and through consultation after its first decade of existence, the community is, in many ways, a direct manifestation of Morgan's utopian vision and his belief in the significance of the small community as the primary center of cultural evolution.

NOTE

1. Language between the brackets was added by the community in 2018 and is the only revision to the constitution since it was first adopted in the 1940s. Celo Community is currently revising language throughout their governing documents to make them more gender-inclusive. As of this writing, those revisions have not been completed and I have retained the current language throughout this book.

Chapter 2

Cultivating Intentional Community Commons

A History of Celo Community

In the wake of the Great Depression, doubts about the viability of "the new economic era" were widespread in America (Morgan 1957b: 1). Unemployment was rampant and many people's livelihoods, built up on Wall Street, had come crashing down. In addition, more and more people, especially young people, were moving from their hometowns and small communities to industrial and urban centers seeking economic opportunity and cultural variety. In Morgan's perception, small town, community life was disappearing and along with it, the small farm heritage. One of Morgan's biographers notes that "for [Morgan] . . . the depression was clear evidence of the failure of a ruthless, competitive society and indication that the country needed another kind of foundation. The very survival of modern society seemed to him to require a new system" (Talbert 1987: 123).

For Morgan, this economic and sociocultural climate suggested that his philosophies regarding the importance of small community be put into action through the creation of a cooperative intentional community. In the mid-1930s, Morgan was approached by William H. Regnery[1] of Chicago, a wealthy industrialist and owner of a textile mill, who wanted to use some of his fortune "to endow some project of substantial social value" (cited in Miller 1990: 71). Morgan suggested that they buy some land where they could "provide a physical setting in which young people might undertake to get footholds in self directed activities" (Morgan 1957b: 2) and where they might

> maintain a considerable degree of freedom from the pressures and compulsions of the going economic regime, with the aim of using that freedom to try to orient themselves to the economic world in ways that would be in harmony with what they considered to be fundamental ethical considerations. (Morgan 1957b: 1)

Although Morgan and Regnery did not have "any formal ideology in mind," their desire was to allow for a place where like-minded people might live in self-governing proximity and where children might be raised to acquire "personal integrity, considerateness and simplicity of taste" through their social and economic environment (Morgan 1957b: 8). In their endeavor to find such a place, Morgan and Regnery were joined by Clarence Pickett. As executive secretary of the American Friends Service Committee, a Quaker relief and service organization that Morgan had become involved with, Pickett shared their concerns about economic trends and community life. He also had appropriate experience, having been involved with the Division of Subsistence Homesteads and the Independence Foundation, respectively government and private organizations dedicated to promoting cooperative community homesteading and self-sufficiency in the aftermath of the Great Depression.

CELO AS EXPERIMENTAL COOPERATIVE COMMUNITY: UTOPIAN RESPONSES TO THE GREAT DEPRESSION

Where could these three men find a setting for their envisioned community? Where could they translate Regnery's financial endowment, Pickett's concerns, and Morgan's vision into a community project that would address the needs of the time? Among the main considerations for the location of his envisioned community were climate, natural setting, and character of the local residents whom Morgan wished to be honest, hardworking, and independent. But most important were the feasibility of agriculture and the possibility for local economic development. Morgan wanted to be sure that the experimental cooperative community would not be so close to any urban or industrial centers so as to come under the sway of the economic currents and attendant social disconnection prevalent in the cities and not so far as to impede all commerce and communication. He wanted the participants in his community to develop their own patterns of life and livelihood as much as possible, without outside influence. Mainly through the efforts of Arthur Morgan's son Griscom Morgan, a search for suitable land culminated in the purchase of approximately 1,200 acres in the Appalachian Mountains of western North Carolina in 1937.

Arthur and Griscom Morgan located Celo's land with the help of S.T. Henry, one of Arthur Morgan's acquaintances from the nearby town of Spruce Pine, North Carolina. Henry was a local dairy farmer who was, according to Morgan, "well informed on land conditions in the locality" of the South Toe Valley (Morgan 1957b: 2). Morgan relates that people in the valley were reluctant to part with their land.

With very high birthrates in the mountain area there was great pressure for cultivable land. Every nook and corner of such ground was valued. The steep mountainsides were still being cleared for the four or five crops which could be produced before the soil would be washed away. . . . The little flat patches of farm land in the valleys were being sold at about the same price per acre as the broad, fertile farms of Illinois. During the depression this was about $100 to $150 an acre. . . . The abandonment of thousands of these mountain farms, which has since taken place, was not in evidence at that time. (Morgan 1957b: 3)

Celo's 1,200 acres were purchased from three local families. One 1,023 acre parcel had been in the Erwin family for over a century. Ten to fifteen percent of this land had been cleared for agriculture and "the usual farming methods of the region had resulted in considerable deterioration" of the soil (Morgan 1957b: 3). Some of the rest had been cut for timber, but much of it remained undeveloped. Griscom Morgan located Mr. Erwin in eastern North Carolina and convinced him to sell his property for $20 an acre. "It was the fact of ownership of the Erwin tract as a unit, by a nonresident family which was down in finance, with the present owner growing old and with no son interested in carrying on, and with the buildings and cleared land run down, which caused the land to be available" (Morgan 1957b: 3). Upon selling their land to Arthur Morgan, the Erwin family retained a one-acre plot of land and a small cabin for use as a summer home, a property that remains with the family to this day near the geographical center of Celo Community.

The remainder of Celo's 1,200 acres was purchased from the Autrey and Ballew families and the number of acres would have been higher had negotiations with the Patton and Hall families not failed. Two members of the Autrey family parted with approximately 153 acres for an average price of $48 per acre. The Ballew family sold four of their eight lots totaling 36 acres for slightly under $8 per acre. The price paid for the Autrey tracts was much higher because they were cleared, flat bottomland whereas the Ballew land was steep and uncleared terrain in the foothills of the Blue Ridge (Ohle 1957).[2] The title to the land and the operating budget for the community enterprise were held in trust by the American Friends Service Committee, under the direction of Clarence Pickett, until the community was sufficiently organized to receive title and take control over the budget. This took place in the early 1940s. In the meantime, the community organization received a certificate of incorporation as a nonprofit corporation from the state of North Carolina in 1938.

Looking back at the purchase of Celo's land in 1957, Morgan recounted the advantages and disadvantages that he and Griscom considered. Under advantages, Morgan included size, contiguity, and price of the land, aesthetic context, availability of fresh water, availability of timber for community needs and revenue, climate, and the character of the neighbors. Disadvantages included the fact that the soils were in poor condition due to unsustainable farming practices and timber extraction, susceptibility of the area to frost and fog, and perhaps too great a distance from railroads or cities, although Morgan thought it important that some such distance be maintained. Morgan was also concerned about the land tenure arrangements between current tenants and absentee landlords under which

> the usual terms of lease commonly resulted in sharp conflict of interest between owner and tenant. It was commonly to the tenant's interest to take everything possible out of the land, and not to go to any expense in putting anything back. On the whole, the prevailing tenantry practice was degrading, both to the tenant and to the land. (Morgan 1957b: 5)

Thus, Morgan recognized early on that developing an alternative form of land tenure would be a fundamental undertaking of the new community were it to be sustainable. Although Morgan originally intended to include local families as participants in the experimental community he envisioned, it soon became apparent that their land use practices and goals did not coincide with his vision for the community nor with the values and goals that people from outside the region brought to the cooperative endeavor he envisioned. The idea of an experimental, cooperative intentional community was foreign to local families, most of whom saw involvement in the community as an opportunity for upward economic mobility. Indeed, many of the locals referred to the community as "the company" during its early years and viewed their relationship with it in terms of employer and employee (Hicks 2001). However, Morgan saw the community as a moral alternative to predominant economic trends and did not want participation in it to be used as means of individual financial gain. Although one local family did formally join and remain in the community for many decades, arrangements were ultimately reached with all tenant families for their removal from land that the community now owned.

UTOPIAN VISIONS AND PRELIMINARY STRUGGLES

Morgan's visions for an experimental intentional community that would provide solutions to the problems of the Great Depression and of modern industrial society in general did not immediately gain momentum in the South Toe Valley. There were a series of fits and starts in Celo Community in the late 1930s and early 1940s. Morgan had trouble recruiting participants and those that did participate during this period, be they local residents or people who came from outside the area, did not share his vision. Agricultural equipment was purchased but the participants were not especially successful in either cultivation or marketing of agricultural products. Initial member recruits were inexperienced either with agriculture or with cooperative enterprise, and there was little market for their products within a reasonable distance over difficult roads. Working out a land tenure arrangement that would bind individual members into a cooperative whole was an issue that occupied significant time and energy.

Morgan's designs for the community were grand and visionary. In the increasing pace and large-scale organization of American life, Morgan saw the destruction of small community ideals and interaction that he believed were the foundation of human civilization and cultural development. He wanted to provide a place where a small community could be created that would serve as a model for the establishment of other such communities. Eventually, he thought that through networking, these communities might be a major source of social and cultural revitalization. In a letter, Morgan articulated that he saw Celo as a beginning.

> To a large degree the small community is the key to the future of culture and civilization. In view of the great importance of small communities to the destiny of our country, it is important that there should be a deliberate and conscious design and planning of community life and organization, to the end that the innate great possibilities of the small community be realized. . . . Celo Community aims to be one such undertaking. (Morgan 1939: 3)

Morgan's designs for Celo Community were vague but not without some detail. In the document quoted above, he describes numerous components—the types of people, the kind of social environment and the numerous options for economic activity with an aim of economic self-sufficiency—that he envisioned for the community. He suggested that working out new forms of governance and land tenure would be necessary in order to balance community and individual interests. Morgan (and Regnery and Pickett who were less directly involved) left the working out of the practicalities of this vision to the people who would live in the community, although he did make suggestions through correspondence and occasional visits.

What awaited the first settlers of the community was mostly undeveloped land and very little infrastructure. A paved highway ran through the valley, but there was relatively little commerce, even in agriculture; while wage employment was increasing, most local household economies were still based to a significant degree on subsistence agriculture accompanied by hunting and gathering in the de facto forest commons on surrounding lands. The purchased land had been poorly managed by the tenants of absentee landlords and there were only about 70 acres of cleared land and two habitable buildings to begin with (Ohle 1957: 16). At this point, the provisions of any tenure agreement were vague, but Morgan saw the development of such an agreement as a primary concern. In a letter to Regnery's son Henry in November 1937, Morgan stated, "Just now I am trying to find time to write out my idea of plans for [Celo's] development, and land tenure looms as one of the important elements" (Morgan 1937). The original tenancy agreements of 1938 reflect the idea of rewarding tenants for the improvement of their landholdings in terms of agricultural productivity and habitability by paying for their labor in such efforts and for any improvements that they made if they were to leave the community. Morgan's vision for the community did not include the granting of deeds to private individuals. The land was to be both site and source for community building and not for individual financial benefit.

In his letter to Henry Regnery, Morgan elaborated on his ideas about land tenure in Celo, indicating that the community should have significant control over the development of the land tenure experiment based on experience as the relationships between individual community members and the community as a cooperative whole is worked out:

> The problem as I see it is to . . . formulate a set of general controlling principles, and then to allow a common law of tenure to develop, case by case, in conformity with these general principles. . . . The general principles of land tenure would be subject to modification and development in the community. . . . The overall aim would be to remove arbitrariness and caprice in exercising both rights and privileges of tenure on the one hand, and responsibilities and limitations of tenure on the other; and to justify confidence in the security of reasonable tenure, while also establishing the dominance of general or community interests over private or personal interests. (Morgan 1937)

As with resource-based commons anywhere, Morgan wanted to guide the community toward an arrangement that balanced the meeting of individual needs with group interests and control. He suggested that "the tenure should be secure enough to justify investment in the land" by individual community members while also indicating that "all tenure should be under final servitude to the public interest" of the community as a whole. He saw a need for individuals to have enough security of tenure to know that any improvements they made on the land in order to meet their needs for economic production could not be usurped by the community. But he also wanted to give the community the power to ensure that individuals were held to standards of "excellence of use" such that they were not degrading the land in pursuit of short-term profit. He thought that certain "zoning rights" should be reserved to the community and that "certain kinds of . . . lands might be held in common by the community and perhaps leased from year to year" by individual members (Morgan 1937).

He stated that such community lands might serve a variety of purposes. Among these were "recreation grounds, for water supply sources, and as 'little wildernesses' where solitude may be available for those who crave it" (Morgan 1937). Morgan had previously pointed out the need for land stewardship in Celo as a way to ensure sustainable economic production by, for example, limiting the soil erosion and unsustainable timber harvests that characterized previous land use in the valley, especially by tenants renting from individual, absentee landowners. He stated that "there should be considerable tolerance in deciding what is a good use of land. A writer or a business man or a farmer might want to keep a piece of unspoiled land as a setting for his home or for his life. Physical productiveness might not be the only measure of good use" (Morgan 1937).

In this way, Morgan helped shape the unique common land tenure arrangements that characterize Celo to this day. In doing so, he recognized the uniqueness of the arrangement the community was creating and his hope that it might serve as a model. In a memo dated September 1940 entitled "Some Notes About the Plan for Celo" and apparently intended to be sent to specialists in the field of land tenure as an introduction to Celo's working land tenure contract, Morgan stated:

Since most people have no experience with land holding except for outright ownership or renting, they may not at first see what we are arriving at. While we have given a great deal of thought to the most desirable arrangements for land holding, and are continuing to study the matter with specialists in that field, the land holders may have suggestions that will be helpful. They can go ahead in the development of their properties knowing that any value they add by their work is an investment which they will not lose if they should leave for any reason. We have tried to work out arrangements that will make the interest of the individual holder be the same as the interest of the community as a whole. If we do a good job in this we may set a standard that can be used over the country. (Morgan 1940)

At first, Morgan included both local families and people from outside the area in his experiment. The first participants included three or four local men and three families who came as a result of Morgan's association with the president of an Adventist college in Tennessee. By the end of 1939, all but one of the original participants had left the valley or withdrawn from membership in the community. This chain of events repeated itself again over the next several years; both local families and those that came from other areas did not appear to understand Morgan's aims and became dissatisfied with life in his experimental community. Community managers were brought in to directly oversee the affairs of the community and to provide direction, but there were conflicts over the nature of the community and over the extent and nature of the managers' authority. Morgan and others, including the community managers, recruited people to join the community, but most left either because of an inability to get along as a community, or because it was unfeasible to make a comfortable living. The community farming business was unproductive, not due to lack of effort, but rather to lack of knowledge and experience and because of the relative absence of a market for agricultural products and the vagaries of nature. Beyond agriculture and due to the low population density and minimal reliance on a cash economy in the area, there just wasn't much of a market for easy start-up business ventures in the valley (Ohle 1957).

Morgan asked his community managers to recruit people of differing backgrounds and abilities when he could not do the recruiting himself. He wanted people with complementary skills and abilities to join the community. He also suggested that they create a type of labor exchange system whereby members of the community could trade their skills, services, labor, and products among themselves to compensate for the inability to establish a solid monetary income. The labor exchange did not last long due to conflicts about the varying quality of work and reliability of various laborers. Most of the people who were convinced to join in the enterprise, especially recruits from the local population, saw the community as an opportunity for their own economic betterment. While Morgan was dedicated to making the community economically viable, he did not want it, and the money he and his cofounders poured into it, to serve as a welfare institution for local people or for settlers from more distant areas. Celo was an experiment in cooperative community that required sacrifice and dedication. These were largely absent in the early years as recruits to the community, lacking Morgan's vision, continued to draw down the remains of William Regnery's original endowment. They made little progress in terms of economic self-sufficiency or the development of cooperative governance or land tenure institutions.

Repeatedly, Morgan's idealistic, theoretical vision for the community, grounded as it was in his own relatively privileged position, came head-to-head with the sociocultural and political-economic realities on the ground. Morgan's expectations were unrealistic for local residents, many of whom were scrambling for an economic foothold following generations of poverty associated with the ongoing enclosure of the de facto commons around them and, more recently, with the Great Depression. For them, wealthy outsiders coming in and buying up the land around them was part of the problem, not the solution and their desire to take advantage of the opportunities Morgan offered makes perfect sense from their relatively disadvantaged perspective. It was unrealistic to expect them to make sacrifices and dedicate themselves to an abstract cooperative endeavor dreamed up by a privileged outsider who spent very little time in the area and was inexperienced with their daily realities. On the other hand, while Morgan's relatively abstract ideas about cooperation and community may have been appealing to some of the recruits that he and his community managers brought in from outside areas, the realities of making a living from the land were challenging, especially to those inexperienced with working the land and with no experience working with each other. Morgan's theoretical ideas about cooperative community did not magically translate into workable models as quickly as he had hoped.

As the United States prepared to enter World War II, the national economy began to recover from the dark times of the Great Depression. As more economic opportunities opened up around the country, it became difficult to attract the type of industrious and ethical person that Morgan sought, people who found themselves unemployed during the Great Depression and eager for opportunities. As the community's previous ethnographer George Hicks notes,

> The Community, a child of the Great Depression, was stunted in its anticipated growth by the sudden recovery from that depression. Those who wanted to disengage themselves from industrial work and its attendant social life failed to respond to the alternative [Morgan] offered. Changes wrought in United States society by the approaching war, however, were to have important consequences for Celo Community. (Hicks 1969: 41)

Celo Community would soon provide a nexus for people who were critical of the direction of American society and saw in the community an opportunity to live according to their values, to create alternative social institutions and to support each other in their endeavors. Some of these newcomers more closely shared Morgan's vision.

QUAKERS AS CULTURAL CRITICS: PACIFISTS HELP BUILD CELO COMMUNITY

Just as World War II initiated a recovery in the economy, it also instigated a civil movement of conscientious objectors against involvement in the war and the "war system." Over 13,000 of these conscientious objectors were sent to Civilian Public Service (CPS) camps where they exchanged their labor for their service in the American military. One of these camps was located at Buck Creek Gap in the Blue Ridge Mountains near Celo Community. Arthur Morgan visited this and several other such camps and engaged in long discussions about his ideas regarding community with the men he found there. He liked the character of these men and invited several of them to participate in the activities at Celo Community when they had free time, and to come join the community when their service was completed. The longest-standing member of Celo Community at the time of my initial research there recalls,

> I was one of the last C.O.'s [conscientious objectors] to come here after the war. We spent about five years in other things. These other guys came as soon as they got out of the Civilian Public Service, the alternative service. They had had their aim on coming over here and as soon as they were out, they came right over. It was '46 or '47 they sort of dribbled in. But we didn't get here until '51 because of these other things we had done. (Interview with author in Celo Community on April 17, 2001)

The pacifist stance of many of the conscientious objectors grew out of their Quaker heritage; peace and nonviolence were fundamental components of their spiritual beliefs. When their terms in the CPS camps were up, some of these conscientious objectors arrived in Celo. Those that brought their Quaker heritage and values to Celo during this time provided a foundation that anchors the community to this day. As Morgan himself was a converted Quaker, many of their perspectives were congruent with his. At this point, in Celo Community's development, the critical stances that Quakers adopted toward the predominant culture join Arthur Morgan's philosophies as fundamental cultural building blocks of Celo Community. A brief discussion of Quakerism is thus appropriate at this time.

Quakerism is an emancipatory body of spiritual beliefs and practices whose history dates back over 350 years. Like the Anabaptists, the Seekers, and the Diggers, the Quakers emerged as a critical response to the Protestant theocracy that ruled in England in the mid-seventeenth century. The Quakers, or Religious Society of Friends as they call themselves, sought emancipation from religious dogma and hegemony. They believed that direct connection with the divine was available to all.

> Although firmly rooted in Christianity, Quakerism has never had a fixed set of theological creeds. Friends have generally felt that it is the reality of a person's religious experience that matters, not the symbols with which she tries to describe this experience. A direct experience of God is open to anyone who is willing to sit quietly and search diligently for it, Quakers believe. There are no prerequisites for this experience, neither the institution of the church, nor its sacraments, nor a trained clergy, nor even the wisdom of the Bible, unless read and illuminated by the Christ Within, or Inner Light. (Bacon 1999: 3–4)

Quakers were persecuted in both England and in the New World, but they persisted in their beliefs. They saw the hypocrisy of the church and the disjuncture between religious ideals and empirical realities and they sought to overcome them in their lives. As a result of their beliefs and experiences, Quakers developed strong values of peace, democracy, equality, religious and civil liberty, social justice, and simplicity. They seek to put these values into practice in their daily lives. They champion the causes of oppressed groups including Native Americans, other racial and ethnic minorities, and women. They work to improve the lots of prisoners, the elderly, the poor, and the mentally ill and they organize to deliver relief to people displaced by wars and political instability (Bacon 1999).

The attempt to live according to their values leads them to protest, to experiment, to assist, and to seek to empower those whom they wish to help.

> The programs run by the Quakers are almost all very small. They can properly be regarded as pilot projects, experiments, which, if successful, can be turned over to community groups, to the government, or to the schools for implementation. . . . This fact permits Quakers to experiment with new ideas in social change and keeps them in the pioneering frontier of social reform. (Bacon 1999: 150)

These experimentalists and pioneering social reformers were just the sort of people that Morgan sought for Celo Community.

A willingness to reform and to experiment were not all that the Quakers brought with them to Celo Community. The Quaker custom of simplicity also fit quite well with Morgan's romantic vision of a small community free from the encumbrances of modern industrial life.

> Quakers avoid conspicuous consumption. . . . To move one's family halfway across the country in search of a slightly higher salary, a slightly better status, a slightly bigger car, is to be trapped by the unimportant material aspects of life, many Quakers believe. Quakers feel they can keep themselves free—free from making compromises, free to speak their minds . . . free to devote themselves to spiritual rather than material growth. (Bacon 1999: 222)

These ideals took strong hold in Celo and continue to resonate to this day.

Perhaps the most significant innovation that Quakers brought with them to the community was a tradition of democratic, consensus-based decision-making through which they govern their organizations. This tradition blends spirituality with business in that the process of making decisions that will affect all is felt to be spiritual in nature. The Quaker concept of consensus grows from their belief that the right course of action will be chosen through the process of discussion and debate in which everyone is involved on an equal plane. In this scenario, a minority of one may be justified in preventing consensus from being reached because that one person may hold the right answer (although that person should feel very strongly that this is the case on fundamentally principled grounds). Quakers do not vote; rather they reach "unanimous consent" or a "sense of the meeting," through an "attitude of openness toward other points of view, the patient search for unity beneath diversity, the avoidance of polarization—and the voting that leads to polarization of opposing views" (Bacon 1999: 197; for an in-depth, ethnographic and historical account of Quaker consensus decision-making see Sheeran 1983). This process of consensus decision-making soon became the basis for community self-government in Celo Community.

A belief in the deeply personal nature of religious experience, commitments to peace, democracy, equality, social justice and simplicity, a willingness to experiment in order to live by their values and a tradition of cooperative, consensus decision-making are some of the things that Quakers brought to Celo Community. Through their ongoing presence in the community and through the embedding of their values in the institutions of the community, the Quaker tradition has become a part of Celo Community. While being a Quaker is not a prerequisite for community membership and while the majority of community members today are not in fact Quakers, a Quaker meeting house located near the geographic heart of the community has been used continuously for worship since 1949, and Quaker-inspired values and practices continue as bedrock foundations of community culture.

THE 1940s AND 1950s: A COMMONS COMMUNITY TAKES SHAPE

The early to mid-1940s were pivotal years for Celo Community. Men that had been released from the CPS Camps came with their families and created a stable population for the community for the first time. Most significantly, it was during this time that community members began striving to take greater responsibility for their own finances and self-government. To this end, they devised systematic processes for screening potential community members, organizing land tenure, and conducting community governance. The issues that were raised reflect a growing concern with making the community a viable entity and giving it some direction, of creating a balance between individual freedom and mutual responsibility and cooperation in community affairs. To some extent, the fact that these were issues at all reveals the fact that a community was indeed beginning to take shape. Many of the developments of these years created the foundation upon which the community still rests to this day.

By 1943, the first members who would have a lasting presence in and impact on the community had arrived in residence and some of them had established a cooperative buying club. In 1944, the new membership, now consisting of five families, took some tentative steps toward self-organization and self-government. The first community meeting was held on May 17 of that year with all members participating. In that and subsequent meetings, the members discussed a number of fundamental issues related to the issue of self-governance. These included necessary steps toward taking over decision-making from the board of directors (as per Morgan's original intent), specific procedures for conducting community meetings including the taking and approval of minutes, designing contracts for members to sign, constructing a sound landholding agreement, possible zoning policies, and the creation of community documents such as a constitution and by-laws (Ohle 1957).

In 1945, the institution of community manager was terminated in favor of self-government under the direction of a board of directors composed of Morgan, Regnery, and Pickett. The community organized a committee of five to replace the manager and decided to hold community meetings once every month. By the next year, the committee of five had been disbanded in favor of involving all community members in managing community business, making decisions as a group of equals. By 1946, the community's monthly general meeting had adopted a set of by-laws and was delegating some business to individual committees including those dedicated to zoning issues and the construction of a health center. In 1947, the community established a regular expectation for community members to contribute one day of labor per month to a project of value to the whole community, a community workday tradition that continues to this day (Ohle 1957).

The issue of land tenure was also taken up in 1944. It was clear from several past experiences that allowing for the granting of simple deeds to tracts of community land would not be viable as it provided incentive for defection from the community, resulting in the fragmentation of community land. At least two early member households, in disagreement about the direction of the community or seeking security prior to a long trip abroad, ended their memberships but retained individual possession of the landholdings that they originally obtained from the community, resulting in a small subtraction from the community's collective acreage. This was seen by members as a threat to the community's ongoing viability and stability and prompted them to follow up on Arthur Morgan's concern that the community's land tenure arrangement strike a balance among the advantages of outright individual ownership, maintaining an intact collective land base as a foundation for cooperative community, and providing incentives to not use the land in abusive manners. This required the creation of a new form of land tenure (Ohle 1957).

Work on a landholding agreement progressed, albeit slowly. Morgan, along with some community members, consulted with lawyers, economists, and rural sociologists in their efforts to devise a workable landholding agreement. The document that resulted reflected a balance between the rights of individuals and the interests of the community. This document, the Celo Community Holding Agreement, was adopted by the community in 1946 and revised several times since. To this day, it still functions to define the goals and nature of the community. Hicks attests to this:

> It thus gave visible form to their stated goals of Community Organization. . . . Its provisions against exploitation of the land and natural resources and the general belief that exchanges of land between members and the Community should not contain speculative and immoral elements, added some increment of permanence to the Community's boundaries. Far more than defining the geographical boundaries of their experimental group, the Holding Agreement aided in marking off the ideological and cultural borders of the Community. To belong to the Community was to be party to the Holding agreement. (1969: 109)

In 1945, at the behest of Morgan and Regnery, a cooperative medical care center was created to serve both the members of the experimental community and the residents of the valley. To facilitate this, Morgan recruited a doctor then serving with the U.S. Public Health Service to join the community and staff of what became the Celo Health Center, organized under a separate nonprofit called the Celo Health Education Corporation. The doctor was the last person for whom recruitment to and membership in the community was accompanied by a paying position, as had been true for previous community managers. Arthur Morgan's insistence that he be added as a community member came just at the time that existing members were forming membership selection procedures and seeking independence from the board of directors on which Morgan served. This, combined with the doctor's forceful personality and occasional paternalism, would be a source of some controversy in the community in the coming years.

As part of their striving for political independence from the board of directors and for economic independence from Regnery's funding, community members made a number of decisions regarding financial matters in 1947, decisions that would all have a lasting impact on the community. As they were working on the landholding agreement it had become clear that there was a need for members to know what kind of financial settlement they could expect should they choose to depart from the community. To this end the community decided to limit the community's liability for members' equity in their homes and landholdings, although the specific limits were to be worked out later. They also made the decision to collect rents and per-head assessments from themselves in order to generate funds to pay property taxes and supply their annual operating budget. Additionally, they made the decision to use the remaining portion of Regnery's original endowment—about $7,000 by this time—to supply funds for paying departing members and to make loans to community members for home construction and starting businesses. Finally, recognizing that a former hired community manager had badly mismanaged funds generated from allowing outside parties to cut timber on community land, in 1946 the community decided to reserve timber harvests only for internal needs (Ohle 1957).

By the end of 1946, there were eight member families, including one local family from the valley, all the community houses were full and membership in the community continued to grow. A pamphlet titled "About Celo Community" was printed and distributed. The pamphlet described the purposes of the community:

> To live and work in a small progressive community. To rear children in a wholesome environment where they could become acquainted with nature. To raise some of their own food. To work for themselves—or in small organizations—at callings that would provide simple but adequate living. To cooperate with friends and neighbors in creating a satisfying community life. (Celo Community 1946: 2)

It also reflected the fact that the community was still developing, that the members were not committed to any particular ideology or group enterprise, that they were flexible and experimental in nature.

> No hard and fast plan has been made. Given a careful selection of members, questions of what the community will do, what plans it will make, how much of cooperative effort there shall be and how much individual enterprise—such problems should be worked out by those living in the community. . . . The community does not desire as members persons who are committed to social dogmas and who would try to force them on the community. (Celo Community 1946: 7)

It is difficult to tell what effect this pamphlet had in terms of recruiting new members, but by 1947, the number of families had swelled to fifteen, initiating a discussion about the number of people the community could accommodate while still maintaining its town meeting style of governance. Ten of the twelve male community members in 1947 were conscientious objectors to World War II who came from the CPS camps. In the late 1940s, Quaker community members started a formal Friends meeting and a summer camp for children on community land, both of which remain in the community to this day and have had a lasting impact. It was clear that after ten years, the vague outlines of a community that might resemble what Morgan envisioned were beginning to take shape. The community was growing and prospering.

However, the growth and prosperity that did occur was not in terms of tangible financial success, but rather the sentiment that there was a sense of community beginning to take root. Many of the members shared common values and they undertook to manage their affairs and their assets in a more structured and efficient manner. They sold off much of the farm equipment and livestock that they were maintaining at a cost, although a few individual community members continued to experiment with agricultural production as a way to make a living. They continued to systematize the collection of assessments and rents that they charged themselves rather than relying on Regnery's trust when these could not be met. For the most part, they decided not to pay themselves for their duties to the community as a social entity and corporation or to the land on which it was based. By 1952, the community had achieved financial independence from Regnery's trust fund and in 1953, the membership took over all nominations to the board of directors of Celo Community, Inc., essentially exerting their full control over community affairs.

The community continued to define itself in the 1950s. Part of this involved solidifying their manner of self-government. They used the concept of consensus, in the Quaker sense, to reach a sense of the meeting decisions during community meetings. This allowed all community members equal participation in community decision-making. They also continued to refine their land tenure mechanisms as indicated in another brochure that the community produced to recruit new members. "Members hold their land under a standard form of agreement with the Community that confers most of the rights of ownership but reserves essential social controls, such as zoning, to the Community" (Moody and Toness 1950).

Consensus decision-making in community governance and Celo's unique Holding Agreement, as they developed during this time, became defining aspects of membership in the community. They provided a means to balance the common good with individual aspirations. The collectively held land provided a common focus. Managing it through the consensus decision-making process required that everyone's perspective be considered equally, at least in theory. In order for collective ownership and consensus decision-making to work, the members would have to develop the mutual regard and sense of responsibility that Morgan believed were such important components of small community life. This was not always easy, especially given different personality types and paternalistic attitude of the doctor who ran the health center, but a viable forum for community self-governance took shape.

The brochure produced by the members of the community at the time gives an idea of their developing sense of community identity. The vision for the community included such things as mutual trust, personal sacrifice, intellectual freedom, simple but adequate living, raising food, economic self-sufficiency, and land conservation. It was clear that the community did not believe that they had achieved utopia: "Anyone expecting to find Celo Community a neatly finished product ready to go on display as a model of the perfect community will be appalled by its unfinished roughness" (Moody and Toness 1950: 1). However, they were also forward looking: "As to the future, the pattern remains flexible, leaving individuals and small groups within the Community free to experiment" (Moody and Toness 1950: 3). Celo Community was following Morgan's lead in adopting experimentation and utopian striving for a better kind of community.

Despite the apparent coalescence of Celo Community in the years following World War II, for several families, the new community that was taking shape was not what they were looking for. Indeed, it did not accommodate the more strictly communal and intensely spiritual focus that they sought. Conflicts over control of the newly established Celo Health Center and the nature of the landholding agreement contributed to the tension. This precipitated an exodus from Celo Community in the 1950s.

EXODUS AND DISILLUSIONMENT

In 1954, four families who had been focusing on creating a more materially communal organization and a more spiritually focused life within the community terminated their memberships and left to join other intentional communities including the Bruderhof, or Society of Brothers, and Macedonia in Georgia which was on the verge of converting to be a part of the Bruderhof organization. The Society of Brothers had a historical connection to the Anabaptist Hutterite Bruderhofs, although they were of different and more recent origins in Germany. They also emphasized more spiritually and economically communal characteristics and a greater degree of separation from the broader society than did Celo Community. Celo was still trying to establish an economic basis for itself that would balance communalism and individuality; in its economic communalism, the Bruderhof was more firmly economically grounded. Those searching for a way to support themselves financially and materially in Celo during this time found life difficult due to the lack of solid economic opportunity and they found hope in the Bruderhof with its more established communal economic enterprises. In addition, because Celo lacked any common ideological or religious mandate that defined community membership, the consensus by which the community sought to reach decisions was often hard to come by. It created dissension within the community at times. After a short period of apparent harmony and prosperity during the postwar years, this lack of unity was certainly a contributing factor to the exodus from Celo.

Because several other families left in the early 1950s as well, the exodus of the four families that left for the Bruderhof in 1954 put a serious dent in community membership. A community member who came to Celo in 1951 talks about why people were leaving the community in the mid-1950s:

> Why they left had something to do with their inaccurate idea of how it was going be to live down here. Most of them were educated people and they'd tell tales of growing this great field of beans and picking them and taking them to market in Asheville and then bringing them all home at night and having to can them. I mean it was like they were trying to do something that they weren't really educated to do. Some of them left to get more education and then try to get jobs elsewhere. Some of them left because they wanted more community. There were four families who left to join the Bruderhof. They didn't all stay there, but the Bruderhof is a Christian community that's communal. (Interview with author in Celo Community on April 17, 2001)

Her husband adds that because of the nebulous nature of the community, "the energy in the early 50's when we were just getting started was [focused on] survival and where do we go from here?" (interview with author in Celo Community on April 17, 2001).

In a dramatic memoir written for *Liberation* magazine in 1959 and published under a pen name, a former Celo resident recounts a similar sentiment—the alternating buoyant optimism and demoralizing disenchantment that coursed through the members of the community as they attempted to create their own social entity, to live out Arthur Morgan's experiment: "It was the people who lived there . . . who made Celo a delightful place that first summer. There seemed to be no adequate way to make a living and yet far too much to do. No one had any money, nor was anyone much concerned about it" (Greenbough 1959: 14). By the time she left a few years later, her tone had changed significantly:

> It is sad to think of the gradual disillusionment and bitterness that overtook nearly every one of us. There was perhaps not a single community member who did not know at the end of his first year, that his private utopia would never work. Yet most of us stayed five years—some more—some less, for to leave was the bitterest defeat of all. (Greenbough 1959: 16)

Such disillusionment is reflected in the community records and demographics as well. In 1958, eight community houses sat empty. In the years following World War II, community members had been forced to build houses to keep up with the influx in membership. Now, however, the members were forced to confront the possibility of the community's demise if the community could not keep up with the expense of maintaining vacant, community-owned houses. In 1956, they adopted a provision to their by-laws which declared a state of emergency if the membership were to drop below twenty members. According to this provision, at such a time, the board of directors would assume control and divide the corporate assets among the remaining community members and several charitable organizations.

Hicks believes that the depopulation and disillusionment led to the sentiment that "the utopian optimism which pervaded the community in the few years before and after 1950 had disappeared" (Hicks 1969: 160). However, the defeatism expressed above by Hicks and the former community member was not universally subscribed to by community members. A relatively lengthy article on Celo Community in the December 1957 issue of *The Carolina Farmer* presented a positively upbeat portrait of the community. Based on a day-long visit to the community by the author and a number of interviews with community members, the lead-in to the story read "This little bit of heaven was planned, but there's no standard design for the angels" (Brown 1957: 10). The article is full of optimistic quotations from community members. Clearly not all members of Celo had become disillusioned with the community. Twenty years into his experiment, Arthur Morgan was not ready to concede defeat either. He wrote,

> It takes more than one generation to develop the possibilities of community life and it would seem to be unfortunate if boys and girls growing up at Celo should feel compelled to leave because the home environment has little economic opportunity. . . . It was our belief . . . that if sincere, normal people will work together in reasonableness they will make day by day and year by year decisions which will tend to emerge into something like a desirable pattern. (Morgan 1957b: 8)

Despite all of the discord of the 1950s in Celo and probably little known to the community members at the time, something like a "desirable pattern" had begun to emerge in the community. Cultural currents in the United States over the next two decades would lead to the emergence of a group of people who very much appreciated Morgan's experiment in community. For them, the ideas of stewarding the land rather than speculating on it, of living simply and disconnecting themselves from the modern, industrial political economy and of cooperating with one another, were central tenets. The two longest-standing community members at the time of my initial research spoke with me about the transition that occurred between the 1950s and the 1970s:

> B: Of all those early people, one thing or another led them to leave. Except us and the doctor and his wife and family. So within our first fifteen years the

original community was just about changed. There were very few of us left. There would be temporary people. People coming in and renting a house and seeing how it would go, but they never really committed themselves to it. And then about 1970 or maybe sooner came this shift of younger people wanting to come to this type of an environment and bring their craft with them. Or for some other reason to join in.

P: It was all over the country—the back to the land movement. (Interview with author in Celo Community on April 17, 2001)

BACK-TO-THE-LAND UTOPIANISM
REVITALIZES CELO COMMUNITY

The early 1960s were relatively slow years in Celo Community. A major event was the opening of the Arthur Morgan School in 1962 as a boarding school for grades seven through nine, an initiative spearheaded by Arthur Morgan's daughter-in-law Elizabeth, who moved to Celo and joined the community at this time. The curriculum was imbued with Morgan's educational philosophy regarding the importance of combining the development of practical skills with broad-based knowledge and critical thinking. In the early years of the school, the students were boarded in the homes of community members. Some staff came to the school in the 1960s as conscientious objectors to fulfill their selective service agreement. Some of them decided to stay in the community, thus filling some of the gaps left by those who departed during the previous decade and initiating a pathway to community membership that remains prominent today.

Review and revision of the documents and policies that governed the community had been ongoing within the community since the 1940s, and intensified in the late 1950s and early 1960s before culminating in 1965. The unique aims of the community and the unique nature of their landholding agreement continued to make it difficult to precisely define processes and policies the community wished to formulate given its status as a nonprofit corporation. In 1965, a membership agreement was formulated and added to the landholding agreement that new members were expected to sign when they joined the community. A defined process for becoming a member of the community and an agreement to abide by the community's unique conceptualization of land tenure were both seen by existing members as defining thresholds for participation in their cooperative experiment. The legal advice they had received, while sometimes contradictory, suggested that they would do well to define membership and land tenure in separate documents and to add these to the existing corporate charter and corporate by-laws, the latter of which was still being revised. In addition, community members decided to codify the growing list of rules and guidelines for community member behavior, expectations, and land use that they had made in community meetings by creating a Procedures and Rules document that all members would agree to abide by when they signed their membership and landholding agreements.

Major changes started to take place in community membership around 1970 when the back-to-the-land movement arrived at Celo's doorstep. Frustration with modern, urban, industrial, capitalist society and the political and cultural directions of American life led to a fluorescence of social movements in the late 1960s and early 1970s. Many in these movements, critical of the direction of American society, sought to reestablish the connections and relationships of community life that they felt were missing, connections whose loss Arthur Morgan lamented over a generation previously. Added to this were concerns regarding the environmental destruction and social injustices that resulted from the ascendance of an increasingly global, capitalist political economy. While some responded by joining urban communes, others sought to escape the cities. Either in intentional communities or individually, they sought to live more simply and self-sufficiently, to recreate the small farm agrarian lifestyle of American historical mythos.

> The back-to-the-land movement was, in its own quiet way, a broad-based protest against what the spirit of the sixties saw as the irrational materialisms of urban life. Starting in the mid-1960s and on through the 1970s, each year thousands of urban émigrés found their way to the countryside to set up individual homesteads on a few acres of land. (Jacob 1997: 3)

As Phillips (2019) has documented in his account of the back-to-the-land movement in the Ozarks of Arkansas, back-to-the-landers are an oft-stereotyped group. Frequently portrayed as starry-eyed utopians unprepared for what they encountered in their moves back to the land and as a group who had little lasting impact, the reality is more complex. While some who went back to the land did not endure long, many of them stayed and worked diligently at finding a way to make a living from the land. Many of them, like those who came to Celo, remain where they landed in the 1960s and 1970s, making ongoing contributions to the shape of their broader communities. In their efforts to educate themselves, they often turned to long time local residents, either in the Ozarks or the Appalachians, in whom they recognized a wealth of skills and knowledge that could be useful to them. As such, and as in Phillips's account of the movement in the Ozarks, back-to-the-landers' interactions with local residents belie simple descriptions of juxtaposition, conflict, and opposition. Many local families recognized a kindred spirit and desire for independence among back-to-the-landers even if it might have been embodied in a physical presentation that was out of keeping with local customs. Ultimately, the back-to-the-landers who stayed recognized that the cultural transition that they sought to embark upon would be a long one, starting with their own personal transformation and radiating out from there across the generations in what Phillips describes as a "deep revolution" (2019).

For a number of people, Celo Community proved a congenial place to live out their back-to-the-land ideals. In Celo, they joined the remaining conscientious objectors, the deep revolutionaries from a generation before, in seeking to enact personal and social transformation in a small, cooperative community context. An interview with one couple who came to Celo in the early 1970s is revealing. Both were raised in big cities on the East Coast and trained as artists. They met in school in California, but moved back east seeking jobs and a way to start their life together. They were unsatisfied with the prospects for livelihood in the city; and they were enamored of the back-to-the-land ideals.

> We had gotten caught up in the back-to-the-land idea when we were in California. It was the big thing in the air, that the idealists would move out to communes and communities out on the land . . . looking for a different way, a better way. I think that is what I gravitated to. I always loved being out in the woods and there was something so basic about building your own house, raising some of your own food. Getting back to basics was real appealing to me. (Interview with author in Celo Community on September 22, 2004)

A series of fortuitous coincidences eventually led them to Celo. Reading in *Mother Earth News*, a key publication in the back-to-the-land movement, they happened across a story of a uniquely designed, energy efficient house that had been built in Celo Community in the 1950s. While visiting Penland School of Crafts in an adjacent county, the couple were introduced to a member of Celo Community and invited for a visit. They soon realized that it was the community they had read about in *Mother Earth News*.

Upon further examination, they found that the community neatly matched their desires. "We wanted to be living amongst like-minded people in the country. . . . We wanted people that shared our values—simple living and caring for the land, people that shared our ideals about stewardship of the land and not abusing the land, not speculating on the land" (interview with author in Celo Community on September 22, 2004). Reflecting on their time in Celo Community, this couple finds that the community enabled them to live by their ideals. "Celo really enabled us to be able to start living out our dream, which was to build a little house in the country . . . and to have a garden and raise a family. That's what we wanted and that's what we've done" (interview with author in Celo Community on September 22, 2004). This story encapsulates the experiences of several other community households that came to Celo Community in the late 1960s and early 1970s.

The back-to-the-landers who came to Celo Community revitalized the community and provided a new sense of purpose to the experiment that Celo was designed to be. But they also continued trends that had already begun to manifest themselves within the community. Quaker ideals of simplicity imbued the community beginning in the late 1940s with the arrival of the first lasting community members. The values of land stewardship were already present in the community in Morgan's early conceptualizations and were promoted as part of its purpose as early as 1950 in promotional materials designed by community members. One member of the community had already designed and built two houses that received widespread recognition, including the aforementioned article in *Mother Earth News*, for their innovations in energy efficiency. Most of the houses in the community were small and simple compared with urban standards and many of them were accompanied by home gardens. The back-to-the-landers merely brought these trends to the forefront. As environmental awareness and critical perspectives on the wasteful materialism of American society increased in the 1970s, the values of simple living and self-reliance became common denominators in the community. While over the last two decades there has been a significant undercurrent of self-criticism about growing affluence among community members (often referred to among themselves as the "Celo country club syndrome"), a focus on simple living, a do-it-yourself approach, and shared values and practices of land stewardship remain fundamental community characteristics to this day.

CELO COMMUNITY SINCE THE 1970s: BALANCING ON A COMMONS

Few events as significant as the exodus from the community or the arrival of the back-to-the-land movement have taken place in Celo over the last four or five decades. Most of Celo's current institutional structure was established by the time the back-to-the-landers arrived in the late 1960s and early 1970s. Celo's major institutions—collective land ownership and stewardship, governance by consensus, and the process for being accepted as a member in the community, and the requirement that community members take a landholding and live on the land—have been subject to periodic revision as community members adapted to changing social and environmental contexts, but in their basic form they are products of the Celo's first three decades. Before moving on to an overview of Celo today, I will discuss a number of changes that have occurred over the last four plus decades.

Celo has witnessed a fairly steady increase in membership since the 1970s although this increase is purposely kept to a slow trickle. A long waiting list of potential members has accrued as people have recognized a desirable alternative social arrangement in Celo Community. Celo deliberately restricts the number of member households that may join the community in a given year. As Celo's members come from diverse, albeit mostly racially and ethnically homogenous, backgrounds, the slow process of admitting members is seen as a necessary precaution because Celo's unique governance process and land tenure arrangement require high levels of familiarity and trust among members.

Two particular demographic characteristics of Celo's membership add complexity to this situation. First, a growing number of children of community members, people who grew up in the community, have decided, as adults, that they wish to apply for membership in the community. While second generation members started joining the community some decades ago, this trend has picked up pace in more recent decades. As of this writing, approximately 10 percent of community members (eight total) are second or third generation community members. A second demographic factor affecting community membership is the fact that a significant percentage of community members are reaching old age. An internal analysis conducted by a community member in 2019 indicates that approximately 60 percent of community members are aged sixty or older. Both of these factors have led the community to enact or consider changes to the process for admitting new members. These changes and considerations will be discussed at some length in a subsequent chapter.

When asked about noticeable changes in the community, members who have been in Celo since the 1970s often refer to increasing levels of affluence.

> When we first came here [in the 1970s], it seemed like most of the houses were pretty rough and when I walk around now and look at houses in the community, it seems like they're all rather large and lavish by comparison. Not all, but certainly the mean has gone way up. The economic status of community members in general seems to have gone up considerably. (Interview with author in Celo Community on May 4, 2001)

Greater material affluence along with greater levels of socioeconomic inequality is also reflected in the broader, mainstream society, from which most new members are coming. However, the levels of affluence and inequality characteristic of Celo is not a mirror of the levels of affluence and inequality in the broader society. When one visits Celo, it is apparent that Celo's members are living more modest lifestyles than is true of most suburban, middle-class Americans. While houses in Celo have increased in size and new automobiles are more common than they ever were, most members of Celo maintain a relatively simple standard of living and signs of conspicuous consumption and attendant keep-up-with-the-Jones attitudes are almost completely absent. Given the lack of communal economic enterprises in the community, the financial viability of potential members has long been a concern for existing members. However, this is balanced by the community's repeatedly rearticulated desire to make land accessible to those of lesser economic means by keeping the costs associated with signing a landholding agreement below market value.

An issue that has been of continuing significance in Celo Community since the 1970s is the development of a comprehensive land use plan for their commonly held 1,200 acres. While this topic will also be discussed at length in subsequent chapters, a brief overview here is appropriate given that it was an ongoing topic of discussion in the community in recent decades. This focus on land use planning arises from a desire to determine how many people they can accommodate in their community while maintaining a context of mutual support, a smoothly functioning governance process, and a commitment to ecologically sound land stewardship. With regards to social issues, there is a perceived conflict as to how increasing size will affect social intimacy and governance processes. While not all community members are familiar with each other on equally intimate levels, they do all know each other and provide care and support to each other in times of need. Some believe that including more people in the community will lead to more mutual support and more intimate social relationships while others believe that the opposite will occur. As the community grows, there are more opinions and perspectives to account for in making decisions about community governance. As a result, the process of consensus governance, which requires that all perspectives be considered, can become more challenging and has been experienced as such by a number of community members.

With regards to land stewardship, there is a perceived conflict between increasing community population and the continued ecological integrity and beauty of the land. The community has chosen to set aside over one quarter of their land as wilderness, to protect watercourses and ecologically unique pockets of land and to provide effective wildlife corridors. More people in the community means more development, more encroachment upon the land whose integrity they wish to maintain and whose beauty they all enjoy. This trio of interrelated issues—the desire to preserve land from development, the desire to maintain an effective consensus governance process, and the difficulty of determining how many people can effectively constitute an intimate, self-governing social community—is a topic of ongoing debate within Celo, a debate that has manifested itself, in part, through the development of a land use plan.

In 1994, Celo attempted to address these issues by surveying themselves in an effort to determine if community members placed a greater priority on people or land. The results revealed that both people and land were of equal importance among members, with some members strongly favoring increased growth in community population and others favoring placing emphasis on stewarding the land while maintaining minimal growth levels. Subsequent discussions indicated a collective desire to strike a balance between ecological and community integrity, although finding that balance has been elusive and subject to ongoing community debate and discussion. Over the last three plus decades, discussions about establishing elder housing in a cluster pattern to accommodate the community's aging demographic has added another layer of complexity to this issue. Where would such a project be built and how would it fit into their land use plan?

These perceived conflicts and the differing perspectives on these issues reveal fundamental issues that lie at the heart of Celo's intentional community-building endeavor. Significant time was devoted to the intertwined issues of land use planning, social intimacy and community size in the early 1970s, the mid-1980s, the mid-1990s, and again in the 2000s when a comprehensive land use plan was finally adopted. This land use plan was the result of years of debate, neighborhood and community meetings, and group land walks. The community came together in an attempt to determine where they could accommodate more people and what parts of their land should be protected from development. The outcomes of this process will be discussed at greater length in other chapters of the book. The basic point is that Celo Community has devoted a significant amount of time and effort in seeking to strike a balance both among people and between people and land stewardship. That they have identified only a small number of new building sites interspersed with areas to be preserved for ecological and aesthetic function and that they have not reached consensus regarding an ideal community size indicates that these are issues that the community will continue to confront.

For most of its history, Celo Community lacked a specific place that could serve as a central gathering area, a community center. A room in the health center building that was constructed in the 1940s long served as a space for community meetings, but the building itself was clearly the domain of the health center, its staff, and its patients. A number of other places in the community served as gathering sites—the food co-op along highway 80 that was established in the 1970s, the Quaker meeting house (which only in the late 2000s moved into a space more substantial than a converted goat barn), Granny's Beach where people gather to swim in the river on hot summer days, or the community soccer field—but none of them provided facilities for a community center, an indoor place where people could gather for meetings, celebrations, or other activities. Beginning in the 1980s, the desirability of a community center became an ongoing topic of debate at community meetings. Some felt it would provide a focal point for the community and lead to more interaction, more group activities, and more intimate social bonds. Others felt that it was a financial and maintenance responsibility that the community should not take on. The construction of a community center also became entangled with issues related to the land use plan discussed above including where on their land they would be willing to sacrifice open space for development.

In 2000, the issue came to a head. The Celo Health Center received grant money to build a new facility on an adjacent piece of community land and would be vacating the building it had used for almost sixty years. Possession of the old building reverted to the community and they were forced to decide what to do with it. Although not everyone was equally enthused about it, consensus was ultimately reached to convert the old health center building into a full-fledged community center. During community meetings about the new community center, concerns were expressed about a variety of things: the cost of renovation and maintenance, who would provide labor for renovation and take responsibility for maintenance, how the building would be used and how its uses might or might not meet the needs of Celo Community and other local constituencies, the potential duplication of activity spaces that already existed resulting in an unneeded burden on community resources, and the potential for the building to generate revenue for the community.

It was decided that the community center building, now called Celo Community Center (see figure 2.1) or CCC (and sometimes referred to as the Ohle building after the doctor community member who came to staff it in the 1940s, now deceased) would serve as a location for meetings and other Celo Community events as well as a social center for the wider community in the valley. A committee of community members was formed to conceptualize and oversee the process of building renovation and use and to bring their recommendations to the community's general meeting for discussion and approval. Funds were appropriated for the building's renovation and a community member was hired as a building manager to oversee and complete renovations. As is common with most construction projects in Celo, renovations were completed using mostly community labor and expertise. A small minority of community members carried the process of conversion forward, although a larger number of community members participated in several monthly community workdays that were devoted to the renovations.

Community workdays are a regular occurrence in Celo, and I participated in several of these workdays at CCC during my research. As is the regular pattern, a predesignated workday project involving either community or individually held property is announced at Celo's general meeting. It usually falls on the Saturday morning and early afternoon following the first Wednesday

Figure 2.1   Celo Community Center. *Source:* Photo by the author.

of each month when the general community meetings take place. On CCC workdays, members of the community—usually about ten in number—showed up in work clothes, carrying gloves and tools, knowing that they were bound to get dirty. This is part of life in Celo; maintaining community property or helping other community members build and maintain their property requires elbow grease, a bit of blood, sweat, and tears. Such work is valued in Celo Community culture. As we tore up old linoleum and emptied out dusty closets, other community members, older people or those with physical disabilities, showed up with refreshments, appreciations, and encouragement for the hard work we were doing. Although many of Celo's members do not participate in workdays regularly, it is one way that the community develops a sense of camaraderie and mutual support. Even those who don't attend workdays get a feel for this when workday projects are described, and often cheered, at community meetings.

A little over fifteen years after the Celo Community Center became a reality, it is clear that it is a multifunctional asset to Celo and to wider communities in the valley. It continues to provide space for the community's governance meetings including the monthly general community meetings on the first Wednesday of each month as well as meetings of individual committees that deal with issues such as membership, property, and finances. The community center itself has its own committee that, like other committees, meets monthly and sees to issues such as scheduling, maintenance, and policies regarding use of the center. The center also provides space for a community office where records are kept, a small room for community historical archives, a children's play room, and a library. There are several small office spaces that are rented to both community members and noncommunity members for their business enterprises and as a way of generating funds for the community center. A large portion of the downstairs includes an industrial kitchen and adjacent dining and sitting area for large events.

The community makes this space available not only to community members but also to others from the surrounding area who need a place for an organized event or fundraiser or who simply need a quiet place to read or access the Internet. The Celo Community Center regularly hosts any number of events including fundraisers for a variety of local organizations, events that often include food prepared in the center's kitchen along with live music. At the end of the 2010s, the community added an outdoor pizza oven and adjacent covered space for outdoor events during the warmer months. In 2019, I attended Celo Community's annual meeting, a combination of business with its board of directors and a celebration of the community's achievements that included events held in both the indoor and outdoor spaces associated with the community center. It is clear that the Celo Community Center has become a thriving heart of the community, a part of the commons shared not only by community members but by others from the area.

NOTES

1. William H. Regnery was, like Arthur Morgan, a prominent Progressive. Originally a strong supporter of FDR's New Deal, he later became disillusioned with it. He was a founder of the America First Committee and his son, Henry Regnery, created the conservative publishing company now known as Regnery Publishing. William's grandson and Henry's nephew, William H. Regnery II, is today a prominent white nationalist. None of the Regnery family, and particularly the later generations, were ever directly involved in the formation of Celo Community outside of William H. Regnery providing funding for the purchase of land, although William and, in at least one instance, Henry, both consulted via mail with Arthur Morgan about the community during its early years. However, it is interesting to consider the ways in which their views, in combination with those of Arthur Morgan as a Progressive, may have precluded other possible paths for the community in subtle ways. It should also be acknowledged that the Progressive, sometimes racist stances of the Regnery family were counterbalanced by the involvement of Clarence Pickett who was also involved in supporting Morgan in forming Celo Community. As executive secretary of the Quaker organization, American Friends Service Committee, Pickett's views on racial equality provided a counterbalance to those of the Regnery family.

2. The total acreage purchased appears to be slightly greater than 1,200 acres. In the early decades of the community's existence, two tracts were deeded to departing families prior to the establishment of the community's collective landholding agreement. In addition, a five-acre parcel was sold to a neighbor. Thus, the total community acreage today is probably somewhat less than 1,200 acres. For convenience and following the regular practice of the community and Arthur Morgan in his writings, I regularly use the figure of 1,200 acres.

Chapter 3

A Commons Community Today

Celo through the Lens of
Transformative Utopianism

Who are the people that make up Celo Community? Presenting a precise picture of Celo's membership in print is challenging due to ongoing flux in membership. In the two or three years prior to this writing, four members passed away, three resigned their memberships, and another four joined the community. At the time of this writing, Celo Community is composed of eighty adult members, including at least one member who is on an extended leave of absence from the community. In addition, there are four trial members nearing the end of their trial membership and twenty-three people on the community's waiting list for trial membership. The gender balance among Celo's current members is approximately equal. Celo's members are not particularly racially or ethnically diverse. One African American and one Japanese American are the only members that are not of European American ancestry. Of the current members, none joined as part of the influx of Quaker conscientious objectors following World War II (with the last members from this group passing away during the 2010s), and only a small minority arrived during the influx of back-to-the-landers in the 1970s. If I include current trial members, eight community members are the second or third generation of their family to join the community. Arthur Morgan's great granddaughter is currently a third-generation community member. Community members vary widely with regards to age, the youngest members being in their early 30s and the oldest in their 80s. There is a high concentration of people in their 60s and early 70s, but there has recently been an influx of new members and people waiting to join the community who are in their early 30s.

Precisely dating any individual member's involvement in Celo Community can be tricky because many lived in the area and participated in community-related events well before they became formal members of the community. Some of them grew up in households where their parents were members, and other worked at or attended the Arthur Morgan School or Camp Celo for some years before joining the community. Both of these institutions are located within Celo's geographic boundaries and can only be reached by driving through the heart of the community. Since the 1950s, the camp has been run by two generations of the same family and a third generation from this family, along with his wife, has just taken over its operations. Staff and students from the school and the camp are frequently in attendance at community meetings, community workdays, and at the Friends Meeting in the community. Thus, noncommunity members attending or working at the school or camp are directly involved with both the people and the places that are Celo Community. Many of them develop an attraction or attachment to the community and decide to stay and become members.

Most of Celo's members came as couples and have families, although there are some singles included in the community's membership and it was more common for single people to join in the past. Celo Community is family-oriented; children of member families have always been a significant part of the community scene and the community acts as an extended family. Children of similar ages often play together, traipsing across the community's land. Both children and parents feel safe in the knowledge that there is a large number of adults who will watch out for them and attend to their needs if their parents are not immediately present. Some of these children attend the Arthur Morgan School and Camp Celo and some attend the county school system. The elementary school is only a quarter mile from the community while the middle and high schools are farther away in the town of Burnsville. Reflecting the changing relationship between the locals and the community and the changing demographics of the region, where community children once reported a high degree of antagonism between themselves and local children in the county schools, this seems to have diminished significantly.

Most of Celo's members moved to the community from urban or suburban settings, although this is certainly not true for all of them, especially the eight members who are the second or third generation of their family to join the community. However, of this small group, the majority spent some time in their early adulthood living away from the community, often in some other part of the country, before deciding to return and apply for membership. Still, it is hard to generalize about Celo's members because, despite the relative homogeneity of their ethnic, social, and economic backgrounds, they have brought with them to the community diverse experiences, attitudes, and perspectives on the world. A brief, purposive sample of Celo's members and their backgrounds can be used to illustrate this diversity.

Peter Holder grew up in Madison, Wisconsin, in a professional, upper middle-class household. He attended Antioch College when Arthur Morgan was president there and took two classes from him. Morgan encouraged

Peter to come to Celo Community in the late 1950s and, although he did not formally join the community until the 1980s, he maintained an association with it from that time on. Peter received his PhD in astrophysics from the University of Michigan and eventually became an international development consultant. Before his retirement, his job required him to maintain an apartment in Washington, DC, and to travel around the world. His experiences and education have given him broad perspective, contributing to his cynicism about Celo Community. In contrast to most other members, he does not think that the consensus process functions particularly well and he does not believe that the community is a good model of community sustainability. Peter, like two other community members before his time, is known for his insistence on strict adherence to community policies and he likes to point out when the community is falling short of its ideals or when it has potential problems on the horizon, albeit with an aim of improving the community. Peter conducted and distributed a recent demographic analysis of the community that suggests its aging membership could present a challenging situation for community finances in the near future.

Julie Singleton grew uin a poor and devout Catholic farming family in a small Iowa town and joined a convent directly after high school. As a nun, Julie got involved in social justice work around the United States and in Latin America, including spending time working with the United Farm Workers Union and the American Friends Service Committee. After some time she realized that she couldn't realize the full extent of her activism within the confines of the church. She left the clergy and became a full-time peace and social justice activist and spent some time in a Christian intentional community in Georgia named Koinonia that has a long commitment to racial justice. Following a tradition in Celo Community that extends back to some if its first lasting members, Julie lives a lifestyle of resistance. In an interview with me, she described herself as a "war tax resistor" or a "peace taxpayer." She intentionally keeps her income below the poverty line in order to avoid paying taxes to support the war system. Her house is simple, spartan, and meticulous. She is an idealist, but is somewhat uncomfortable with her idealism. When I asked her if she would like to do an interview with me she replied that she would but worried, "what if I say something really idealistic? Then I will have to live up to it." Julie is a quiet but forceful presence in Celo Community. When she speaks at the Friends Meeting or at community meetings, people listen because they know that serious thought and principle stands behind what she says.

Bonnie Licht grew up in a conservative Christian family in a small Alabama town where both sides of her family had deep roots. In high school she got involved in the Civil Rights movement and, as a political science major at the University of Alabama, she helped organize anti-Vietnam War demonstrations. After college, she and her husband moved around various big cities in South Carolina and Florida where he worked as a lawyer and she as a jeweler, eventually finding themselves in a fast-paced, money-driven life that did not suit them. Seeking a move to the southern Appalachian region, fortune led them to stumble upon the South Toe Valley and Celo Community, a place and a group of people that she says immediately felt like home. However, a divorce and a desire for life change led her to resign her membership in Celo and start a period of wandering which included graduate school in Georgia in humanistic, transpersonal psychology, time spent studying shamanism and healing with indigenous peoples in Peru, Mexico, and the American Southwest, and being among the group of people who founded Earthaven Ecovillage on the other side of the Blue Ridge from Celo in the mid-1990s. Finding that Earthaven did not feel like home in the same way that Celo did, she applied again for membership in Celo and rejoined the community in 2002. Bonnie's experience with multiple intentional communities gives her a unique perspective and that, along with her near perpetual positive attitude, are valued contributions to Celo's ongoing endeavor.

George Farris was born and grew up in Celo Community, the son of Quaker conscientious objectors who came to the community in 1951. He went to the Arthur Morgan School before going away to a Quaker boarding school and then on to Earlham College, a Quaker school in Indiana. He met his future wife and current community member Annabelle when they both worked at Camp Celo, a children's summer camp in the community run by George's parents. After travelling in the United States for a time when they both graduated college and doing volunteer community development work in Honduras, George and Annabelle landed in Chapel Hill, North Carolina, where Annabelle went to nursing school and George worked as a carpenter and teacher at a local Quaker school. They frequently returned to and always maintained contacts in Celo, but it was not a foregone conclusion that they would settle there. When George's parents decided to retire from running the summer camp, George and Annabelle realized how much they valued the community, the rural setting, and the value the people in the community placed on land stewardship and they decided to apply for membership so they could take over running the summer camp. George worries about the rapid development of the land around Celo and appreciates the efforts Celo Community makes to account for the needs of the other-than-human inhabitants of the land. With his wife, George has followed his parents in being core participants in the Celo Friends meeting and running the summer camp (George's sister's son recently finished his trial membership and has taken over running the summer camp as a third generation community member). For the last two decades, George has been one of the lead organizers of the community's monthly workday events. He is recognized as a person of integrity who adheres closely to Quaker values and his family's long-standing contributions to the community are valued by other community members.

Marleen Ito-Wilson was born in the United States to parents of Japanese ancestry and moved back to Japan when she was one year old. She returned to Pennsylvania for her last year of high school before meeting her future husband Bob when they both attended Warren Wilson College in western North Carolina. Bob and his sister Roxanne had grown up in an intentional community in Georgia and his sister had already moved to Celo Community when Marleen and Bob came to work at Camp Celo and the Arthur Morgan School. When Marleen gave birth to her and Bob's first son, they were overwhelmed by the positive support and caring they received from community members and decided that, in addition to being near Bob's sister, the community would be a great place to raise children. Along with the community providing a rich and caring environment for raising a family, Marleen appreciates the community for its commitment to caring for the land and for the broad and varied skills and expertise that other community members are able to share. She and Bob built their own house in the community once they joined and Bob continues to work in construction in the local area while she works in childcare. Marleen is not one of the most outspoken community members but through time she has developed a confident knowledge of the community and a widely recognized aptitude for caring for all people, especially community children.

John Stephenson spent his first thirteen years growing up with expatriate parents in Caracas, Venezuela. At age thirteen, he returned to the United States to go to a Quaker preparatory school in Pennsylvania before going on to college in Louisville, Kentucky, and graduate school in art in Oakland, California. In California, he met his future wife who was an undergraduate art student and, in addition to sharing their passion for art, they got caught up in the back-to-the-land movement that was taking off as the revolutionary idealism in the San Francisco Bay area began to fizzle. After moving back to his future wife's home state of Rhode Island, they began searching for rural areas in which to pursue homesteading or start a community. When one of them went to western North Carolina to further develop their artistic skills at the Penland craft school, they were introduced to Celo Community. Realizing that the rural, homesteading community they sought already existed, they soon moved to and joined Celo where they were able to live simply and devote their energies to developing their artistic crafts, with John becoming a well-known artist at the national level. Recognizing the unsustainable trajectory of land development in the broader society, John resonated especially with Celo's dedication to land stewardship. He has spent the last two plus decades shepherding the development of the community's land use plan through the community's governance process and has also been involved in broader movements to conserve forested landscapes in the region, including being on the board of the Western North Carolina Alliance as it fought to protect forests and public access to them in the region. His commitment to preserving open spaces in the community rankles some other community members who would like to see the community add more members and be open to building more houses to accommodate them. His stance on this issue even led him to question his daughter's plans for starting a farm in the community when she joined the community as a young adult.

Celia, daughter of John Stephenson, was born in the community in 1978. Growing up in the community, she recalls feeling watched both in terms of knowing that there was a community of neighbors who cared about her well-being, but also in terms of those neighbors having high expectations of her. As a kid, she remained relatively aloof from community governance but when she attended the Arthur Morgan School where students work with their teachers to design the curriculum and manage the budget, she had her first direct experience of community process. Feeling that the community was too insular a bubble, Celia went across the country to attend Evergreen State College in Washington to study agriculture. After college, she and her husband farmed in Maryland for several years, but they decided to return to Celo to raise a family in what she knew was a child-friendly environment. She says it was a "leap of faith" for them to move back to the community, knowing that the community as a whole would have a lot of say regarding where, how, and whether they farmed. Unable to farm where they had originally envisioned, through the community process, they ended up with a better option that wasn't obvious to them when they were first looking. For Celia, this has shaped her view on the importance of letting go of your expectations while asking for what you need, placing faith in the Quaker-based principle of community governance that the best solution will emerge from the wisdom of the group. Celia was not a very active community member when she first joined since she was busy raising children. However, as the kids grow older and her appreciation of the community deepens, Celia has taken on more leadership, including serving as the chair of community meetings. Celia is part of a small but growing trend of children who grew up in the community returning to take up membership on their own. She feels very fond of this community which has been such a positive part of her life.

Tom Golden lived in the San Francisco Bay Area until age fourteen when his family moved to a New England college town. He grew up in a liberal-minded household of Jewish ancestry that highly valued education and curiosity; most of his relatives are teachers or doctors. At a young age, he developed a curiosity about the natural world and, as a young adult, became a passionate amateur naturalist. He met his wife at Haverford College, a place where he first encountered Quaker thought and principles. Though he majored in history, much of his professional life has been devoted to some form of experiential education. After a few years working in Durham, North Carolina, while they started a family, Tom and his wife both took positions at the Arthur Morgan School in Celo. As they quickly fell in love with the mountains and slowly got to know the community, they decided to build a life in Celo for them and their two children. Tom continued working at the Arthur Morgan School for several more years after they joined the community and has since founded a naturalist guide business. As one of the junior members of Celo's "Jewish brushcutters" crew, he enjoys participating in workdays, especially those that involve clearing and maintaining the community's series of footpaths. He loves exploring Celo's hundreds of acres of forest and he has developed an agreement with the community that allows him to guide groups to some of Celo Community's protected natural areas. He considers himself a student of the forest, and believes that, as precocious as we are, all of humanity is only in about fourth grade when it comes to understanding the world around us. Along with Celia, Tom and his wife are in the vanguard of a group of younger members who have joined the community over the last two decades. His energy for community work and his enthusiasm for reinforcing the community's values of land stewardship are much appreciated by other community members.

As this brief sample shows, Celo's members bring a diversity of perspectives and experiences. Their backgrounds, interests, and worldviews vary greatly and it is hard to generalize about them. Some of them work full time at jobs located fully in the community (at the summer camp for example), some are self-employed as artists or builders, and others hold more regular jobs, sometimes in other states. Some are more involved in the broader communities in the area and some focus most of their attention on Celo. Some are overt political activists and others are simply trying to make a satisfying life for themselves. They do not always see eye to eye and they are not all intimately connected with each other on a personal level. Indeed, there are distinct antagonisms among some of them. The extraordinary thing is that they have all found common cause in the community and in its commitment to land stewardship. They have deliberately bound themselves together through Celo's institutions of membership, land tenure, and community governance. Although they conceptualize it in a variety of ways, being a member of Celo Community enables them to live closer to their values.

Celo Community may be entered from either the northwest or the south along North Carolina State Route 80 which bisects community land. Only two other points of access are available along two small asphalt country roads: from the north along Hall's Chapel Road and from the east by Seven Mile Ridge Road. It is not apparent that one has crossed onto Celo Community land as there are no distinct boundary markers. As indicated before, one must look below surface appearances to see the community as a bounded entity, in this case defined by property lines. Fisherfolk and families often use the main road through the heart of Celo Community, Hannah Branch Road, to access the South Toe River. Most of them are probably unaware that their recreational activities are taking place in the heart of an eighty-year-old intentional community. Like most other properties in the United States, Celo's collectively owned land is bounded by distinctly geopolitical lines. Celo's property is defined by property boundaries that have been drawn and redrawn over centuries of land speculation rather than by the contours of landforms or watersheds.

Celo Community's households are relatively dispersed across significant portions of their 1,200 acres, although eleven different "neighborhoods" are recognizable by loose clusters of households and by neighborhood names that reflect the community's geography: Firefly Ridge Neighborhood, Laurel Cove Neighborhood, Mac Hollow Neighborhood, and Upper and Lower West Side Neighborhoods. Community land is bisected by a stretch of the South Toe River (see figure 3.1) and by North Carolina State Route 80 which runs alongside the river as it passes through Celo's property.

Most of the community's land lies to the east of the river, but the best and largest extent of agricultural land is to the west. The population of the community follows this pattern, with most residing on the east side of the river. There are two neighborhoods totaling nine households on the west side of

Figure 3.1   The South Toe River in Celo Community. *Source:* Photo by the author.

the river. The west side of the river also contains a small area designated as a business district that borders Route 80. This area includes an art studio, a cooperative crafts store, a cooperative organic foods store, and the Celo Inn, a bed and breakfast that is owned and operated by one community household. Celo Health Center and Celo Community Center are both located directly across the river from the business district. Celo Friends Meeting (see figure 3.2), the community soccer field (see figure 3.3), and the Arthur Morgan School (see figure 3.4) are all located along the community's main street, a two lane, county maintained, dirt road that runs along the east side of the river. Although the community is rather large, it is feasible to walk almost anywhere within the community in a reasonably short period of time (see figure 3.5). This opportunity is valued by community members who have constructed and maintain a series of trails to facilitate this.

The geographical layout of the community influences, but does not determine, the social relationships within it. Adjacent households tend to associate with each other more frequently and may even choose their homesites based on preexisting relationships. When the land use plan was being developed, meetings and "land walks" were conducted within specific neighborhoods in order to locate appropriate spaces for new homesites and other areas to be protected from development. However, the proximity of Celo members'

Figure 3.2   Celo Friends Meeting House. *Source:* Photo by the author.

Figure 3.3 Celo Soccer Field. *Source:* Photo by the author.

Figure 3.4 Arthur Morgan School Graduation. *Source:* Photo by the author.

Figure 3.5   Foot Trail in Celo Community. *Source:* Photo by the author.

homesites to each other does not determine the strength or extent of personal relationships within the community. People who live on opposite sides of the community may be the closest of friends. For example, the couple that lives on the site of the Celo Inn, the business that they operate at the northern boundary of the community, share an intimate relationship with the couple that, until recently, lived on and operated Camp Celo near the southern boundary of community land. However, the locations that serve as gathering places for the community—the food co-op, the Friends Meeting house, Celo Community Center, and the community soccer field—are all centrally located. Yet, despite the availability of connecting footpaths and central gathering places, Celo's households are dispersed and isolated enough that one may spend weeks without direct personal contact with other community members, especially if they choose not to participate in community governance processes.

It is difficult to see Celo Community as a whole and distinctly bounded social entity today. The coming together of all of Celo's members for a single event in a single place at one time simply does not occur. The closest approximation of a full community gathering occurs at Celo's general meetings which take place at the Celo Community Center on the first Wednesday night of every month or at their annual meeting there every October. During these times, the large, red brick building is full of people and it echoes with animated discussions about community history, people, and business. However, the entirety of Celo's membership is never present at these events as at least several community members are bound to be away from the community traveling, visiting relatives, or engaged in work or activism in the nearby towns of Burnsville, Asheville, or places much further away. Others may simply be too busy with their daily lives and their jobs outside the community or be too burned out on participating in the arduous process of consensus decision-making to participate. It is not uncommon for a community member to decide they need to take a year or more away from community meetings where participating in the process of consensus decision-making can be challenging to one's patience. While the majority of Celo's members gather, some of them will be tucked away in their homes or art studios attending to personal business, or perhaps as far away as India on a spiritual retreat.

Celo's members sometimes gather to celebrate the life of a person who has recently passed away or to help repair flood damage to the home of a community member or neighbor. During my research, I attended a memorial service that was held for a recently deceased neighbor of Celo Community at the Celo Friends Meeting House. Well over a hundred people attended this standing-room-only event, joining together in silent meditation and outpourings of grief and joyous remembrances of the dearly departed. While many of Celo's members walked to this event, friends and relatives of the deceased arrived from sometimes great distances by air and car. Many of them appeared to be quite at home in Celo Community, rekindling old friendships, apparently quite unselfconscious of the fact that they were in an intentional community with relatively deep and extensive utopian roots. At times like this, it is clear that the social boundaries of Celo Community are blurred and indistinct. The same could be said for many of the events that take place at the Celo Community Center, a place where the boundaries between the intentional community and the wider community of neighbors sometimes fade to near insignificance.

The remnants of two Atlantic hurricanes caused severe flooding in the community during some of my most intensive field research there in the fall of 2004. Immediately afterwards, Celo's members were joining their neighbors, community members or not, marshaling their forces to clear away downed trees, mend driveways that had washed away, and repair massive damage to the Ten Thousand Things food co-op that sits on Celo's land and across Route 80 from the swollen South Toe River (see figure 3.6). Repairs to Ten Thousand Things' building and inventory were swift; water-logged boards, shelves, cabinets, and inventory were repaired or replaced by spontaneously composed teams of people and without central guidance. Seeking authoritative direction as to how I could help, definitive responses were lacking. The message seemed to be "just take ownership for it and do it." In their responses to this event, Celo's members and their neighbors joined together in cooperation and mutual support and they expressed the sentiment that "this sort of cooperation is what community is about." However, this sort of coming together in response to an emergency situation did not seem unique to Celo as an intentional community. As we can see on the news, most any group of neighbors will join together to help each other in response to death and tragedy, creating what Solnit (2009) described as "the extraordinary communities that arise from disaster." Even though times of death and tragedy may draw Celo's members together in one place and one time, these are not the definitive expressions of the uniqueness of Celo Community.

While at least some of Celo's members invariably are not present for these events, those that do participate are joined by many of their neighbors, people who live nearby and share many of Celo's values but have not taken official community memberships and do not live on community land. Indeed, the membership of Ten Thousand Things, a unique, entirely voluntary, cooperative institution with no paid positions that has existed on community land since 1972, is comprised of a majority of noncommunity members. Tuesday and Thursday afternoons as well as Saturday mornings when the co-op is open for business are boisterous times. Co-op members staff the checkout counter, subtracting the totals of items purchased from members' accounts

Figure 3.6   Ten Thousand Things Food Co-op and Toe River Crafts Artists Co-op. *Source:* Photo by the author.

maintained in handwritten ledgers rather than by computer. Jovial banter-
ing and laughter are interspersed with more serious discussions such as the
sharing of advice regarding techniques for personal construction projects and
the scheduling of appointments for cooperative work on them. Although Ten
Thousand Things was initiated by Celo's members, it has become the domain
of a much wider community. Many of Celo's members maintain closer personal relationships with people from this wider community than they do with
most of Celo's official members.

A wider community of like-minded people has grown up around Celo
Community. Some of them came to the area in their quest to go back to
the land. Many of them were attracted to the area by the presence of Celo
Community, although they have chosen not to become official members. Some
in Celo follow an earlier community member, Arthur Morgan's son Ernest,
in referring affectionately to this wider community as "our sane fringe." On
the surface, this label presents a contrast with the common phrase "the lunatic
fringe," and could be interpreted as it was by previous ethnographer George
Hicks (2001), as a condescending attack by community members on local
families and residents of the area. My conversations with community members suggest that this way of referring to the wider community of like-minded
neighbors that has grown up around Celo is an ironic, self-deprecating reference. It calls attention to the fact that people in the wider community have
created lives that resemble what the members of Celo Community sought
without being party to the painstaking processes and sometimes cumbersome
arrangements that characterize Celo Community: its membership, land tenure, and governance institutions. These people too are committed to simple
living, but their individual decisions are not bound by the restrictions of collective land tenure and consensus decision-making. They share interests with
Celo's members with whom they cooperate on a variety of projects focused
on building local food networks and creating locally based education, entertainment, and mutual aid initiatives. They participate in projects initiated by
Celo's members such as the Ten Thousand Things food cooperative and the
community-supported agriculture farm operated by two of Celo's members
on community land, but they do not go to community meetings and they are
not required to have their building designs and uses of land approved by the
community. They go to events at the Celo Community Center but they don't
have to participate in meetings where management and budgeting decisions
are made about the building (although they can if they wish as community
members have designated one spot on the community center committee for
noncommunity members).

There is a high degree of interaction between members of Celo Community
and the wider community. In some senses, Celo Community is only dif-
ferentiated from this wider community by their commonly owned land and

their processes of community governance and membership screening. The wider community participates in and, by sheer numbers, dominates some of the local institutions initiated by Celo's members. The congregation at Celo Friends Meeting, the weekly Quaker service held on community land, is often composed of a majority of noncommunity members. Cabin Fever University is a three-month long series of events that occurs every winter and involves a good mix of Celo Community members and those from the wider community. Announced by the publication of a calendar every January that lists all of the events, Cabin Fever University is an opportunity for an individual or group to invite people to participate in an event of their design. These events may be educational, political, culinary, social, entertaining or any combination thereof. Cabin Fever University events often include plays, dinner events, political discussions, slide shows, and how-to sessions through which participants can share their skills, opinions, experiences, and expertise. The participation of the wider community in Cabin Fever University and these other institutions reflects Celo's porous boundaries and its influence beyond its political and geographical borders.

Similarly, the presence of Celo Community has made the valley a fertile place for noncommunity members to cultivate a variety of initiatives focused on local food, conservation, education, and self-empowerment. Across the valley, a former teacher at the Arthur Morgan school established the Appalachian Institute for Mountain Studies (AIMS), a nonprofit organization that defines itself as "a living laboratory for modeling sustainable human ecosystems and [that] envisions a society where traditional knowledge from mountain cultures is combined with appropriate technology to provide innovative solutions for a transitional world" (Appalachian Institute for Mountain Studies 2020). AIMS has placed particular emphasis on developing relationships with local families in order to promote the preservation and sharing of agricultural biodiversity and the associated knowledge and practices that have grown up around it in the region. Paralleling AIMS' work in the areas of biocultural diversity conservation, permaculture, and the cultivation of traditional knowledge and practice, the nearby Mountain Gardens organization has, for the last twenty-five years, developed the philosophy and practice of "Paradise Gardening." The founder of Mountain Gardens says that Paradise Gardening aims to "find a way to live on earth which promotes our health and happiness/is conducive to the full development of our innate potential, and at the same time is 'democratic', that is, available to all/not using more than our share, and harmonious with the biosphere's evident drive toward increasing diversity, complexity, stability" (Hollis 2020). Combined with a wide variety of other, similarly oriented initiatives, organizations, and businesses that have sprung up in the valley, this wider community adds up to what Haluza-DeLay and Berezan have called a "distributed ecovillage," which they understand as "a social field productive of an ecological habitus, that is an orientation that generates lifestyle practices and institutional forms that effectively fit the ecological conditions of place" (2013: 131).

Some people in Celo Community say that their relationships with people from the wider community are more intimate than their relationships with other community members. The presence and growth of this wider community, in addition to the long list of people waiting to become members of the community, is an indication that Celo Community has manifested a lifestyle that many value and aspire to. Despite the fact that one can participate in many aspects of Celo Community without actually taking formal membership, there is a long list of people waiting for the opportunity to undertake the trial membership period and join the community. Although such membership entails significant limitations on one's freedom to develop and profit on personal property, and although Celo is no longer actively seeking new members through announcements and advertisements in intentional community communications networks, the community still attracts a large number of people who seek membership. This is an indication that Celo's commoning endeavor holds wider resonance.

In addition to referring to their like-minded neighbors as "our sane fringe," another way that Celo Community's members conceptualize the difference between themselves and the broader society is through the use of the label *the mainstream society*. This label manifests juxtaposition; it implies a contrast between themselves as members of a unique social community and the mass of people living "normal" lives in American society. Another way that Celo's members perceive of their difference is with reference to "the local" people, the families that have lived in these mountains for generations and were here prior to the establishment of Celo Community. These labels are not necessarily used normatively; rather they are simply an expression of difference. However, despite this perceived difference, Celo's members are very much engaged in both the mainstream and local components of the wider society.

There are a number of ways in which the wider society overlaps with Celo and in which Celo Community spills out into the wider society. One manifestation of this overlap is the ways in which people who are not members of the community proper or of the wider community of like-minded neighbors engage in activities that take place within the boundaries of Celo Community. During my research in Celo in 2004 just prior to election season, Yancey County Democratic Party representatives and candidates held a meeting with their constituents from the South Toe Valley at Celo Community Center. In addition to the representatives and candidates and Celo Community members themselves, the constituents in the audience included people that Celo's members might refer to as "our sane fringe," locals, and participants in the mainstream. This event was representative of the ways in which Celo Community's relationship with the wider world has changed historically. In the community's early years, Celo Community members were sometimes ignored and even shunned by local politicians. The fact that a county Democratic Party would hold a campaign meeting at Celo Community Center reveals both that Celo's influence in the area has grown and that Celo's utopian idealism has been tempered enough that they recognize the necessity of engaging in mainstream politics rather than adhering strictly to their original utopian visions.

Most of Celo's members engage in many activities outside of the community's boundaries, especially on an individual level. Some of Celo's members are active in the local Democratic Party and the local chapter of Habitat for Humanity for instance. Other members are active in the Toe River Arts Council, a group of artists committed to cooperatively promoting the work of artists in several local counties. Some have worked with activist organizations like the Western North Carolina Alliance, a group committed to shaping public lands policy to ensure multi-use access to what amounts to a broad public commons (see Newfont 2012). Although most of Celo's members value simple living and eating food that has been produced by themselves or other local agriculturalists, most of Celo's members make semi-regular trips to the nearby towns of Burnsville or Spruce Pine or slightly farther to the city of Asheville for shopping and entertainment. In this sense, Celo is far from the self-reliant community that Morgan once envisioned.

Celo's relationship with people in the local communities has also changed, even as the composition and worldview of these local communities have themselves been transformed. In Hicks' account of Celo Community (2001), he characterized Celo's relationship with the locals as almost entirely antagonistic in nature. He points out that the nature of the community was confusing to local families who could not understand their values or what they were attempting to do. The vociferous pacifism of some of the community members during World War II was seen as unpatriotic by some, the fact that the community owned their land together ran counter to values of rugged individualism, and the eccentric behavior of some of the back-to-the-landers was just plain offensive. At various points, some of the local suspicions and misunderstandings about the community and a lack of communication between the two groups led to the community being labeled variously as German spies, Jewish communists, or hippie holler. The removal of local tenants from community land in the early years of the community and their being asked to dissociate themselves from community business added to the strain. At one point during World War II, a group of local men, led by a disgruntled former community member, barged into a community meeting, threatening violence if the pacifists did not leave the area. Although nothing came of these threats, it is indicative of the fact that there has been a good deal of tension between the local communities and Celo Community.

However, it became evident during my research that antagonism and strained relationships between Celo and its members and local communities and families, while they no doubt existed, were not as broadly characteristic as Hicks's account leads one to believe. Indeed, at least one local family joined the community and maintained their membership despite some disdain from their local brethren. In fact, a second generation of this family joined in community membership, although the relationship between the community and the second generation family member was strained and he ultimately resigned. Some of Celo's members developed relationships with local families. Celo's longest-standing members at the time of my initial research, in addition to their regular participation in Celo Friends Meeting, had been attending local church events for decades. The father of this family taught for many years in local schools and is fondly remembered by his local students who, until his recent passing, recognized and thanked him when they saw him. Before the local schools were consolidated, when local children were taught in a number of one-room school houses throughout the valley, the students from the school house closest to Celo attended school in the basement of Celo Health Center when their regular school building burned down. And the Celo Health Center itself was explicitly conceptualized and established to be of service not only to Celo's members but to the residents of local communities as well and continues to serve in this capacity today. One of the local families even named their son after the community member doctor who delivered him at the Health Center.

As time has passed, any antagonism between the two groups that did exist has softened considerably, although a certain level of ambivalence remains. The wider world has made inroads into what was, at the time the community was founded, a relatively isolated geographic area. Improvements in transportation routes, intrusions of television and Internet, and the proliferation of chain businesses in the area have changed the local culture. People in local communities have become more cosmopolitan and more appreciative of Celo's presence, if still somewhat guarded. This is indicated by a quotation from an interview I conducted with a long time local resident:

> The community has, in my opinion, been a tremendous asset to Yancey County. It's been a positive effect. The only thing, it took me thirty years to get any of them to work in the political scene much. They was afraid that somebody'd think they was a-meddling in affairs. And I said, look, you've been here almost as long I've been here. . . . The people on the Celo Community is just—they had some funny ways, we thought. You might could find somebody who maybe would smart off a little bit because they don't want them to cut timber in the mountains. They call them tree huggers. That's just a difference. But still it's

their business what they do on their property. (Interview with author in Celo Community on October 15, 2004)

At the same time Celo's members have become more appreciative of the ways in which local families had long lived largely self-reliant lifestyles characterized by informal networks of cooperation, reciprocity, and the passing on of basic subsistence skills. This was alluded to in my interview with Celo's longest-standing members.

> B: We had some very warm relationships. If we had felt antagonism and hostility on the part of the local people, I don't think we would have stayed. The Silvers up here . . . they were very close to us.

> D: We depended on Alonzo Silver, because he had so much knowledge of agriculture and stuff and he helped with the garden. And Isabelle Ballew up on the mountain, Seven Mile Ridge, was just a wealth of earthy knowledge about cows and chickens and corn and all sorts of things that we didn't know much about. We depended on those people. . . . We feel we have a lot in common with the people who go to the Baptist church across the river. We don't define things in the same way, but they have a spirit of caring for each other and caring for us that crosses all sorts of lines.

> B: But, it's just that there is this psychological boundary. (Interview with author in Celo Community on November 11, 2004)

Celo's members recognize that a certain estrangement still exists between themselves and local families and communities. This is likely an inevitable outcome where the formation of intentional communities is the result of a diaspora of people from one context to another, in this case, from the cities to a traditional rural area. However, after eight decades, the community and its ongoing commoning endeavor has become a permanent part of the social and ecological landscape in the South Toe Valley.

Thus, one has to look beneath the surface to gain a perspective on Celo Community as a distinct social entity, an ongoing project of intentional community building and commoning. While Celo Community and its members are unmistakably integrated into broader local, regional, national, and even global communities, Celo is distinctly defined by a set of bounded social institutions and the values that they encode and enact: Celo's membership process, its land tenure arrangement, and its process of community governance by consensus decision-making. If one approaches Celo hoping to find a concisely bounded utopia, they will be disappointed for Celo's social boundaries with the wider world are unmistakably porous. However, within these porous boundaries, Celo is circumscribed by unique social institutions that continue to enact utopian strivings, cultural critiques, and commoning endeavors whose roots stretch back to the founding of Celo Community by Arthur Morgan, to those first Quaker conscientious objectors who put down roots in the community, and to the back-to-the-landers who came to the community a generation later.

In his dissertation, *Ideology and Change in an American Utopian Community* (1969), ethnographer George Hicks paints a picture of Celo Community that portrays it as a failed social experiment, a fallen utopia, whose promise was not to be realized. He speaks of there being little business to conduct at community meetings, meetings which were taken up mostly by gossip. He portrays the community as a disappointment to its own members, a social endeavor that failed to realize its potential:

> That Celo Community is not destined to lead a major social overhaul has gradually impressed its members since the intense disputes of the early 1950s. (1969: 176)

> Celo simply was not radically different from an ordinary neighborhood; it had not developed, as they had hoped, into a unique experiment in social design. (1969: 177)

> The residents no longer see the Community as offering to the matrix society an example of a better social order. Even the Holding Agreement, once thought of as a grand example of improved land tenure relations [has lost its significance for most members]. As a whole, the Community has lost its transcendental vision; it merely furnishes a context for the diverse activities of its residents. (1969: 304)

Perhaps this was how it appeared in the mid to late 1960s when Hicks conducted ethnographic research in Celo Community. There is no doubt that the community was shaken by the dissension and defection of the 1950s. The remnants of this were what confronted Hicks during his stay. There is no way he could have foreseen the impact that the back-to-the-land movement would have on the community in the 1970s, the revitalization that resulted from the ideals of the countercultural movement. For people who were part of these movements, Arthur Morgan's experiment in cooperative intentional community, growing as it did out of a critique of modern industrial society and culture along with the utopian writings of Edward Bellamy, provided a place where they could live out their own ideals in a supportive social environment, where they could join together with others and respond to their cultural critiques by creating and participating in alternative institutions. Celo's experimentalism was revived by their presence.

Even after returning to Celo for a few weeks in 1979 in preparation for turning his dissertation into a book (published posthumously in 2001), Hicks continued to insist on characterizing the community as a utopian failure.

Although Celo Community fell short of creating a model of a new society and culture, it persisted as a haven for those who felt themselves outcasts and misfits. Members came and went, worthy causes altered from one era to another, opposition to the direction of American life took new forms and Celo did offer a beacon of hope for some Americans. In the end, however Morgan's dream of its destiny as a "master community," a model to be emulated far and wide, remained just that: a dream. (2001: 172)

Hicks suggested that the community's increasing emphasis on land stewardship starting in the 1970s represented a turn away from utopian endeavor, a desperate attempt by members of a dying utopian community to define their relevance and reshape their own identity in the wake of their failure to create the exceptional community that Morgan envisioned.

[A]s Celo gradually lost its mark of strangeness and exclusiveness, the expansive promises of its earlier years fell away. The grand reformist dreams faded, becoming something of an embarrassment to those who joined in the 1970s and afterward. Careful stewardship of communally owned land—always part of the members' definition of the Community—took hold as the primary object of the enterprise. (Hicks 2001: 211)

Much has changed in the world, the nation, the Upper South Toe Valley, and Celo Community since the late 1960s, the time during which most of Hicks' research in Celo Community was conducted, and since 1980, the time at which Hicks's account of the community stops. Most prominently, environmental degradation has increased exponentially and, at the same time, scientific consensus regarding the necessity of stewarding both local and global commons in more sustainable manners lest we be faced with a number of social, ecological, and economic crises has become almost complete. This context necessitates the cultivation of human subjects who are able to see like a commons and to effectively engage in acts of commoning. This is exactly what my analysis suggests that Celo has done as it has become a multigenerational commoning endeavor whose impacts and influence have spread far beyond its spatial boundaries. In any case, more than a generation later, it appears that the time is ripe for a reanalysis of Celo Community.

My assessment is that Hicks exaggerated the disillusionment that he says characterized community members toward the end of the twentieth century and that he evaluated the community using the measure of utopia as an end rather than employing the concept of utopianism as a frame for understanding an ongoing transformative process. Judging Celo Community with regards to whether or not it had achieved utopia, whether or not its members had managed to completely transcend the dominant reality, Hicks inevitably found that it had not. While some community members might have believed they would find utopia in Celo Community and were disillusioned and left when they did not, it is clear that most people who came to the community were more pragmatic in their expectations. Community documents from various eras indicate that the community saw and advertised itself as an ongoing social experiment, but never as a finished product, much less a utopia. The community did back away from actively promoting itself as a model community, as it had during its early years when it was among a small number of member communities in the Fellowship of Intentional Communities and sent updates about developments in the community for inclusion in the organization's newsletters (see, for example, Morgan 1959). However, my research indicates that this is due to a growing level of interest in the community that became overwhelming and that began to impede the practicalities of community functioning rather than to a realization that "the community is not destined to lead a major social overhaul."

Whatever the case may be, I found that community members were well aware that they were part of a social experiment characterized by unique institutions for community governance, membership screening, and land tenure, the very same institutions that Hicks points to as characteristic of their "utopian" undertaking. There may be different levels of excitement about the experiment in community and different levels of commitment to the community's ideals. There may be different degrees of satisfaction with life in the community and with the perceived effectiveness and fairness of community processes, but I did not come across a single community member who believed that they were living in "an ordinary neighborhood." Even though many members of Celo Community are not vociferous, broadly engaged social activists and are not guided in their lives by a forceful utopian vision of establishing the perfect model community, they are well aware of their community's unique history and cooperative structure. This is a manifestation of the process of transformative utopianism that I have described elsewhere (see Lockyer 2009). Although the community's idealism may have diminished relative to the early years and in response to the practicalities of everyday life, current community members still recognize and carry forward the community's roots in utopian experimentalism and cultural critique and the community's very existence has had an impact far beyond its borders. This attempt to understand and interpret Celo not by the yardstick of achieving a perfect utopia but through a focus on ongoing change and adaptation is part of broader scholarly attempts to understand the significance of intentional communities without holding them to impossible standards of achieving the grand visions of their founders (see also Pitzer 2013).

In any case, as the baby boomers age today and as younger generations, both those raised in the community and those from elsewhere, become members, Celo Community's vitality is evident. Community meetings are well attended, their agendas full and the tone serious but light and punctuated by laughter and camaraderie. Celo Health Center has moved to a new building and the community and its like-minded neighbors are energized by the collaborative opportunities and activities the new community center affords. The community continues to receive requests for information from potential members and others who want to set up or revitalize intentional communities elsewhere. People who go through the formal process of expressing a desire to join the community may face a wait of ten to twenty years before their names reach the top of the list. Yet, interest in the community has not waned. It seems that Celo's stability is part of what attracts so many people to it. It no longer has to struggle so ardently to implement cooperative endeavors or act on cultural critiques for Celo has already established successful, alternative institutions that function well and can adapt to changing circumstances. Because of this, the community does not appear, on the surface, to be utopian in nature. Indeed, in some respects it is "not radically different from an ordinary neighborhood." Other than collective land ownership, membership screening, and consensus-based community governance, there is no other communal enterprise in which all members are involved. However, employing the lens of transformative utopianism, we can see that these institutions are the outcomes of the hard work of previous utopians and cultural critics and their confrontations with the tension between the real and the ideal. In Celo, their utopian endeavors live on through the everyday commoning endeavors of community members both within and beyond the community's boundaries.

The idealism of the 1970s and earlier periods has faded considerably in the face of the practicalities of raising families, resolving disputes, and stewarding the land. Yet, in many respects, Celo Community is much more than just a neighborhood. It is a community whose strength grows, in part, out of a symbiosis with the land, a symbiosis that is facilitated by governance and land tenure institutions that were created by previous utopian communitarians and cultural critics and by which all current community members are bound. These members are diverse in background experiences, current livelihood strategies, and the ways that they perceive of and participate in the wider world. It is thus difficult to generalize about them. However, all of the members of Celo Community recognize that they are participating in a unique social experiment and their community documents, including those they pass along to interested inquirers, indicate this.

> CCI members have no common political ideology or religious conviction, rather its central focus is stewardship of the land held "in trust." Arthur Morgan's plan was for Celo Community to be an experiment, an adventure in community

building. Working together with good will, the members would cultivate basic value patterns, social and ethical standards, free and open-minded inquiry, and a network of customs and relationships to create what he called "The Great Community."

Members express the desire to avoid prevalent value patterns of urban and suburban America, to cooperate in creating a satisfying neighborhood, to develop relationships of honesty and mutual trust, to appreciate and care for the natural world, to raise some of their own food, to participate directly in making decisions affecting their lives, and to rear children in a wholesome environment. (Celo Community, no date)

[We] have come here to share and cooperate with others in creating a satisfying neighborhood, attempting to live [our] lives somewhat free of the stresses of modern American society and to participate directly in making decisions which affect [our] lives. No common political ideology or religious conviction binds this group of people together. Rather it is stewardship of the land held "in trust" which is the center point of CCI. The members carefully consider issues which effect use of the land and make decisions by the process of consensus at regular monthly meetings. (Celo Community, no date)

Though coming from diverse backgrounds, most Celo Community members are motivated, at least in part, by a desire to avoid the prevalent value patterns of urban American life. Hence, variations of income and life style within the Community carry neither prestige nor stigma. . . . Each contributes to the viability of the Community in his own way. . . .

The original intent was that the Community be an evolving experiment whose people, free from the pressures of urban society, might explore the possibilities of rural living, social change and social cooperation and interaction. (Celo Community 2012)

These long quotations are included in introductory materials sent to people interested in joining the community. They are the way that the community represents itself and they provide one lens for viewing Celo Community as it exists today as a product of its own history. Celo Community is the outcome of the decisions, intentions, and actions of all who have been part of the community over the last eighty plus years. As we have seen, three particular strands of utopianism and cultural critique have significantly affected the community: Morgan's idealization of the small community, Quaker commitments to peace, equality, democracy, and simplicity, and the back-to-the-land movement's desire for simplicity, community, environmental conservation, and self-reliance.

It is apparent that Celo Community is an outgrowth of Morgan's cultural critique of modern society and his utopian vision of the small community.

Morgan's efforts in founding the community and his aims for it are acknowledged by current members. Many community members still recognize the community as an experiment, one that was designed to determine how people could cooperate, develop mutual trust and responsibility and a collective vision of the common good in juxtaposition to predominant cultural trends that emphasized individualism and material competition. Although in daily economic life Celo Community has not managed to detach itself from the political-economic system of industrial capitalism that so worried Morgan, it has developed a unique set of social institutions that continue to attract people seeking alternatives to mainstream life. These institutions assert a greater degree of local, collective control over the political economy of land ownership, the constituents that compose the community, and the way they relate to each other and govern themselves. This control manifests itself in terms of the ethical values of mutual care and respect and ecologically sensitive land stewardship that characterize Celo's ongoing commoning endeavor.

Although there is no official requirement that community members share Quaker values or participate in the Friends meeting at Celo, the Quaker heritage is a significant part of Celo Community. Some see the Friends' meeting, a regular Sunday gathering for silent worship followed by a potluck, as the heart of the community. Indeed, the Friends' meetinghouse does lie almost at the geographical center of the community and a significant percentage of community members participate in it to some degree. The Celo Friends Meeting is also a nexus for cultural critique, utopianism, and commoning. It is a place where peace, justice, and other social and environmental concerns are earnestly discussed. It is a place where cooperative endeavors to improve the world are conceptualized and planned and a place where people come together to share food and fellowship after each period of worship.

In many ways, Celo Friends Meeting is a node for the larger cultural critiques and utopian striving for a better world that underpins the history of Celo's intentional community-building endeavor. Most people in Celo Community, even if they do not attend the Friends' Meeting, adhere to Quaker values of simplicity, equality, social justice, and egalitarian decision-making. Perhaps, most significantly, a process of Quaker-inspired governance by consensus, of seeking unity and truth among a diversity of opinions, of encouraging all to participate in governing the community of which they are part, continues to serve as the model for conducting community business. This model stands in stark contrast to predominant political institutions that result in apathy, disenfranchisement, isolation, and low voter turnout. It is a means of bringing people together in the process of utopian striving for a better world.

The back-to-the-landers who came in the late 1960s and early 1970s built upon latent themes of environmental stewardship and simple living that already existed in the community and brought them to the forefront. Today most community houses are owner-built, relatively small, simple and energy efficient, especially in comparison with the average suburban American home. Many of them include alternative energy systems and home gardens. Many of the older houses are named for their original builders; they bear the names of earlier community members—Leveridge House, Reed House, Wyatt House—reflecting a strong sense of history and rootedness in the land and community. Social interaction, cooperative gardening, hikes in the woods, and cooperative work projects often substitute for television and high-priced, high-technology entertainment for many community members. Organic, locally grown food is a staple and fast food, largely unavailable in the area anyway, is disfavored. Although Celo Community is far from self-sufficient, most households in Celo Community are much more self-reliant than is true of the average American household. In all of these senses, Celo's earlier utopian cultural critics have succeeded in creating viable cultural models that stand in juxtaposition with dominant cultural values and social institutions.

CONCLUSION

At a fundamental level, Arthur Morgan was right. For most of human existence and in many places to this day, humans have lived, met their needs, and developed their individual characters in small communities. For much of human history, people in small communities cooperated to use, manage, and otherwise interact with the physical environment around them in order to obtain the things they needed. Managing the commons is an ancient human practice, one that over recent centuries and millennia has been increasingly encroached on by empire building, state-making, and processes of industrial and neoliberal development. As global capitalist empire encloses and erodes both local and global commons and enforces its high modernist logic which conceives of humans as *homo economicus*, the task is to find ways of reconstructing the commons and cultivating other kinds of human subjects who are capable of relating to each other and to the earth in more cooperative manners.

Celo's commoning endeavor, like many others over recent decades, is an experiment in commons design and intentional community building that has been constructed as a deliberate response to the cultural ruptures created by empire. Like other intentional communities in American history, it aims to provide an alternative sociocultural setting that can address some of the shortcomings created by rapidly increasing enclosure associated with the spread of industrial capitalism. In terms of longevity, stability, and desirability to at least some subsets of people interested in alternative ways of being, it is a commoning endeavor that has proved successful. At its founding, Arthur Morgan suggested that it might be a model that could offer lessons for other such endeavors.

The scholarship on the commons, and particularly Ostrom's design principles for successful commons functioning, offers one lens through which to view Celo's utility as a model. Has Celo, like other commons, manifested the factors encapsulated in the design principles in the process of becoming a viable commons? If so, how? If not, why not? What other factors might be relevant? While fairly ubiquitous in American history, a history whose narrative is defined by efforts to address the tensions between the individual and the collective and between the real and the ideal, intentional communities have received relatively little serious attention and no study has viewed them systematically through the lens of the commons. A case study analysis of Celo Community framed around Ostrom's design principles may provide additional support for or refutation of those principles, but that is not my main aim; a large volume of scholarship has already been devoted to this. Instead, my aim is to use the commons design principles as a tool to inform and help empower the construction of other enduring commons communities and of more people who can see like a commons through the telling of the story of one of the United States' longest extant intentional communities.

In his overview of Ostrom's life work and the ways in which the insights she generated might be used to help devise solutions to the sociocultural, political-economic, and environmental challenges we face in the early twenty-first century, Derek Wall stated:

> If we feel neoliberalism has failed, we should look at why alternatives might seem impossible. Strange as this may sound, it was very much Ostrom's technique. She saw common pool resources as a problem and a challenge. She noted that collective solutions were dismissed as impossible and then worked with great effort and imagination to show why this was not the case. We need to put the same kind of energy into examining potential alternatives that work. (2017: 55)

Arthur Morgan and those who followed his lead in creating and cultivating Celo Community over the last eighty years have done just this. In the following chapters, I will use Ostrom's design principle as a framework for telling the story of Celo as a commons alternative that works.

Part II

DESIGN PRINCIPLES FOR A COMMONS COMMUNITY

Eight of the nine chapters in this part of the book are structured around the eight "design principles" for successful commons stewardship originally identified by Elinor Ostrom and subsequently confirmed and refined through further analysis, often conducted in dialogue with Ostrom, by other scholars and practitioners. Each chapter elucidates how one of the principles, or subprinciples in several cases, is manifested in the governance institutions and processes of Celo Community. To supplement the often technical descriptions of community governance and to bring the community to life for the reader, each chapter begins with or incorporates one or more ethnographic vignettes[1] based on composite descriptions drawn from data collected during my field research in the community or from research I conducted in the community's extensive archives. Each of these vignettes is accompanied by one of the "eight points of orientation for commoning" identified by the German Commons Summer School. These points of orientation were developed collaboratively by a diverse group of commons practitioners and activists who gathered in Germany in the summer of 2012 and translated Ostrom's design principles into a set of statements that might better reflect "the personal perspective of commoners themselves" (Bollier and Helfrich 2015b: 48). These statements stand in contrast with the more analytically phrased, academically oriented principles articulated by Ostrom and other scholars. Beginning each chapter of this part of the book with these points of orientation for commoning, combined with ethnographic vignettes of the community, seems a good way to bring my description of Celo Community down to earth.

During the process of writing this book, I presented the analytical framework for the book, oriented around commons design principles and points of orientation for commoning, to community members in open discussion forums. Five current community members also reviewed my ethnographic descriptions of Celo Community contained in chapters 4 through 12 of this book. While Celo's members do not usually describe their community in terms of commons design principles or points of orientation for commoning, during the discussion forums and in comments based on their manuscript reviews, they indicated broad agreement that these are appropriate ways of conceptualizing their community-building endeavor. The discussions at the open forums were lively and informative and helped me refine and sharpen my perspective on and descriptions of the community.

One additional note about methodology seems in order here. I have been visiting and collecting data on Celo Community for over twenty years. My most intensive periods of data collection took place as part of my doctoral dissertation research in anthropology at the University of Georgia. During spring and summer of 2001 and for over eight months from spring 2004 to spring 2005, I lived in the community and collected data primarily through participant observation, semi-structured interviews, and research in the community's archives. Since then, I have returned to community for brief visits on average once per year. Beginning in 2016, I started spending more time in the community in anticipation of this book project. While on sabbatical leave during calendar year 2019, I spent approximately six weeks in the community across three different trips during which I engaged in intensive participant observation, informal interviews, conducted a survey, spent a lot of time in the community's archives, and presented the basic framework for the book to the community in the aforementioned discussion forums. I believe that the familiarity I have developed with the community and its members gives me a unique perspective from which to describe the community as I attempt to do in the following chapters.

The following accounts and examples of commons design principles as manifested in Celo Community include descriptions of policies and interactions drawn mostly from the last twenty years or so during which I have been actively engaged with the community. In a couple of cases, I've had to delve deeper into the community's history to identify the most appropriate examples. In these cases, I've drawn on the extensive minutes of community meetings in the community's archives and on the memories of longtime community members. Rarely if ever do I present descriptions from before the mid-1960s which was the last time the community added significantly to the group of documents that govern their commons endeavor. Unless otherwise identified, when I quote a particular community policy, it is the policy in effect at the time of writing. Thus, what follows should be a current account of commons governance in Celo at the time of publication. However, as I note in what follows, flexibility and the ability to adapt to changing circumstances is an important part of what makes Celo work. The community is thus a moving target that can't be fully captured in a written work.

I'd like to make one final note about the themes and issues that populate my examples of commons design principles in action in Celo in the following chapters. In reviewing the notes I took and other data I collected over the last twenty years, combined with a study of community meeting minutes and other historical documents in the community archives, it is remarkable how much the community's governance conversations have repeatedly returned to or continuously revolved around some of the same themes and issues. Especially since the mid-1960s when the community took the basic institutional form it maintains today, issues of membership size and trial membership process, holding site selection, consensus decision-making, the development of a community center, use of herbicides on community land, tree cutting, and community finances among a few others have been ongoing topics of discussion, debate, and policy adjustment in the community. The reader will be introduced to many of these issues most prominently in the following descriptions.

NOTE

1. For clarity, these vignettes are indicated by italicized text throughout.

Chapter 4

Common Land and
Community Membership

Celo's Social and Spatial Boundaries

As community members, we are tasked with the stewardship of Celo Community land and shared property. This year, with tremendous individual and group effort, we've faced that weighty responsibility solidly. In the realm of land stewardship, we gave thoughtful consideration to the Department of Transportation's offer of paving Hannah Branch Road, and decided no in keeping with our desire to maintain the slow and rural characteristics of our shared land. We gave thoughtful consideration, also, to the comprehensive US Forest Service management plan for the Pisgah section, and sent an avalanche of letters supporting continued designation of adjacent lands for multiple use and non-clear cutting. With Paolo at the helm, our own forest management has stepped up this year with continued emphasis on the protection and preservation of our forests to the benefit of the whole community by means of creating a knowledge base about our forests and relevant issues, long range stewardship planning, possible selective harvesting and timber stand improvement in designated areas. We decided that all forestry actions will be taken with an eye towards balance between forest as natural habitat and forest as usable resource for the community. With Justina leading the charge, we addressed concerns regarding riparian effects of the logging on the Marshall tract adjacent to Celo. A tireless ad hoc committee has continued the work of keeping the brush cut back on our powercuts to avoid the French Broad Electric Co-op's new herbicide spray protocol. . . . We've begun considering how to address increasing user traffic on our roads and wilderness areas with more work to come. . . . At the same time, we've continued working at—and thinking about—the stewardship of our buildings. We've replaced the Celo Community Center roof, refinished all but the last of its floors save 2 offices and bathrooms, and pursued outdoor lighting. And, we've continued to give attention to how we may make land accessible and affordable to those wanting to join us and to our aging members in search of accessible elder housing. All that and we've still made time for stewarding our Procedures and Rules and other governing community documents. (Celo Community 2015)

H: *If I look specifically as to why I joined the community, the two main reasons would be for community and because I believed that land ownership is not the way to go. I think an alternative to land ownership is one of the most important developments that needs to happen in our world.*

I: *Why?*

H: *Because ultimately with land ownership, it creates a division between the rich and the poor and there will be a world landless class developing more and more all over the world. I mean, I've seen how that works in other countries. I did a lot of work in Central America, where it's devastating, where it created a violent, distorted culture, an impoverished culture. That hasn't happened in this country yet because there's so much land and so much wealth, but it'll come. I mean, it's already getting that way right now. The ability of the poor to buy a piece of land is extremely limited. And then the other reason is, this community protects the land. I believe in cooperative ownership and stewardship of the land. So stewardship of the land is a vital issue. A really key environmental change issue now is that we don't own the land. I think one of the basic reasons for environmental problems is this whole psychology of owning the land which means, if you own it, you can do whatever you want with it. You can trash it, you can cut down every tree on it, you can poison it. It's yours. Whereas here, that is not acknowledged at all. You can't do whatever you want with it. And so, talk about a clear way to positive environmental change, to move away from owner- ship and move towards stewardship is a key element. (Interview with author in Celo Community on November 17, 2004)*

The parcel of land that Celo's members own together and the entire South Toe Valley that surrounds it are possessed of rare beauty. A dark green forest blankets much of the land and, where there are breaks in the trees, awe-inspiring views of the Black Mountains and the Blue Ridge open up. Creeks with waterfalls cut through the forest and cascade into the South Toe River which bisects the valley and a portion of community land between the high-peaked Blacks to the west and Seven Mile Ridge to the east. Located at significant arm's length from any major urban center, the area maintains a rural character and hosts the most biodiverse temperate forest in North America. For those who appreciate nature, it is a place that is easy to fall in love with. For those who have wished to develop a different, more coopera- tive relationship with the land, a relationship grounded in a commitment to environmentally sensitive land stewardship, it is a place that has drawn them into common endeavor.

Nestled into this valley is a collection of about seven or eight dozen individuals that compose the official membership of Celo Community, Incorporated (Celo, CCI, or the community for short). For a variety of reasons, each of these individuals has decided to go against the grain of prevailing American culture; instead of pursuing the proverbial American dream of an individually owned suburban home filled with consumer goods and surrounded by a white picket fence, they've all chosen to throw their lot in with others in a unique endeavor of joint land ownership, stewardship, and governance. They all did so despite knowing the challenges and disadvantages it entailed: limited equity in one's home and the inability to obtain a mortgage along with the requirement that most decisions about individual land use practices and building construction fall under cooperative governance processes that dictate group interests prevail over those of the individual only two among such challenges and disadvantages. Having in place a deliberate process for choosing new community members is an important component of how this community has made this unique arrangement work for over eighty years.

All commons arrangements involve a defined group of people who work together to use and steward a defined communal resource be it land, a fishery, a pasture, or a water source among many other possibilities. The first point of orientation for commoning states that "as a commoner I clearly understand which resources I need to care for and with whom I share this responsibility. Commons resources are those that we create together, that we maintain as gifts of nature or whose use has been guaranteed to everyone" who is part of the group (Bollier and Helfrich 2015b: 48). While the statement by one of Celo's members at the beginning of this chapter situates common ownership of land in Celo within a broader context of global social and environmental justice, it also points very specifically to the ways in which Celo's members conceptualize membership in the community as a group endeavor of land stewardship that stands in stark contrast with patterns of individual land ownership that predominate in the United States. For such an endeavor to work in this context, it must be approached quite deliberately; careful attention must be paid to developing a collective understanding of what resources are being stewarded, who is to be involved in processes of stewardship, and how the participants are to be selected for inclusion in the group. Celo Community has crafted this deliberateness by creating a defined process for joining a community of co-owners and co-stewards of a contiguous, 1,200-acre parcel of land that was purchased as a site for Celo's communal experiment in the 1930s. The vignettes below offer a window on how these deliberate processes of community-making and land stewardship work.

Celo's meeting room is particularly full this evening as community members come together for their monthly community meeting. I've arrived with the community members with whom I'm staying during my research. Our flashlights sit on the floor next to us, ready to help us navigate through the dark along the community's footpaths as we make our way home after the meeting. Having discussed, debated and approved items of business introduced to the general meeting by the members of the property committee, we move on to matters raised by the membership committee. Tonight, there is a prospective community member in attendance. The chairperson of the membership committee introduces her and she stands to read her letter of interest.

"Thank you for having me here tonight to express my interest in becoming a member of Celo Community. I have been working at Arthur Morgan School for three years now and I've been blessed with the opportunity to learn about and experience the uniqueness of Celo Community. Through friendships I have developed with community members and through my participation in community workdays, I've gained an appreciation of the sense of community and environmental values that imbue this beautiful place. I am impressed by the way that you cooperate with one another and by your common commitment to stewarding the land together. Your values match my own, but until now, I have not experienced a context in which I could live by them on a daily basis. Celo Community is so different from the neighborhood I grew up in outside of Charlotte. I finally feel like I've found home. Please accept my application for membership in Celo Community. Thank you and blessings to you all."

This speech is met with a hearty round of applause from Celo's members, but soon it is back to business. Through previous experiences, Celo's members are well aware that good intentions and expressed coincidence of values do not always translate into positive outcomes for new community members nor for the community. In fact, the next item of business on the agenda involves a current trial community member who, in many senses, seems a good fit for the community. She has lived in the valley for a long time and is well known to many community members. She is an organic farmer who is clearly committed to environmentally sound land stewardship. Further, many in the community wish that more community members made a living from the land in line with Arthur Morgan's original aims for the community. She is also, like some current community members, a war tax resistor who deliberately lives below the poverty line so as to not pay taxes into a system that perpetuates not only outright violence but also structural violence associated with what she sees as unjust foreign policies.

However, as discussion in the community meeting proceeds, it is clear that a number of community members have significant reservations about whether or not this person is a good fit for the community. While there is almost universal support for her organic farming endeavors, some people are concerned about the unkempt appearance of her current operation on rented land across the valley; their desire for idyllic, pastoral viewsheds in the community may include food production, but not widely scattered plastic planting containers, deteriorating temporary greenhouses, and weedy crop rows. When a contingent of concerned community members approached the trial member to discuss their concerns, her reactions were emotional and defensive. That this has not changed much during subsequent mediated discussions does not bode well for the trial member's perceived ability to conform to community decision-making processes that are dependent on deep listening and temporary displacement of individual perspectives. A related and additional, albeit lesser, concern is the trial member's vocal opposition to U.S. foreign policy including via letters published in the local newspaper. While many share her desire for more humanitarian policies, they are also concerned that her outspokenness on these matters may draw unwanted attention and ire from the local community residents who tend not to share these views.

A small but significant contingent of community members believe that these actions on the part of the trial member are outward indications of deep personality traits that will be disruptive of the delicate balance of power and decision-making processes that the community has achieved through many challenges and much deliberateness over the years. A straw poll called for by the meeting chair suggests that the trial member would not receive the necessary 85% affirmative vote to be admitted into community membership when the vote is scheduled to take place in two months. A few moments of silence pass as community members weigh the gravity of the situation, expressions of angst and exasperation clear on many faces. No one wishes to cause hurt feeling by turning down a trial member who has clearly invested a lot in joining the community but, equally, no one wants to add a disruptive force to community social interactions and governance processes. Two or three community members leave the meeting early, continuing the conversation out to the parking lot. The meeting chair calls for all interested parties to pick up this discussion at the next membership committee meeting next Wednesday and report back at the next monthly community meeting. Note: the trial member in question was ultimately denied admittance to community membership in a vote that caused great and lasting tension in the community. While a number of trial members have chosen to exit the community's trial membership process of their own accord, this is the only example of a trial member being denied membership through community vote in the twenty years I have been working with the community. The individual in question still lives nearby and participates in community events; hard feelings seem to be slowly fading into the past.

Today I joined some of Celo's members for a "holding walk." A couple, Celo Community's newest members, have been renting from two community members on leave of absence to return to the site of their Peace Corps work in Lesotho for the last year. This new couple has been working hard to choose a holding site and develop a design for their new home in the community. The father, a computer technician who works in Burnsville, and the mother, a stay at home mom taking care of three young children, have been up late at night developing the design for their home. On weekends, when their children have been playing with other community kids, they have been walking through the woods attempting to demarcate a piece of land on which to build their new home and talking about their plans with other community members who would soon be their neighbors. They presented their plans at the property committee meeting last Wednesday and all seemed to go well.

Now is their chance to show community members in person and on site how they plan to make their home. They are nervous, but confident that they have thought of all contingencies. As they walk through their site, designs in hand, explaining their plans, it becomes apparent that there are concerns among those present. One community member points out that their home does not have a large southern exposure to accommodate passive solar gain. Further, were it to be so oriented on this particular site, it would require the cutting of a large number of trees that are not within the boundaries of their landholding as they have them marked out. Another community member points out that their proposed driveway runs through a patch of rare and mature black locust trees. Even if they plan to incorporate the lumber from these trees into their building design, she is not sure that she can countenance their removal. They're slow growing hardwoods.

As the group walks back towards the community center, the chairperson of the finance committee asks them if they have considered the financial implications of their building design. He points out that their building, while modest, will probably cost over a hundred thousand dollars to build. Do they have that kind of money available? They will not be able to obtain a bank loan because they don't own the land on which they are building and the community limits construction loans from its common fund to a maximum of $65,000. Finally, do they realize that if, God forbid because he really likes them, they have to leave the community and they cannot find a new holder from within the community and agree on terms for transferring the holding, the community will only guarantee a portion of their equity in the building. This guaranteed equity is, by the way, well below the estimated $100,000 building cost. As a young family with three children could they afford this? Perhaps they should reconsider their design.

As the land walk wraps up and the other community members depart in small groups, the couple looks at each other deflated. This wasn't what they had hoped for. They had witnessed other holding walks that did not raise nearly as many concerns. Perhaps they shouldn't have joined the community. But they knew what they were in for; they will persevere with the understanding that they *are abiding by the consensus process and the community's shared values of environmental stewardship and simple living. Note: this couple ultimately built a small and cozy house on another site that they took as a holding. It is fully oriented for passive solar gain, did not raise any concerns regarding the land that was cleared, and cost only $75,000.*

Ostrom's first design principle for successful commons stewardship is split into two parts which reference clearly defined social and spatial boundaries of the commons. Commons design principle 1A states that there are "clear and locally understood boundaries between legitimate users and nonusers are present" (Ostrom 2010: 653). In other words, there are clear criteria, clearly understood among the commoners themselves, regarding who is and who is not permitted to use and make decisions about the use of the common resource in question. In a related manner, commons design principle 1B states that "clear boundaries that separate a specific common-pool resource from a larger social-ecological system are present" (Ostrom 2010: 653). The clearly bounded group of individuals who share use and governance a resource must also have a clear understanding of what specific resource they share and where it begins and ends. In summary, the foundation for any physical commons is a clearly identifiable, bounded communal resource and a clearly bounded and identifiable group of stewards who share use and governance of the resource. In the following, I outline the ways in which the land whose purchase was facilitated by Arthur Morgan in the 1930s has turned into the foundation for the provision of a variety of commons resources and how membership in the community of commons stewards is determined.

CELO'S SPATIAL BOUNDARIES

A basic feature of the Community is its landholding agreement. All the land belongs to the Community. The individual or family evaluates and states his/its need for land, then pays for that much land and any existing houses or buildings at a fixed price (based on annual assessments). Then a Holding Agreement is signed by which the holder assumes responsibility and all essential privileges of ownership. No deed is ever bestowed. Since the individual does not own the land, he may never use it for speculation purposes, but within Community structure he may pursue his business or homelife as he wishes. On the holder's departure or death, his holding reverts to the Community for re-use, but it may pass by sale or will to another Community member if the Community approves. (Celo Community 2012)

In the case of Celo Community, the primary commons resource is a 1,200-acre parcel of land with clearly demarcated property boundaries. While the

contours of these particular property boundaries took shape long before
Celo existed and while they were laid out according to American jurisprudence aimed at facilitating individual land ownership, they have nonetheless become a container for a unique experiment in commons design. This
parcel of land provides community members with a variety of more specific
resources: home sites, fertile land for producing food for subsistence or for
sale, access to other goods such as water, firewood, or lumber, and spiritual
nourishment through interaction with relatively intact landscapes and ecosystems. While Celo's property is clearly legally bounded, the ecosystemic
properties of the land do not conform to these boundaries. Celo's communal
property was, long before it was purchased for the community, defined by the
straight lines typical of private property boundaries. It is also contiguous with
adjacent properties managed by a variety of owners and stewards, both public
and private. The old cliché about what happens upstream is clearly applicable
here and, as we will see later, has direct implications in terms of some of the
other principles for successful commons stewardship as manifested in Celo
Community.

A large number of maps of community land are on file in the community's
archives (see figure 4.1) indicating that clearly identified boundaries are a
salient issue to community members. These maps demarcate the boundaries of community-owned land relative to surrounding parcels as well as the
boundaries of individual landholdings taken by community member households relative to the remaining common land and to the landholdings of other

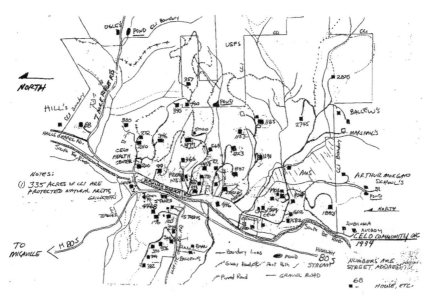

Figure 4.1   Example of Celo Community Sketch Map. *Source:* Courtesy of Celo Community.

community members. Within the physical landscape itself, the boundaries of community land are not always clearly marked, although a small number of community members have taken on the job of occasionally walking the boundaries and marking them at intervals. In addition, there are occasional organized "land walks" and most community members spend some time individually walking at least portions of the property and getting to know the land of which they are co-owners and co-stewards.

The common ownership of this 1,200 acre parcel of land has also provided a context for other acts of commoning, for the development of additional commons resources, not only by Celo's members but also by residents in the wider communities that surround Celo. For example, community members have developed common infrastructure in the form of roads and footpaths that provide access to the land including small, individual landholdings and larger common areas. They have also developed a community center building and associated grounds that are used for community governance meetings and social events. The community has accumulated a financial commons; they have a reserve fund that is used to reimburse departing members for their equity in their buildings and individual landholdings. The fund can also be used to make loans to individual community members who wish to build homes, make improvements to existing homes or landholdings, pursue educational opportunities, or start business ventures. Additionally, there is a cultural commons of knowledge and wisdom held by community members. This includes knowledge about the land, the community's history, and the rules and procedures for community governance. These are embodied in the community archives stored at the community center building as well as in the brains of longtime community members. The cultural commons also includes the sharing of individual skills, experiences, and expertise among the members of the community. Sharing of this information and wisdom is facilitated via organized events, including the annual Cabin Fever University series, that are often held at the community center. Finally, there is a labor commons manifested in the form of monthly community workdays during which community members volunteer their skills, energy, and labor for a group project. Sometimes these projects focus on maintaining or improving commonly held land or infrastructure, but they may also involve making repairs or improvements to an individual community member's home or landholding. In this book, the primary focus will be on the land as a commons, but reference will also be made to some of the other commons described above (see also Table 4.1).

Celo Community's common resources also serve as a venue for other commons institutions that Celo's members have developed in cooperation with residents of the surrounding area who are not community members. In some cases, these institutions have been granted a landholding by the community on which to operate. For example, the Celo Friends Meeting, a local gathering

Table 4.1   Celo's Commons Resources

Commons Resource	Description
1,200 acre contiguous land parcel	Provides individual home sites, wilderness areas, timber and other resources
Infrastructure	Roads, trails, Celo Community Center building, individual homes not currently occupied by community members
Financial commons	Reserve funds for holding transfers and loans of various types to community members
Social commons	Interpersonal social relationships, networks, and support
Cultural commons	Shared knowledge and wisdom; Institutional memory
Labor commons	Monthly volunteer workdays
Commons institutions physically anchored within community boundaries but governed or used by groups that include noncommunity members	Celo Friends Meeting Quaker worship house
	Ten Thousand Things food cooperative
	Toe River Crafts artists' cooperative
	Arthur Morgan School middle school level boarding school
	Cabin Fever University events, many held at the Celo Community Center

for Quaker worship has, for almost the entire life of the community, had a landholding and building in which to worship located in the heart of the community's common land. Over the last twenty years, the membership in this group has been composed of about half community members and half noncommunity member residents of the surrounding area, although it is trending toward a majority of noncommunity members. Similarly, the community provides land and buildings for a food co-op and an artists' co-op, both of whose memberships are composed of majority noncommunity members. In addition, the Celo Community Center acts as a venue for many wider community events, including many of the events in the aforementioned, cooperatively organized Cabin Fever University series.

CELO COMMUNITY AS A LAND TRUST

In some of its documents, Celo Community describes itself as a private land trust or private stewardship trust. While Celo does not have official legal standing as a land trust, it functions in a similar manner with many land trust principles present within the community's institutions, procedures, and rules. According to Gilman, "a land trust is a non-governmental organization, frequently a non-profit corporation, that divides land ownership rights between immediate users and their wider communities" (Gilman 1990: 112). There are a number of different types of land trusts but within each, "the immediate users (non-human as well as human) have clear rights which satisfy their legitimate use needs" (Gilman 1990: 113). That these needs are met is ensured by the process through which the land trust is governed and administered. This process usually involves a board of trustees within which the needs of the various stakeholders—leaseholders, the trust community, the wider community, nonhuman species—are represented by board members. "By dividing ownership into 'stewardship' for leaseholders and 'trusteeship' for wider community representatives, land trusts are pioneering an approach that integrates the legitimate interests of the individual with those of society and the rest of the natural world" (Gilman 1990: 113). While official community members are the only ones who may participate in daily decision-making about land use, I will show later how Celo's members take into account the interests of the wider community and even the other-than-human inhabitants of the land.

The idea of land trusts is fairly radical when considered in the context of American society where individual ownership and control of land is sacrosanct. By vesting individuals with political and economic power, partially through individual land ownership, the United States attempted to overcome systems of feudalism and theocratic control that characterized Europe. Traditionally, private land ownership in America was seen as the basis for individual security, earned equity, and a family legacy. It was the mechanism through which one could build a home and a livelihood that could be passed on to one's family. Increasingly, ownership of land is seen as source of profit and the inequitable distribution of land underlies larger patterns of social, political, economic, and racial inequality in society. Land is developed, subdivided, and sold as property values increase. Alternatively, the resources contained on the land, resources that may have accrued over many years prior to the establishment of current individual ownership, are extracted and sold as commodities for profit. Increasing percentages of land are used in these ways as a source of profit by corporations and individual landowners that control large amounts of land and that do not have any direct interest in the integrity of the land, local communities, or the utility of land and resources to future generations (Institute for Community Economics 1982).

The idea of the land trust is radical because it is an attempt to institutionalize recognition for the broader interests of a broader number of stakeholders—human and nonhuman, past, present, and future—for whom the land is a source of livelihood, flourishing, and security. Proponents of land trusts

talk about "decommodification," of changing the way people look at land and housing—not as a commodity for speculation and exploitation, but as a resource to be shared. Land trusts counterbalance the American taboo about inviolability of private property by stressing the historic social rights of the community [and the rights of non-human communities as well]. (Naurekas 1990: 115)

The land trust concept is an attempt to remove the idea of land ownership from the strictly economic realm and to bring broader political and ethical concerns of social equity and ecological integrity into the institutions that govern land ownership.

The development of the land trust concept is well over a hundred years old. This development grows from Henry George and his Single Tax Theory, the single tax colonies of Fairhope, Alabama and Arden, Delaware, the work of Ralph Borsodi at the School of Living in Suffern, New York, and the work of the Institute for Community Economics. Celo Community's land trust model and the work of Arthur Morgan and others at Community Service, Inc. are cited as examples in a long line of development of the land trust model (Stucki and Yeatman 1990, Questenberry 1990). In Celo's model, the interests of the wider community and nonhuman species are dependent upon the values and ethical integrity of the residents of the land trust. Whereas other land trusts are governed by an outside board designed to represent outside interests, the members of Celo Community retain control of the selection of members of the board that oversees the trust. This is one reason why coincidence of values in Celo, a coincidence maintained through their membership screening and consensus governance processes, is so important.

The community land trust is a more recent innovation in the land trust concept, one that goes to greater efforts to institutionalize the interests of the wider community, especially those in need of affordable housing, and natural ecosystems. It does so by separating control of the board of trustees from the leaseholders of trust land (Further discussions of the community land trust model can be found in Moore and McKee 2012, Campbell and Salus 2003, Stucki and Yeatman 1990 and Institute for Community Economics 1982). Celo Community combines features of the land trust and community land trust models into the unique arrangements, contracts, and agreements that structure members' relationships with each other and with their 1,200 acre parcel of land.

Celo's Holding Agreement is the legal contract, the institutional form, that manifests Celo's model of land tenure and trust. It encodes the mutual relationships that exist among the community as a social entity, its individual members, and the entirety of its land that it holds in trust. Celo Community Inc.'s Holding Agreement is a fairly complex legal document. It spells out the rights and responsibilities of both the holder (the individual community member taking temporary individual usufruct of a specified tract of community-owned land) and the community as an organization committed to mutual benefit and land stewardship. The Holding Agreement institutionalizes a unique form of land tenure and property rights. In the community's words, "The Holding Agreement is neither a deed nor a lease but a legal contract defining the legal relationship between Celo Community, Inc., and the Holder in regard to the use of real property within the Community when taken as a Holding" (Celo Community 2018b). The Holding Agreement balances individual and community interests in favor of "mutual benefit" and "common welfare."

Membership in Celo Community is synonymous with residence on land owned by the community and, more specifically, with the signing of the Holding Agreement and the taking of an individual landholding. The Holding Agreement confers regulated usufruct rights to a specific landholding on community land to the individual community member and her household and dictates the terms under which any transfer of an individual holding and associated usufruct rights may be conducted. Celo's institution of membership-based group land tenure is unique and it is worth quoting Celo's conceptualization of this arrangement at some length.

> A basic feature of the Community is its landholding agreement. All the land belongs to the Community. The individual or family evaluates and states his/its need for land, then pays for that much land and any existing houses or buildings at a fixed price (based on annual assessments.) Then a Holding Agreement is signed by which the holder assumes responsibility and all essential privileges of ownership. No deed is ever bestowed. Since the individual does not own the land, he may never use it for speculation purposes, but within Community structure he may pursue his business or homelife as he wishes. On the holder's departure or death, his holding reverts to the Community for re-use, but it may pass by sale or will to another Community member if the Community approves. (Celo Community 2012)

> The Community operates for the mutual benefit of all holders of lands under agreements with the Community for land holdings. . . . This Agreement is not a deed, but is a cooperative agreement between parties that have mutual interest in the development and welfare of Celo Community, Inc. Because the Holder and other members of Celo Community, Inc. are mutually interested in maintaining the common welfare of the Community, and are agreed to forgo some elements of private control in order to promote their common welfare and in order to develop the greatest and best use and value of the Community's resources, the Holder accepts the conditions of possession and use of this Holding as set forth in this Agreement, as part of the general program of mutual benefit to all holders in said Community. (Celo Community 2018b)

In their literature, Celo Community is careful to articulate the implications of their Holding Agreement for incoming members who may be accustomed to the model of private land ownership that prevails in the United States. Below, I discuss a number of these specific implications.

One thing the community wishes to make especially clear to potential members is that upon joining the community, they will be party to a unique land tenure agreement that provides the advantages of partial ownership of a large property and associated community buildings while reserving to the community many of the specific rights that would otherwise accrue to the individual landowner. In the interests of land stewardship, the community has designed an institution through which the advantages of access to and joint ownership of a large piece of rural land are traded for usurpation of particular property rights that would otherwise be assigned solely to an individual owner. Specifically, Celo's Holding Agreement disallows speculative gain and development of land or extraction of associated resources that is not conducted in a socially and ecologically sensitive manner.

In some senses, Celo's model of land tenure functions in a manner similar to local zoning laws, but in many ways Celo's rules and procedures go much farther than do most zoning laws in regulating land use. The community must consult on and approve holding sites, the placement and design of individual houses, the construction and placement of any outbuildings, the clearing of land and the cutting of any trees over six inches in diameter. The procedures for taking a holding once one is accepted into the community appear fairly straightforward, but the approval process and the regulations contained in the Holding Agreement can be convoluted and complex when submitted to the process of consensus decision-making (discussed in another chapter) and considered within the context of Celo's land use plan. The community has recently developed a comprehensive land use plan (also discussed more fully in another chapter) that delimits all designated holding sites. These sites have been deemed appropriate for individual holdings based upon a number of considerations defined by Celo's members including potential for solar gain for purposes of energy efficiency; spatial relationship with other holding sites; and noninterference with other community land uses including wilderness areas, greenways, wildlife corridors, communal use parks, wood lots, agricultural fields, business sites and trails.

Individual holding site selections and building plans must be approved by Celo's property committee and their general community meeting through the consensus process. All interested community members can participate in this process. It can be extremely time-consuming to account for all perspectives and reach consensus on a holding site and building design. After appropriate approvals, surveys, appraisals and payments, the new community member may take up residence and begin building on his holding. Alternatively, he may choose to take an existing holding that was made available by a departing member, in which case the process is simplified because the holding was previously approved and the buildings already exist. Designated holdings may also be taken for agricultural use in which case it is expected that no house will be built there. With regard to individual holding sites a number of other regulations contained in the Holding Agreement or in other community documents are binding on the individual holder. These include stipulations regarding the holder member's responsibilities to the community and vice versa, stipulations that the holder agrees to abide by community rules regarding property use described in other community documents, descriptions of how the value of the holding is to be determined and the process by which the holding may be transferred upon termination of the holder's membership or upon the dissolution of the community, and rules that regulate timber harvesting, extraction of other natural resources and the use of chemical sprays. All these regulations are designed to ensure that the community's land and infrastructure remain intact as a commons.

Perhaps the most significant component of Celo's Holding Agreement is the part that concerns the transfer of a holding upon termination of community membership. The regulations governing this eventuality are designed to prevent the possibilities of subdivision of community land and speculative profit on real estate development and sale and they have the effect of encouraging commitment to community and place and to simple living. In the event that an individual member decides to terminate her relationship with the community, her landholding, including any buildings and improvements, cannot be placed on the open market. Rather, the holding can only be transferred through the community to another member of the community. This other community member may be the child of a community member or another member of their family who has been accepted as a community member and to whom the holder has designated in writing that the holding should pass. More often, the other community member is someone who was recently accepted into membership who is in search of a holding to take. In the event that an appropriate transferee cannot be found within the community within a certain number of years, the community will only guarantee return of a certain portion of the holder's equity in the property up to $65,000. In addition, this guaranteed amount may only be paid over a period of ten years. As such, one must be fully aware that they are making a financial investment in a property that they may never fully recover in monetary terms as they likely would if they possessed an individually deeded property. One community member, expressing to me a desire to more effectively communicate the implications of this agreement to potential community members, described the arrangement to me as "the opposite of equity."

Although Celo Community only guarantees a certain portion of one's equity in their holding, Celo endeavors to make their land affordable and easily available to prospective members. The monetary values assigned to landholdings reflect this. The amounts that community members pay for their individual landholding acreages ($2,500 per home site acre, $2,000 per acre of additional cleared land, and $1,000 per acre for additional wooded land) are significantly lower than the going market rates for comparable land in the area. This stems from the community's desire to provide opportunity, in the form of access to land and supportive community, to those who wish to live their lives and organize their livelihoods according to considerations that are moral or ethical rather than strictly financial. Standing behind these regulations is the idea that a new member is making an investment in a social community and in caring for a large piece of collectively held land. Following Morgan's vision and those of other utopian cultural critics who came to the community, it is believed that this sort of investment should be more highly valued than any financial gain that might accrue from a transitory and speculative relationship with the land. This broad definition of value speaks to the second principle of commons stewardship discussed in the next chapter, particularly as it pertains to the benefits of participating in a commons arrangement being commensurate with the costs for an individual commons member. It is also a consideration that all potential community members should keep in mind when they enter the trial membership process for joining the community.

CELO'S SOCIAL BOUNDARIES

The aim of Celo Community is to provide an opportunity for its members to enjoy a life that includes personal expression, neighborly friendship and cooperation, and appreciative care of the natural environment. No person is excluded from membership because of national or racial origin or religious belief, disability, sexual orientation, or gender identity.

We encourage personal enterprise among members by making land and money available when needed for suitable productive use. Regarding ownership of land as a trust, we do not sell it, but assign it for short or long periods at as low an assessment as feasible to those who give promise of improving it while living harmoniously with their neighbors. From our revolving fund we occasionally lend money at low cost to a member for the purpose of improving his property.

In the relation of the Community to its members the legal is an instrument of the moral. The relation is not an external one between a soulless corporation and independent individuals. It is the internal relation between one person of a friendly neighborhood group and all other persons including himself. Thus a member consulting in a Community meeting on a course of action is both a private user and (in consensus with others) a public controller of land. A community member through participating in Community government tends to develop a stable and considerate character along with responsible personal expression. (Celo Community 2018a)

In addition to having clear physical boundaries in the landscape, any group that wishes to share resources and successfully steward them needs to be able to identify who is and who is not part of the group. The quotations above from Celo Community documents open a window on the ways in which the community defines its membership and its members' relationship with their collectively held land. Like many contemporary intentional communities, Celo accepts new members—and thus new co-owners and co-governors of their collectively held 1,200 acres—only after a deliberate, structured process that allows existing community members and potential community members to get to know each other. More specifically, people interested in joining Celo Community must complete a minimum six month to yearlong trial membership period during which they are expected to be present at and participate in community meetings and other processes of community governance and social interaction. At the end of this trial period, the community decides at a public community meeting, preferably by consensus but by supermajority vote of at least 85 percent if necessary, on whether to accept the trial members as full community members. Accepted members are then expected, within a reasonable period of time, to take an individual landholding within the 1,200 acres and begin participating in processes of community governance. Community documents describe this process and the rationale for it at some length:

> The purpose of the CCI membership process is to give prospective members an opportunity to experience the CCI land trust form of landholding, to become acquainted with the CCI meeting and decision process, and to get to know current CCI members. For prospective members who have not lived in the South Toe area, we also feel it is essential that they explore the social, vocational, educational and lifestyle implications of choosing to live in this relatively isolated rural area. In turn, the membership process gives CCI members an opportunity to become acquainted with the prospective member and to form an opinion about how well the prospective member will fit into the land trust . . .
>
> To achieve the goals outlined above, the membership process is relatively extended. The minimum period of trial membership is twelve months and may be extended, for one to six months, on the request of the prospective member or

CCI. It is also important that the prospective member live on CCI land . . . or if CCI housing is not available, take up residence in South Toe Township. . . . A family member already living on a CCI holding with a member (i.e. not requiring a new holding) may complete trial membership in six months if they choose. (Celo Community 2019)

While there is no clearly delineated list of criteria for accepting or rejecting a potential community member, the community does have a description of the community and a list of self-evaluation questions it sends to people who express interest in membership. This list outlines some important considerations that potential members are expected to take into account. This document is worth quoting at length. Some of the statements and questions from this document pertaining to common land ownership, governance, and stewardship are listed below:

Celo Community, Inc. is an intentional community of . . . independent households whose common bond is a desire to care for, use well, and preserve for future use its land-holdings.

The original intent was that the Community be an evolving experiment whose people, free from the pressures of urban society, might explore the possibilities of rural living, social change and social cooperation and interaction.

CCI is a self-governing body which makes its decisions by a process called "consensus," a method of reaching general agreement in feeling or opinion without voting. . . . In CCI meetings consensus is often easily arrived at on questions of small property such as cutting of trees or the mowing of fields. On other issues which involve deeper differences of opinion, great patience and self-discipline are called for.

The Celo way of owning house/land is for most people a sacrifice financially. It may even be un-American as it does not generally involve turning a profit if the house is sold. Receiving a fair price is possible, but taking a loss is also probable.

Before dismissing this too quickly, remember that the desire to own land and to be able to do with it as one wishes runs very deep in some people. Even people who have strong feelings about cooperative ownership on an intellectual level, may still have the basic urge for individual ownership and initiative on an almost primal level.

Do you recognize the fact that our land holding arrangement means you can never expect to make a speculative profit on investment here? That you build your house on land to which you have no legal title? That your rights to your land are dependent on your continued membership in CCI?

Are you satisfied to accept the fact that when you die your children might not be accepted into Community membership in order to inherit your holding?

A member must be willing to seek Community permission to make almost any changes on his holding. There are often delays in getting things done, or even started.

If you plan to build or make changes in an existing holding, would you feel that the Community has a right to go over your plans, criticizing and making suggestions?

Can you share control with others?

Living in the Community is time-consuming. The Community has up to four meetings and two workdays monthly. Are you willing to give the necessary time?

Are you able to speak on an issue you feel strongly about in front of an opposition of strong personalities?

Are you tolerant of other points of view and willing to compromise so that the Community can act as a whole?

Are you attracted to Celo because of interest in the structure (our land arrangement and our method of handling CCI responsibilities) rather than primary interest in specific individuals who are here now? (Celo Community 2012)

These questions and statements give a basic idea of how Celo functions as a commons in ways that are often quite different from what most Americans are used to. They also foreshadow some of the issues that will be discussed in subsequent chapters. For our purposes here, they provide a concise overview of some of the basic challenges potential members are encouraged to consider as they approach a trial membership in the community. This trial membership process is an attempt to filter out people who don't share values of and capacity for cooperative community governance and land stewardship. It is also an example of community institutions designed to ensure the coincidence of values that is important to successful commons stewardship, a coincidence of values that many intentional communities have struggled to ensure exists, sometimes leading to poor stewardship of resources or even dissolution of the community (see Gibson and Koontz 1998 for an example).

Generally, the community only accepts two new members or member households per year. There are multiple reasons for this including, primarily, a desire to prevent disruption of community consensus governance processes via the rapid influx of large numbers of new participants who are not familiar with the rules and procedures. While processes of community governance is described in greater detail in a subsequent chapter, suffice it to say that effective consensus governance involves unique rules and procedures that are quite different from systems that most Americans might be more familiar with such as majority voting or Robert's Rules of Order. It also requires the cultivation of trust among participants, the ability to set aside one's personal views and really listen to others, and the patience to allow group wisdom to emerge, oftentimes at a slow pace. In light of this, and combined with the fact that the community is concerned to balance the development of new housing sites with the maintenance of existing homes and the ecological integrity of their land, they have agreed on the policy of considering only two new member households per year via the trial membership process.

One may enter the trial membership process via one of three possible avenues. The first and most common avenue throughout the community's history is through the community's general waiting list. Up through the 1980s when the community was actively seeking to increase its membership and fill its available land, one could move through this waiting list relatively quickly. In more recent decades, due to growing interest in community membership and the implementation of the family waiting list, people who join this list can find themselves with an initial wait time of up to twenty years to start their trial membership. As a number of children who grew up in the community became interested in community membership, the community added a family waiting list that tends to have a shorter wait time and includes a shorter trial membership period of a minimum six months. Generally, one trial member from each of the general and family waiting lists is accepted each year, although if there are no family members ready to join, an additional trial member from the general waiting list may be considered by the community. More recently, the community implemented a "fast track" trial membership process by which a trial member may be added out of sequence with the other wait lists if their membership is uniquely perceived to meet certain immediate needs of the community, such as a promise to fill a community home that has been vacant for some time, to transfer a holding of a recently deceased member to one of their heirs, or to take over a business being left behind by a departing member.

At the end of the trial membership period, the potential member and the community may decide to extend the trial membership or move for a decision on full membership. If a decision is called for, community members are notified at least a month in advance that such a decision will be made at the next general community meeting. Trial members are present at a community meeting during which their membership application is discussed. At the subsequent community meeting, community members attempt to reach consensus regarding approval of the new member. If consensus cannot be reached, a vote is taken. In this case, votes and accompanying rationales for votes against full membership are provided in writing by all present community members. Negative votes and their rationales may be submitted anonymously. A supermajority of 85 percent is required for affirmation of a new membership. (This is the only area in which the community regularly makes final decisions by anonymous vote rather than through the open discussion characteristic of the consensus process, although there is a lot of open discussion in the months building up to the final vote. It is a result of two contentious trial memberships in earlier decades and is a matter of some ongoing controversy in the community). Final membership votes are contingent upon approval by Celo Community's board of directors, although this amounts to a rubber stamp as the community appoints board members, the majority of which are community members including all board office holders. This process of discussion and decision-making on new memberships provides an opportunity for existing community members to express their views as to whether or not and why or why not the prospective member fits within the social, ideological, and institutional values and structure of the community.

New community members are required to sign their membership agreement within thirty days of their membership being approved. The membership agreement stipulates that the new member understands and agrees to abide by community purposes, procedures, and rules as they are articulated in the following documents: Certificate of Incorporation, Code of Regulations of the Corporation, Constitution and By-Laws of the Community, Community Holding Agreement, Community Membership Agreement and the Consensus Decision-Making Process. It further states that community members are expected to reside primarily within the community (requests for leaves of absence of six months or more must be approved by the community), actively participate in community governance, assume their share of the yearly community budget and property taxes and abide by community decisions reached through the consensus process. The Membership Agreement ends by discussing the procedures and grounds for termination of membership by the community. Thus, the membership screening process described above provides an opportunity for a mutual familiarization period between the prospective member and existing community members. It enables all parties to make judgments as to whether or not there is a sufficient coincidence of values among them such that they will all be able to abide by the rules and institutions that put those values into action as they proceed together in their collective endeavor. In Celo Community, the strongest unifying values and institutions are those that concern the relationship of community members to the land and through the land to each other.

Chapter 5

Creating Our Own Commons Rules

Workday Report—October 4, 2014

As I was going through the sign-up sheets for workday for this past year, it was impossible not to notice the name Mike written in Mike's distinctive hand. Throughout this year, Mike was the champion workday participant, both in deed and in spirit.

And then of course there were these last two months with an empty space where his name should have been. I bring up Mike here in the context of this year's workday report not only because he was such a consistent and enthusiastic participant and not just because he was such a believer in creating community on the ground—and our bodies—through shared work. I bring it up because of something he said to me on the workday on August 9th, just ten days before he died so unexpectedly. We were cutting back the edges of the grassy road, and at some point Mike and I got to talking about life choices and the stresses that can come from trying to make a living in Celo. He said, "We may not have a lot of money to put in the bank, but we have social capital—and this is how we make it earn interest." Social capital: the idea is at the heart of how workday makes us rich. And there is a kind of compound interest or positive feedback loop at work in our workdays: what we do together not only gets done, but makes us stronger as a group and better able to handle everything else on which we need to collaborate. . .

Having the Arthur Morgan School students with us on workday always inspires me, and it makes me aware that, in our dogged monthly consistency, we are passing on this ideal of shared work to everyone who witnesses it and joins us. Indeed, I remember the wave of optimism and greater purpose last November as we worked with the school staff to reclaim the solar panels from the Taylor Togs building in Micaville for installation at the school—the sense of giving something to the future. However, the fact is that much of the effort of our monthly workdays this year, as always, is impermanent. While we made great improvements cleaning up Geouge Park last winter, the clearing we did on the edges of the field in September will need to be done again; and undoubtedly, the fine work cutting back brush on the grassy road begun in August and continued today is an ongoing project, as are the drainage improvements we made there in July. The newly repaired foot bridge at the base of Ohle's pond will give way to the mire, our knowledge of the property boundary regained on last winter's boundary walk will fade in memory and need to be refreshed, the bamboo cut for visibility near the bridge will regrow and again foil our sightlines, and we are likely to be locked for generations in a battle against invasive bittersweet.

We know our work is temporary, that our gains are ephemeral, but we work on together. We work on together because on the morning of the first Saturday after the first Wednesday of every month we know our friends and neighbors will be there to make manifest in physical form the precious idea of community. We work on together to say this is who we are. We work on together because we know that in the end, the only thing we actually own is our connection to one another and the land. We work on together because in the midst of impermanence and loss, this love is the one thing that endures.

Respectfully Submitted, Celo Community Workday Coordinators. (Celo Community 2014)

M: I think one of the biggest reasons, really, that we decided to join, is that when people share things, they don't have to be slaves to a job. Most of the people out there have a house that they could sell and probably profit from it, but they give their lives to that house and that car and that's something I've never been willing to do and neither has [my husband]. I've said that people in this area [referring to western North Carolina], I think, still know their neighbors and are friends with them and do help and take care of one another when they're in trouble, but there's still that economic servitude, that people think they have to have so many things. That I guess is something that really attracted us to this place, is the simple living. We never wanted a lot of stuff and didn't want to become slaves to buying stuff and you could see here right away that that's the way people lived here. (Interview with author in Celo Community on February 25, 2005)

D: I think another reason [I joined] was perhaps the realization that in order to have outside the community what I have inside the community would take a great deal of money. It would require me to have probably a full-time job somewhere, spending less time enjoying where I'm living, benefiting from the setting in which I'm living and so again, that was a way to solve that problem.

I: So what I'm hearing is that you saw the community as sort of allowing you to live a different lifestyle than you might have otherwise in the mainstream, in terms of a land ethic and in terms of being able then to enjoy being on the land without having to be part of the rat race to do it?

D: Yeah, I think that sums it up quite well. . . . We're not looking at ourselves in the same way that people living in the cities are looking at themselves, where they have to have the same thing that everybody else has got. They have to live in a big house because all their neighbors or their friends live in big houses or their cousins in some other city live in a big house. Or they have to go make mucho money because that's the only way they can live that way and afford to live that way. My time is more valuable to me than a lot of money in the bank. . . . So [living here I] benefit from the social connections in the community and the natural setting, which is pretty important to me. (Interview with author in Celo Community on September 23, 2004)

The second point of orientation for commoning states that "We use the commons resources that we create, care for and maintain. We use the means (time, space, technology, and quantity of a resource) that are available in a given context. As [a] commoner, I am satisfied that there is a fair relationship between my contributions and the benefits I receive" (Bollier and Helfrich 2015b: 49). This point encapsulates two important dimensions that may be taken individually. First, the commoners as a group are involved in actively creating, caring for, and maintaining the commons using the means that are available to them. This point is particularly apparent in the way the members of Celo not only live on their land but also in the way they collectively re-instantiate it as a commons through communal rituals and work projects designed to maintain the ecological health of the commons and make themselves aware of the land as a unique place that also cares for them. The second point is that the commoners feel that they get benefits from the commons that are commensurate with what they put into recreating and maintaining them in terms not only of finances but also labor, time, energy, and love. Most of Celo's members were drawn to the community because they felt such a move was an investment from which they could gain many intangible returns.

It's a sunny, summer Saturday morning and I'm on my way to a Celo Community workday inside the large portion of land that Celo has set aside as a permanent wilderness area. I'm wearing a pair of galoshes and carrying a pair of gloves and hedge trimmers because today we will be working in a rare patch of Southern Appalachian Bog that Celo has chosen to protect from development. I'm walking with Celo's resident naturalist, a man who came to the area two decades ago looking for a place to complete his research for his doctoral degree in ecology. He found Celo's collective commitment to stewarding their land attractive, was invited to use their land as a study site, and decided to join the community. He explains to me that the bog is an endangered habitat type in

*North Carolina because of the massive amount of deforestation that has taken
place here over the last century and a half. The bog habitat depends upon dense
vegetation to slow the flow of water on the mountain slopes as well as underlying granite formations to force the water to the surface. He indicates that when
he explained the significance of the bog to Celo's members, they took steps to
protect it and the wide buffers of forest that are required to ensure its continued
functioning.*

*As we arrive at the bog, there are already about ten other community mem-
bers at work, laughing and enjoying the beautiful day. I observe them working
with saws and clippers around the edges of the bog. As I witness their feet
sinking into the spongy surface, I ask my traveling companion if we are not
damaging the bog by trampling through it more than we are helping it. He
explains to me that the bog habitat is dependent upon periodic natural fires for
its continued existence. Since natural fires have been suppressed for some time,
woody tree species are increasingly encroaching on the bog and outcompeting
other species specific to this habitat. Today, we are here to cut back these species. Before we go to work ourselves, he takes time to show me which species
should be cut and which should not, noting specifically three endangered plant
species that depend on the bog—the queen-of-the-prairie, the balsam groundsel,
and the marsh bellflower. As we begin to work, cutting back woody shrubs and
trees along the edge of the bog, the voices fade into the background and the bog
and the surrounding forest come alive around me, animated by the knowledge
and values that Celo's members share and use as a foundation for becoming
partners in stewardship of the their collectively owned land.*

*As the fall leaves see-saw to the ground and the first bit of frost touches the air,
members of Celo Community convene at the community center for a special
called meeting to discuss the results of a recent self-study. The survey, designed
to gauge community members' needs, desires, and priorities for the community
as it looks to the future, was initiated in response to perceived tension among
community members about how it should develop. As people hang their coats
and settle into assorted chairs and couches in the large upstairs room, a slight
but palpable tension hangs in the air.*

*The chair of the community's monthly meetings, a Quaker who also chairs
the business meetings of the Friends group that meets in Celo and who has been
a community member longer than anyone else, gives an overview of community
history that led them to this point. "As most of us are aware, the community
finds itself today in unprecedented territory. During the first four decades of our
existence, Celo struggled to attract enough members to effectively occupy and
use the land. In the seventies that changed as many of you back-to-the-landers
came and brought new vitality and energy to the community. As a result, over
the last three decades, cooperative endeavors in the community have flowered*

anew and a new focus has been given to ecologically sensitive land stewardship. However, as you also know, we face new challenges. Interest in the community has grown so much that we've slowed down the membership process; to the chagrin of many of us, people interested in joining the community may now face a wait of up to twenty years. At the same time, many of us are concerned about the amount of land that has been cleared over the last decade to create housing for new members; some of us are concerned to plan for the development of our land in a more deliberate manner. And," he says, pointing to the cluster of community members standing around the double door of the room, "our consensus-based governance process has grown difficult at times, especially when we can't all fit in the same room."

Writing in my notes that this feels like a momentous occasion for the community, I take handouts from each of the stacks of paper circulating around the room. These handouts summarize the results of the community's self-study. John, a member who joined the community in 1972 as a back-to-the-lander and the point person for the survey, steps forward to discuss highlights from the study. "I think we all acknowledge some differences in opinion about community priorities as we plan for the future. While this survey does indicate some division amongst us along these lines, it also demonstrates significant overlap in our perspectives. I'd like to express gratitude that ninety seven percent of community members took the time to complete the survey; at least we know that everyone has had a chance to have their say. Let's review the results and take some time to digest them."

The next morning, I sit down at the dining room table in a pool of sun spilling in through the large south-facing windows in Leveridge house, a home named after the early community members who built it and currently occupied by two community members with whom I'm staying during my field research. The view across the valley to the Black Mountains is really opening up as the leaves begin to fall from the trees. The sounds of Rick, one of the community members I'm staying with, chopping and stacking firewood with help from two other community members reverberates as I take a closer look at the survey result handouts from last night.

As suggested at last night's meeting, the results indicate, simultaneously, division and common ground. In response to one set of questions, almost equal numbers of people indicate that, on the one hand, caring for the people who live in the community is their most important priority and, on the other hand, that caring for the land that the community stewards is their most important priority. In fact, the percentages don't add up; some people clearly marked both as their highest priority. Closed ended survey questions also indicate that a significant majority of community members wish for the community's membership to grow in size but that, on the other hand, there are significant reservations about how new landholdings to accommodate new community members will be identified and in terms of how many people community members would feel comfortable with participating in community meetings. 71% of community members would like to see the community grow in size, including slightly over 50% of respondents who think the community should add fifteen or more community members. On the other hand, 59% of community members believe that the number of landholdings should not be increased by more than 10 (not enough to accommodate all the potential new community members) and 67% of respondents indicate that they are not comfortable with any more participants than there currently are in the monthly community meetings.

Comments from the open-ended question portion of the survey also illustrate the conflicting perspectives community members have regarding growth in membership relative to effective land stewardship and community governance:

"I have been here since 1971 and feel the influx of members has been healthy. I prefer the community we have now—more going on—more vital—new blood keeps us healthy. 1200 acres is <u>lots.</u> . . . With housing harder to come by, I feel we have a moral obligation to keep our doors open at this time. I may feel we are 'crowded' later but <u>not yet</u>."

"Considering the basis on which CCI was established I consider it wrong for the relatively few people we have now, i.e. low ratio of people to acres, to set a limit at this point in time."

"I think we need to see the development of CCI in context with the development of the area as a whole. When I return to CCI I get a feeling of doom lurking, a fear of development getting out of hand in the county as a whole. . . . Development in CCI within this context means we need to be even more careful about preserving the natural peaceful beauty of the place and about developing an even stronger sense of community. I'm not sure how we can do that if we add significantly more community members."

"The last 5 years included lots of new construction—houses, roads, power lines. Let's take a break—let some new roads settle and some power cuts grow over and some new houses get landscaped. A moratorium on new holdings, a moratorium on active trial members who will need to select new holdings—give ourselves some time to get a grip on the big picture."

"I value the community for both the people and our collective commitment to stewarding the land. However, I'm concerned that if we continue to grow, the consensus process will become unwieldy and unproductive."

As I finish reading through the open-ended comments, Rick comes back in from chopping firewood, waving goodbye to the other community members who helped. I ask him what he thinks about the survey. "Well, as you can see, I clearly value the social relationships and mutual support that come with the community. Given my wife's disabilities, this is extra important to me and I think we could use more of it from more people. On the other hand," he says, turning to the window and sweeping his arms across it to indicate the view, "I really like the open spaces we've maintained here and our commitment to managing the land with environmental accountability in mind. And, as you saw last night, it is already getting difficult for us all to fit in a room, much less reach consensus on controversial issues. It's a difficult balance to strike. Some of us talk about the 'Celo country club syndrome,' meaning that those of us who are already here want to keep things as they are and not let others join who may disrupt the balance—and the view. Sometimes I feel that way myself, but then I look to the history and original aims of the community and I know it would be too selfish to stop people from joining."

Later that night, reviewing the minutes from past community meetings, it becomes apparent that these issues are not really new for the community. Although the tone and content of the discussions appear to have been slightly different in the absence of a large group of people waiting to start trial memberships, as early as 1970 community members were engaged in ongoing discussions about how to balance and integrate new members, values of environmentally sensitive land stewardship, and effective governance, cooperation, and fellowship. As I turn my attention to other studies of intentional communities, it is clear that failure to successfully resolve issues such as these has contributed directly to the dissolution of many other communities. What will happen with Celo? Little did I know that twenty years later, the community would still be wrangling with these same issues.

In the relation of the Community to its members the legal is an instrument of the moral. The relation is not an external one between a soulless corporation and independent individuals. It is the internal relation between one person of a friendly neighborhood group and all other persons including himself. Thus a member consulting in a Community meeting on a course of action is both a private user and (in consensus with others) a public controller of land. A community member through participating in Community government tends to develop a stable and considerate character along with responsible personal expression. (Celo Community 2018a)

Do you recognize the fact that our land holding arrangement means you can never expect to make a speculative profit on investment here? That you build your house on land to which you have no legal title? That your rights to your land are dependent on your continued membership in CCI?

Are you satisfied to accept the fact that when you die your children might not be accepted into Community membership in order to inherit your holding?

A member must be willing to seek Community permission to make almost any changes on his holding. There are often delays in getting things done, or even started.

If you plan to build or make changes in an existing holding, would you feel that the Community has a right to go over your plans, criticizing and making suggestions?

Can you share control with others?

Living in the Community is time-consuming. The Community has up to four meetings and two workdays monthly. Are you willing to give the necessary time? (Celo Community 2012)

Ostrom's second design principle, again split into two sub-principles, is that rules for governing the commons are created in accordance with local conditions and that the benefits of participating in commons governance are commensurate with the costs. Commons design principle 2A states that "appropriation and provision rules are congruent with local social and environmental conditions" (Ostrom 2010: 653). As the vignettes above indicate, Celo's members are constantly adjusting their rules as the social characteristics of the community change. I don't wish to overstate this because the basic institutions and principles of cooperative governance in the community have remained largely intact since the 1950s. However, the community is engaged in a constant fine-tuning of specific rules as circumstances change. This fine-tuning requires significant time and energy from community members, time and energy that might be otherwise expended were they individual private property owners. Flexibility in rules and structure and time commitment from members are two things that make Celo Community work as a commons institution.

LOCAL RULES FOR LOCAL CONDITIONS

Once it is clear who is and who is not part of the group, the group needs to determine the sets of rules that structure their interactions with each other and with the specific resources (in this case land) that they hold in common and to make sure that these rules are appropriate to the local sociocultural and ecological contexts. In essence, this means that the rules for managing the land will be unique to the local community, the local economy, and the local landscape rather than a set of abstract rules devised, imposed, and controlled by outside authorities. In Celo's case, these rules are defined by a number of living documents that were originally developed by early community members and that are occasionally revised by current community members. When they are accepted into full membership, each community member becomes a party to and, in consensus with others, a potential initiator of changes in documents including Celo's "Membership Agreement," the "Celo Community Holding Agreement," "CCI Procedures and Rules," and the "Consensus Decision-making Process." Collectively, these documents spell out the specific details, rules, and processes that govern the communal political economy at Celo.

While a full review of each of these documents is beyond the scope of this chapter, suffice it to say that these documents identify and describe each community member's rights, responsibilities, and restrictions in terms of interacting with the community's commonly held land and with the other community members who govern it. Among the rules governing membership in this communal endeavor are that each community member is expected to be thoroughly familiar with all community documents, rules, and procedures; reside within the corporate limits of Celo Community; participate in regular consensus governance meetings and property maintenance duties; and abide by decisions made through the community's consensus governance process including decisions regarding land use and member responsibilities. These rules and procedures have evolved as the community has, over time, become more familiar with each other, with their land, and with the process of balancing intertwined goals of cooperation and land stewardship.

Here, it is appropriate to revisit the community's history to consider how these documents and community governance institutions came into being. A review of the community's early history, as contained in their own documentation and in documents produced by Arthur Morgan, reveals that local residents of the South Toe Valley had a hard time understanding, or at least were not in attunement with, the nature of the experiment in cooperative community building that Arthur Morgan had in mind when he arranged for the purchase of the land that currently belongs to the community. For much of the first decade of the community's existence, Morgan recruited local residents to participate in the experiment but they repeatedly left or were removed from membership because the ways they interacted with each other and used the land did not conform to the kinds of cooperative interactions and methods of land use that Morgan envisioned.

Scholarship on Appalachian communities reveals local communities throughout the Appalachian region had long used undeveloped land, even land held by private land owners, as a "de facto" commons for hunting and gathering (see Newfont 2012 and Stoll 2017). However, as population increased, industrialization progressed, and absentee land owners increasingly focused on extracting value from their landholdings, these de facto commons systems were increasingly enclosed. By the time that Arthur Morgan entered the valley in the mid-1930s, local residents, like most people throughout the country, were increasingly being swept up in a tide of industrial capitalist patterns of land use. Local residents were also required to generate cash to pay ever-increasing taxes (see Stoll 2017). In this context, long-standing patterns of subsistence provisioning, partially based on informal commons norms, were being displaced by a cash economy and increasingly strict enforcement of private property rights, although surrounding public lands did continue to offer an opportunity for hunting and gathering on the commons (see Newfont 2012). Early local recruits to the community often saw Celo as a company, apparently flush with cash, that could provide them with a source of livelihood and a way to get ahead; they did not see the form of commoning imposed from outside and above by Morgan and his community managers as a viable or attractive option. This suggests that the design of the principles for the cooperative community was not appropriate to existing sociocultural conditions in the valley at the time of the community's founding.

Members of local communities did not understand the goals and aims of the community and were focused on protecting their family's economic footholds and negotiating emergent industrial capitalist realities as best they could as their earlier commons practices were being eroded. As this became apparent, Morgan had to resort to recruiting individuals from outside the region whose views and aims aligned better with his own. As outsiders, including most prominently Quaker conscientious objectors to World War II increasingly took up residence in the community and implemented their particular patterns of sharing and cooperation, there arose among the locals some degree of consternation, confusion, and suspicion about the nature of the community. While I do not wish to overemphasize these conflicts, it is an undeniable fact that the vast majority of community members, with one or two notable exceptions, are to this day in-migrants from other parts of the country who brought with them backgrounds and some cultural assumptions quite different than those that characterized local communities. This fact has larger implications in terms of Stoll's proposal for the creation of commons communities in the Appalachian region and for the ability of Celo to function as a model for such a proposal. I will return to these implications in the final chapter of the book.

Turning from local sociocultural contexts to the environmental conditions of the valley and the prospects for long-term environmental sustainability, the cooperative community that Morgan envisioned and the forms of environmental stewardship that came to characterize its land tenure institutions may have been more appropriate, at least when viewed through a strictly long-term ecological lens, rather than a short-term economic one. By the 1930s, the area was suffering from the effects of large-scale timbering and unsustainable patterns of often tenant-based agricultural production resulting in widespread soil degradation and decline in biodiversity (see Davis 2000 and Silver 2003). These patterns threatened the long-term ability of the land in the valley to provide a living directly to any residents whether local or immigrant in origin. Morgan recognized these patterns and, from the beginning of the community, advocated for more environmentally sustainable methods of land use in the community.

Celo's focus on community-based land stewardship, in contrast with top-down, government-mandated conservation initiatives that soon took hold in the region, provided one model by which a local organization could, in theory, slow environmental degradation while keeping land in the hands of local communities. With the arrival of Quakers and, later, back-to-the-landers—people who at the very least had different views compared to longtime local residents if not also more resources and freedom to choose to participate in such an undertaking—a set of institutions and an approach to cooperative land stewardship that has proven durable took form in Celo Community. This was not an easy nor straightforward process; initial design of community rules and procedures was slow, consumed much time and energy, and was accompanied by attendant wrangling over the legal status of the community's documents and institutions. Indeed, this is a process that is still in motion; the community is constantly adjusting to changing conditions both locally and on a broader scale. The commons are always in process. It is not a blueprint approach; some degree of flexibility is key.

Nonetheless, with a relatively stable population of community members in place for some decades now, the community has developed relatively consistent, mostly autonomous local institutional processes for adjusting their rules and norms to the social and environmental conditions that characterize the community if not the wider valley and region. Two examples of relatively recent policy discussions and decisions made by the community indicate how the community's rules have evolved to align with the current sociocultural and ecological conditions of Celo's commons. These discussions and decisions revolved around intertwined issues of the process for joining the community and land use planning.

In the early 2000s, the community had a long waiting list of people wishing to join the community; since they only allowed two individual or household (generally understood as coupled partners and their children) units to join per year, the wait for interested people to begin their trial membership had reached the point where it could take as much as twenty years to get to the top of the waiting list. At the same time, a growing number of children of existing community members were expressing a desire to join the community, often after a period of time spent outside the community going to college or working in other parts of the country. Recognizing the desirability of having the children of community members who were already familiar with the cultural milieu of the community among their membership, the community established a separate family track for joining the community that shortened the waiting period that offspring of community members might be expected to endure. While the effects of this decision are still playing out, it has arguably decreased the costs and energy involved with integrating new community members and reinforced the cultural identity of the community while still allowing the community to be accessible to those from outside its boundaries.

Around the same time, the community decided to engage in a process of comprehensive land use planning for their collectively held 1,200 acres.

This decision reflected their desire to balance home site development for a growing number of community members with protection of especially sensitive natural areas (some of which the community had agreed to protect from any development decades earlier). The community was also interested in the conservation of green space for community members' enjoyment and the preservation of especially fertile agricultural land for use as productive fields. In addition, the community believed that setting limits on the number of home sites available within their common land in relation to other land uses might help them to indirectly address another contentious issue: how large the community could grow and still have an effectively functioning consensus governance process. While the nature of this governance process will be discussed in subsequent chapters, I would like to emphasize here that these examples of rule changes implemented by the community reflect their ongoing efforts to adjust to local sociocultural and ecological conditions and dynamics; the process of land use design and social design are intertwined here.

At the time of this writing, the community is confronting another issue that has implications for the processes of joining the community and adjusting their land use policies. Even as offspring of some community members are increasingly joining the community, the community's membership overall is aging; community members indicate that roughly 50 percent of community members are over sixty years old. This shift in community demographics raises a number of intertwined issues, prominent among them being the need to replace members who die or depart in potentially rapid succession and the need to provide alternative housing options for aging members who are less able to care for or access individual homes that are often situated in remote parts of community land at some distance from other residences and community infrastructure.

As stated earlier, community policies place a limit on the number of new members that may join the community in a given year. They also dictate that a departing member may only transfer their landholding and associated homes and other buildings to other community members or to the community itself. As a large portion of the community's membership ages, a growing number of community members are expressing an interest in alternative housing arrangements that are more accessible and provide greater proximity to assistance and care. For over three decades now, community members have engaged in discussions about designating portions of their land for some form of cluster- or elder-care housing that would accommodate these needs. However, these conversations have repeatedly stalled because the construction of such housing either does not fit clearly within the community's land use plan or it conflicts with the desires of other community members to maintain existing open spaces within the community that have been proposed as sites for such housing.

As the process of creating alternative housing for aging community members has stalled, community members see on the horizon a time when existing members, either unable to find appropriate housing in the community and moving away or simply passing away before the issue is resolved, departing faster than they can be replaced by new members whose influx is limited by community policy on trial memberships. Since departing members can only transfer their homes and landholdings to existing community members, and since the community is obligated to finance the transfer of these homes if the departing member is unable to develop a transfer agreement with another member, the community is beginning to anticipate a time when the number of vacated holdings reaches a level that the community cannot accommodate either through the influx of new members or through community financing. In response, the community is currently experimenting with an additional "fast-track" membership option whereby individual prospective members who are ready to fill vacant community homes on short notice and who are felt to by the community to be a good fit for membership, may be bumped to the front of the line of the trial membership process. These fast-track trial members would be accepted in addition to the standard limit of two member households per year.

How this shift in the community's trial membership process will affect community governance, culture, and finances remains to be seen. It may be disruptive of the slow and steady approach to change that has long characterized the community, but it may also enable them to avoid financial challenges that would accompany a large number of membership departures in a short period of time. And, as with earlier periods in community history, it may allow for a new influx of energy and ideas that could benefit the community in the long run. In any case, this is another example of the experimental approach to sharing and cooperation that has always been a deliberate characteristic of the community. Flexibility, the ability to agree to alter or make exceptions to established rules and procedures in order to meet changing circumstances, appears to be an important, if unofficial, component of community rules, norms, and institutions. Without such ability to adjust, the community and its commons may well stagnate.

Before turning to a consideration of the costs and benefits of community membership, it is worth discussing specific community policies designed to regulate community members' use of common land for purposes of economic production that may be more extractive in nature than just establishing a home site. The community's Procedures and Rules document contains policies pertaining specifically to the use of agricultural fields, harvesting timber, and hunting. Each of these policies place restrictions on user behavior and establish expectations of the user in terms of responsible conduct relative to the larger community of commoners who together own and steward the land that contains the resources. The community considers all of these policies as operating within the larger context of their Land Use Plan which "should be the basis of all relevant decisions" and which provides a "window of opportunity to propose changes" to the plan and all relevant policies (Celo Community 2019).

At the time that Celo Community, Inc. took possession of its land in 1937, it included significant acreage that had been cleared of forest by previous landowners. Following Arthur Morgan's vision for the community, early community members attempted to use these fields to produce agricultural products both for internal consumption and as a way to generate funds for the community. When community members failed to establish any enduring agricultural enterprises, many of these fields reverted to open space with small portions of them being used by individual community members for small-scale production, mostly for home use.

In recent years, interest in using the community's fields for food production has increased. Notes from the community's fields committee meeting speak to this:

> CCI fields are becoming increasingly important to many of us in the community. A large part of this is due to the increasing effort by members to grow our own food. The goal of sustainable agriculture is one embraced by CCI as a whole, not just the individual farmers. As use of the fields for agriculture increases we are made aware of other uses we count on for these spaces. We value our fields for their recreational use, for wildlife habitat and for the aesthetic value of the open space and views they provide. . . .
>
> An issue for future discussion is, what more can or should CCI do to encourage sustainable agriculture by our members. It has been observed that fields committee is mostly made up of members with agricultural interests in the fields. We welcome involvement and input from other members with other priorities. (Celo Community 2013b)

The growing interest in using community land for agricultural production led to revisions of the community's policies on use of their common fields in the mid- to late 2010s, including the establishment of a new category of land use called "community commons" where members might use the fields rent free provided they are following sound land use practices.

A revision to the community's Procedures and Rules states that "these tracts are valued as open land by CCI for their aesthetic beauty, recreational use and habitat for unique flora and fauna. CCI accepts the costs incurred in maintaining these commons, including periodic mowing and application of lime. Members may request permission to use these fields for rotational grazing of livestock" (Celo Community 2019). Further, "recognizing the use of livestock/poultry as a proven means of improving soil, CCI will consider rent-free intensive rotational grazing proposals. Fields committee is empowered to review and approve individual proposals by CCI members, based on a proposal's attention to soil improvement" (Celo Community 2019). Should a member be granted free use of these "commons" fields for rotational grazing, they are expected to abide by a number of other expectations including not building permanent fences, moving stock frequently enough so as not to degrade the pasture, mowing where needed for weed control, not infringing on specially designated wildflower areas or recreational spaces (such as the soccer field which is adjacent to one such field), confirming improvement of soil through biennial soil testing, and paying for the costs of testing and mowing.

When a community member wishes to use a field on the community's common land for other sorts of agricultural production, other conditions apply including paying an annual rent assessment and annual property taxes on the land. Fields rental periods are generally for five years, although the community may notify the renter of the community's intent to terminate the rental agreement if they are misusing the field or are not using the field productively after a period of one year. For those who rent such fields on an ongoing basis, they are no longer charged rent after their accumulated rent charge reaches the assessed property value of the land under use. Those using fields for agricultural production must bring a farm plan to the community's property committee for approval and they are not permitted to build anything other than "agricultural structures" on the land. Finally, requirements of field renters include the following:

> The renter shall pay for seed, fertilizer, fences, etc., and is responsible for keeping the land in as good tilth as when it was taken. Renter is responsible for measuring and marking rented areas; maintaining edges of fields; not creating obstacles to maintenance of any remainder of the field; reporting each September to Fields committee on their rentals: current condition of the fields/pastures, results of soil tests (preferably done annually), and plans for use or return of field, to be included in the annual report. If the land is to be returned, this plan should include removal of personal items, barriers to mowing, fencing, farm tools, and debris. Mowing or cover cropping may also be requested. (Celo Community 2019)

A community Forestry Committee with the following mission statement was established to oversee timbering and forest management activities within the community. The Forestry Committee

> intends to be the official body responsible for matters pertaining to the forest resources of Celo Community, Inc. It will work towards the protection and

preservation of our forests to the benefit of the whole community by means of creating a knowledge base about our forests and relevant issues, long range stewardship planning, possible selective harvesting and timber stand improvement in designated areas. All actions will be taken with an eye towards balance between forest as natural habitat and forest as usable resource. (Celo Community 2019)

Community policies explicitly reserve some rights of tree cutting, including any trees under six inches diameter at breast height, to individual community members on their individual holdings. A request by an individual member to cut up to six larger trees on their holding can be approved by the chairperson of the property committee and requests to cut larger numbers of trees must be approved by the community's general meeting. Reasonable firewood cutting on or near individual holdings is permitted.

Following the undesirable results of allowing outside parties to conduct timbering operations on community land in the community's early years, the community reserved such rights only for community members. Except for the clearing of land for construction of a new house, no large-scale timbering operations have taken place in the community in recent decades. However, policies are in place for members who may wish to engage in timbering on community land outside their individual holdings. These include marking the trees and getting approval from the property committee and the general meeting before commencing timbering operations, stabilizing any access roads they need to build, leaving behind no slash piles, and paying to the community a stumpage fee for any timber that is sold after cutting.

Community policies regarding hunting on community land, whether by members or nonmembers, have long been debated. The community has long recognized that local residents often pursue game across property boundaries in the area. Acknowledging the impossibility of policing this given the large portions of their land that are roadless and free of houses, the community has long posted a "safety zone" in an effort to keep hunters from moving onto the more populated and residential parts of their common property. More recently, the community agreed to allow individual members to hunt or to invite others to hunt on their individual holdings and "adjacent land" provided that a number of conditions are met. These conditions include getting agreement from their immediate neighbors, then from the property committee, and then from the community's general meeting. Once such approval is obtained, hunting may take place only with a bow and arrow, from a tree stand, and in compliance with all North Carolina game regulations. Finally, "an annual registry of 'approved' hunters, including photos of the hunter and his/her vehicle, contact information and also where we might expect such activity to take place, will be posted on google.docs and on the bulletin board in the CCI office" (Celo Community 2019).

COSTS AND BENEFITS OF COMMUNITY MEMBERSHIP

The counter point to any group being able to construct rules that are appropriate to local social and environmental contexts is Ostrom's commons design principle 2B: "Appropriation rules are congruent with provision rules; the distribution of costs is proportional to the distribution of benefits" (Ostrom 2010: 653). A set of rules and policies may be appropriate to the social and environmental conditions of a given place, but they will simply not work if conforming to the rules does not benefit commons participants in ways that are commensurate with the costs of participation. However, the balance of costs and benefits is subjective and they may be defined and conceptualized in a number of ways that fall outside of monetary cost-benefit analyses that most Americans might be familiar with. As indicated in the vignettes and quotations at the beginning of this chapter, there are a wide variety of costs and benefits encountered and commented on by Celo's members, most of whom have their own way of calculating the balance. Below, I provide an overview of some of these considerations.

As alluded to in the previous chapter, one of the most significant potential costs that a potential member of Celo Community must consider is a monetary one: their limited ability to build equity in their home in the absence of individual ownership of the land on which the home sits. In an arrangement that Celo describes as "neither lease nor deed," Celo's members gain limited usufruct rights for building a home and dwelling on a small parcel of land that is part of the larger land held in trust by the corporate body of which they are part. Further, one of the rules regarding gaining access to an individual landholding in Celo is that the landholding and the individual home that sits on it cannot be sold on the open market. Rather, the market for the transfer of a home is the relatively small pool of other existing or trial community members. Not only that, but a member who wishes to depart from Celo has only a limited period of time to find a transferee from within this pool and agree with them on terms before the provision sets in that they must return their home to the community for a limited amount of equity (up to a maximum of $65,000). The effect of this is that the individual community member who possesses a holding may not seek to gain speculative profit from their possession and development of the holding by selling it to the highest bidder. It also has the effect of encouraging the development of small and simple homes that won't put any individual member at risk of loss of significant equity. As alluded to above, one of Celo's members characterized Celo's model of home ownership, a model perhaps better described as home occupancy, as "the opposite of equity."

However, most of Celo's members recognize that in return for this potential loss of financial liquidity, they gain a variety of benefits that they would not otherwise have access to. One of the most obvious benefits is that the individual member and landholder becomes a co-owner, at a quite reasonable price, and co-governor of a 1,200-acre parcel of land in a beautiful setting that they would not otherwise be able to afford and which, due to the community's landholding agreement and process of community governance, will very likely never be subdivided or developed in a way that would detract significantly from its integrity or beauty. It is clear from my conversations with community members that they place a high value on the peace of mind that comes from having access to this land. Indeed, many of them describe the value they gain from access to the land in terms of a spiritual nourishment that is difficult if not impossible to calculate in dollar values.

Further in terms of costs and benefits, Celo's common landholding arrangement prevents holders from gaining access to financial resources such as mortgages that would normally be available to private land or homeowners. Banks simply won't provide credit to people who don't have clear ownership of land or buildings that they can use as collateral. And, while Celo's members may gain usufruct rights to individual landholdings at a rate well below market value, they also have to pay a per-head assessment that is used to pay the property taxes on the large portions of their 1,200 acres that are not assigned as individual landholdings nor set aside as wilderness areas that are exempt from property taxes. However, these financial obligations and disadvantages are counterbalanced by the holder gaining access to common financial resources. The community manages several blocks of money that they set aside and from which they may lend money at low interest to community members for home construction, home improvement, business ventures, educational pursuits, and other needs. As the interest rates on these loans are, like the community's landholding arrangement, designed not to allow for speculative profit but mostly to cover the costs of inflation, these loans are themselves less costly than other, more standard lines of credit might be.

Another impact of Celo's collective landholding arrangement that can be considered a cost is the restrictions placed on an individual's ability to make decisions about land use and building design on their individual landholding. These restrictions and the challenges that arise from them were alluded to in the previous chapter and they have clearly been challenging for people who were enculturated in a context where individual landowners have the freedom to use their land in whatever manners they would like. One clear example of this is the restrictions the community places on tree cutting whereby community members must seek permission from the community for cutting trees on their holding over six inches in diameter. In the two decades I have been working with the community, this policy has caused controversy repeatedly. For example, one community member's desire to cut trees on their holding in order to create a better viewshed for their home might run up against resistance from other community members who wish to maintain a wooded viewshed from the trail they use to walk to the community center. A homeowner with clear possession of the land on which their home is situated would not only not have to seek permission to cut trees on that land, they would also not have to be concerned about the wishes of their neighbors blocking their ability to cut their trees. Such is not the case for Celo's members.

Another example is the fact that the community has the ability to approve or reject the design of any individual member's new build home. This policy is in place not in an attempt to enforce any uniformity of design—indeed, Celo encourages individuality and experimentation—but rather to ensure that community values such as simplicity and environmental sustainability are accounted for in home design. This policy is also an effort to ensure that one's potential loss of equity in their home does not reach such an extent that a disgruntled, and potentially financially devastated, departing community member decides to take the community to court to recover the equity they may perceive they have been unjustly denied access to. Encouraging new community members to build small homes of simple design in a thoughtful manner that accounts for the unique financial circumstances that characterize the community is the aim of this policy. It also has the effect of restricting one's individual freedom in terms of land use and home design. However, it should also be remembered that many existing communities throughout the country place similar restrictions on land use and building design through zoning and building codes; in this sense, Celo is not that peculiar.

In addition, just as working through the particularities of building codes and zoning regulations can greatly slow down a building project in many American communities, so can the process of getting community approval for home construction or holding improvement projects impose significant time constraints and energy requirements on Celo's members. The process in Celo might be significantly different, but the resulting frustration can be an equally palpable cost. For example, while an individual landowner may have to face the often labyrinthine, impersonal bureaucracy of local planning and zoning regulatory agencies, the individual landholder in Celo has to face the quite personal and often intense consensus-based community decision-making process. While this process will be discussed in great detail in a subsequent chapter, suffice it here to say that one may find themselves in front of their neighbors defending a home design that one spent countless hours working on and having to take input from each and every community member that has a criticism of that design. While the consensus process is, in theory, supposed to be principled and not personal, it often has the effect of cutting quite close to one's identity and rousing intense emotions. Even where this is not the case, it can be quite time-consuming.

Time and energy are other costs that anyone considering joining Celo should consider and that any member of the community must take into account. Time and energy are required not only in terms of seeking group approval for one's personal projects, but they are also required of each individual member in the process of ensuring that the commons continue to function. Celo's members are not just a bunch of hippies in the woods sharing land on a de facto basis, but rather an officially incorporated social welfare organization with federal tax exempt status that is required to hold meetings, maintain staff, keep local taxes and other accounts up-to-date, and enforce rules on themselves and outsiders.

As Celo's Self-Evaluation Questionnaire—a document the community gives to every person who expresses interest in community membership— states, living in intentional community can be time-consuming. As a trial community member will quickly learn (and as this researcher did learn while doing ethnographic fieldwork in the community), a significant portion of one's week can be spent in meetings dealing with community business. In addition to the two hour per month general community meeting, there are at least three committees that meet at least once a month for two hours each. At least one evening each week may be eaten up by committee and community meetings if one wants to really stay abreast of community business. Not only that, as will be made clearer below when I delve into community decision-making and conflict resolution, the actual work that goes on in community and committee meetings is often built on the back of many one-on-one or small group discussions that take place between and among members on a daily basis. This is especially true when there is a controversial issue or deci-sion up for debate, in which case the conversations and meetings might be not only time-consuming but emotionally challenging and draining.

Beyond the community and committee meetings and underlying conver-sations, there are also a large number of community jobs and positions that need to be filled, mostly on a volunteer basis, as well as regularly scheduled community workdays and other events to prepare for and participate in. The current list of community job descriptions includes fifty different positions, slightly more than one for every two community members. While some of those jobs don't entail any significant work on a daily or even weekly basis, others are quite time-consuming and many of them are actually filled by two or more persons, sometimes including one person serving as an apprentice-in-training to the person that currently holds the position. Accounting for the small number of community members that may be on a leave of absence dur-ing any given year and for the small amount of at least relative free riding that inevitably characterizes any such collective endeavor, community members will likely find themselves filling at least one community job at any given time.

One community job is workday chair, a position charged with coordinating volunteers, tools, and resources for the monthly community workday project. These projects most often entail the physical labor involved in maintaining community property such as the community center, roads, or trails. They may also involve working on an individual landholding or home that is in need of extra care or upon which the individual holder is undertaking a significant home improvement project. Community members who are unable to provide physical labor for the workdays often show up with food and moral support for the laborers. While this may, on the surface, seem like a cost of participation in the community, this is where community members generally see things differently. Most community members talk about workday as an event they value, as a ritualized occasion whereby they come together to support one another, care for their common (or sometimes individual) property, and reinforce the special bonds they share as a community.

This brings me to my last point about the benefits of participating in Celo Community. As indicated in the quotations at the beginning of this chapter, there are additional benefits that stem from choosing to commit to this collective arrangement. As a member of the community, one becomes part of a larger social community bound together by their collective landholding arrangement. This social community provides a wide variety of intangible benefits to its members. In contrast to someone living in an isolated suburban home who doesn't know their neighbors, a member of Celo knows that they will never find themselves without support in a time of need. Someone who is sick, who has just lost a loved one, or who has just had a baby can count on daily check-ins and meal deliveries. Someone in need of knowledge, tools, or skills to complete a project they weren't entirely prepared for knows they can turn to one of their neighbors for help. Someone in financial need knows they can get temporary help from the corporate body they are part of. Someone grieving the loss of a loved one or struggling with a personal challenge will find comfort in their fellow community members. In addition to all the trying meetings and discussions, there is almost always a joyous celebration of some sort to attend. Even in death, one knows their life will be celebrated and they will be remembered in terms of the best things they brought to the community. It is these things, combined with the opportunity to live on and with this beautiful piece of Appalachian forest, that makes it all worth the time, energy, and struggle that living in community also entails.

Chapter 6

Governing Ourselves
and Our Commons

As I help arrange the chairs for the community meeting tonight, I tune in to the conversations taking place around me. Most of Celo's members present for tonight's meeting are gathered in small groups, engaged in animated discussions. To my right two couples are discussing their children's performances in the high school play the night before. They are proud of their kids' accomplishment, but they lament the fact that the drama teacher is under pressure to resign because her class has chosen to perform plays that address topics that many local parents have found too controversial, in this particular case racism and homosexuality. To my right, two women and one man are discussing their plans to work together in the community's agricultural commons this coming weekend. They are discussing the different crops that they plan to cultivate and share with each other when they are harvested.

Promptly at eight o'clock, the community member who is serving as chairperson of tonight's meeting rings a bell and the conversations die down as people take their seats. We are arranged in a broad circle, two or three rows deep in some places. This arrangement facilitates a sense of egalitarianism; no one, not even the chairperson, is in a position of dominance and each can see the others' faces as they take their turns speaking. Before the meeting gets into full swing, the non-community member guests in attendance tonight are asked to introduce themselves. Having been present at the past four community meetings, I receive a reprieve. Other guests include a trial community member, the brother of a community member and a young teacher from Arthur Morgan School who is here to announce the school's upcoming open house. After these introductions, the minutes from the last community meeting are read aloud and, after a number of minor corrections are noted, accepted by a vocal chorus: "Approved!"

As is customary, the reading of the minutes is followed by a brief period of announcements. Someone begins by requesting a moment of silence to observe the recent deaths of both a non-community member neighbor and a community member whose presence at this meeting is sorely missed. As silence descends, I note that across the room several community members move closer to the deceased community member's husband, placing comforting hands around his shoulders and on his knee. Other announcements tonight are lighthearted and upbeat. A mother announces that her daughter who recently turned fourteen is available for babysitting. Someone else reminds his fellow community members that the Carolina Farm Stewardship tour next weekend will include several stops within the community including a community supported agriculture farm run by two community members as well as several neighborhood and home gardens. Another community member reports on the progress of the Celo Community photo history project; photos will be accepted until the end of next week for a slide show at the community's annual meeting. The Celo history committee and the photo history project have come into existence just since my arrival as a researcher in Celo; my interest in the community seems to have piqued their interest in documenting and understanding themselves.

After asking if there are any more announcements, the meeting chairperson requests the chair of the membership committee to bring forth any business that committee has to discuss. It is announced that two people have requested that their names be added to the waiting list for trial memberships, including a teacher at the Arthur Morgan School. Another community member asks the membership chair if the waiting list has been updated; he knows of at least one person that, having moved to California for a job, has asked to have his name removed. Moving on, two current trial members have their "documents meeting" next week where the membership committee will help to familiarize them with the community's governing documents. All interested parties are invited to attend. Finally, the newest community member has recently signed her Membership and Holding Agreements. Her home site plan proposal and her construction loan proposal were sent to the property and finance committees respectively for discussion and debate. Please attend those meetings in the coming weeks if you are interested.

Next up is the finance committee which doesn't have a lot of business to discuss this time around. It is reported that the committee approved an education loan for a community member, a mother who is returning to school to get her master's in public health now that her children have gone off to college. Hearty cheers erupt all around. The finance committee continues to consider some major restructuring of the community's finances, but will need at least one more monthly meeting before it is ready to make any major recommendations to the general community meeting. One thing that they would like to submit for community approval is their recommendation to transfer Celo's "reserve funds", *now totaling over $100,000, from a standard money-market account to socially and environmentally conscious hedge fund. A brief debate ensues about what change in interest rates might accompany this shift, but consensus is shortly reached that although this will likely result in a small reduction in return on investment, this move is in alignment with the community's collective values. The proposal is approved by voice vote, that is, with no one objecting.*

The hands of the clock on the wall now point to nine and the meeting chair calls for a break. As those present disperse to all corners of the room for smaller discussions, one community member with whom I've not had a chance to interact approaches me. She says that from what she has observed, she believes that I'm taking a good approach to my research, but she's worried because a previous ethnographer's account of the community left a sour taste in her mouth when he characterized the community as a "failed utopia." "This community was simply not set up to be a utopia and that is the standard by which Hicks evaluated it. He missed the point. We are a practical-minded group; we just adhere to different values than do most in our society." I suggest that I share her sentiments about Hicks' work and that my goal is to keep an open mind and portray the community according to the perspectives provided to me by current community members and the community's historical archives. Would she like to do an interview with me? After checking our calendars, we arrange a date for the following week.

The meeting resumes and moves on to discuss matters brought by the property committee. There is an urgent matter of business to discuss and the property committee chair hopes that the meeting and can reach consensus on it. Yesterday, he was disturbed by the activities of the French Broad Electric Company on community land; he was walking along one of the community's footpaths when the silence was disrupted by the noise of machinery up ahead. The electric company was doing its occasional clearing of power line rights of way, cutting away trees and brush that were encroaching on them. The community member was distressed by the destructiveness and waste of this activity, the use of large machines to rip limbs from trees and clear cut vast swaths through the forest, chipping the wood and trucking it away and, in the process, destroying the floral succession that he and other community members had monitored over recent years. They had recently identified some unique plants with beautiful flowers that had not been documented before on Celo's land. He asked them if they would postpone their work here while he discussed a course of action with the community. Aware of the community from previous experiences, the workers acquiesced but indicated that they could only put it off for a couple of days.

The property committee, following informal discussions at an emergency meeting last night, proposes that the community ask the company to allow them to do their own clearing along the power lines. This way the clearing might proceed less destructively, preserving the beauty of their footpaths, many of which run under the power lines, and allowing the community to harvest the cut vegetation for firewood. A discussion ensues. Some in the meeting indicate that they simply do not have time to do the necessary work to clear the rights of way and others suggest that they should not antagonize the power company, fearing that it will result in delayed service in the future. Others, raising their hand to be put in a queue of speakers kept by the meeting chair, back the initial speaker's proposal. The debate continues and it appears that consensus may not be reached as the ten o'clock hour, the designated end point of community meetings, is approaching. Finally a community member offers to devote the extra time to the project himself if some community members will join him in a special community workday this Saturday. He will complete the remaining clearing himself on Sunday if he can keep as much of the wood that he cuts as he needs for firewood. He also offers to join the property committee chair as a liaison to the electric company.

A brief and spontaneous moment of silence follows as the meeting ponders this offer. After about 30 seconds, someone says, "I motion for approval of this proposal." This is followed by a second and then a third motion for approval. The meeting chair asks if anyone has further comments, probing to see if the meeting has reached consensus on this proposal and, as no one else raises their hand to object, the proposal is approved and noted in the meeting minutes. After asking if there is any further business to be discussed in the remaining three minutes, the chairperson adjourns the meeting early.

This is an example of a process I witnessed numerous times in Celo's community meetings. Although difficult issues did not always get resolved as swiftly as this one did, the community does seem to have a process that works. Their meetings take perseverance and they can get heated at times, but community members are committed to working through their differing perspectives in order to govern themselves and manage their collectively owned property. As I walked away from the Celo Community Center that night, a community member approached me and said, "It's mysterious how things work out around here. Despite our differences, we managed to reach an agreement that is in all of our best interests, and perhaps those of the land too." "It is intriguing." I reply. "But I don't think it's a mystery. It's a result of all of your efforts and those of the community members that came before you." "You know, you're right," he says. "Sometimes I get too lost in the present and don't see the larger picture of Celo's uniqueness. Maybe you can put it in perspective for us."

The third point of orientation for commoning states that "we enter into or modify our own rules and commitments, and every commoner can participate in this process. Our commitments serve to create, maintain, and preserve the commons to satisfy our needs" (Bollier and Helfrich 2015b: 49). This cuts straight to the heart of Celo Community and the process of consensus governance by which community members participate as coequals in making decisions and policies about how they relate to each other and to the land on which they live. The vignette above illustrates just one example of how this process plays out in the governance institutions and processes of Celo Community.

On the first Wednesday evening of every month, Celo's members convene in the large upstairs room of their community center to discuss and make decisions about community business using a unique process of consensus-based governance with roots in Quaker spiritual traditions and business meetings. Seated in a circle so that each participant can look all the others in the eye, guided by a fluid understanding of consensus governance procedures, and led in a minimal way by the person serving as meeting "chair," several dozen strong personalities debate issues, draw out tension among divergent viewpoints, and often reach agreement on decisions, policy changes, and, sometimes, the advisability of not making any change at this moment. Such processes of debate can be troublesome just for couples trying to manage a household between the two of them; sometimes such things contribute directly to the dissolution of marriages. One can imagine how difficult it might be for several dozen individuals living in separate households to reach collective decisions on anything from whether to admit a new member into their group to how much to budget for repairs to the community center, to whether or not to allow the cutting of small trees along the edge of their most picturesque field. Yet, more often than not, it works in Celo.

Article 2, Section 1. It shall be the policy of the Community to endeavor to transact all business by unanimous consent rather than by vote. (Celo Community 2009)

Article 4. I accept the privilege and duty of participating in the Community meetings, of actively serving on committees for the management of Community affairs, and of sharing with the other members the responsibility for maintenance, growth, and preservation of all Community land and other property and interests. I also agree to assume my share of the yearly Community budget. (Celo Community 2013a)

Article 5. It is understood that the making of decisions and policies governing the Community and its members is based on an effort to apply the technique of consensus, and that each resident member has an equal voice in determining such policies and decisions. (Celo Community 2013a)

Ostrom's third principle is that members of the commons should have the ability to participate in making and amending the rules that govern the commons. Commons design principle 3 states that "most individuals affected by a resource regime are authorized to participate in making and modifying its rules" (Ostrom 2010: 653). This principle references the ability of members of a commons arrangement to participate in making and changing the rules of the institutions that govern their actions in the commons at a relatively low cost in terms of time, energy, and other resources. Like many intentional communities that have stood the test of time, Celo has established a well-defined and relatively efficient system of community governance; unlike most intentional communities, this system has, for almost eighty years, been based on unanimous consent. In Celo's case, this system involves once-a-month community meetings that operate on a Quaker-inspired consensus decision-making basis with the work leading to specific decisions often delegated to smaller committees that themselves function by consensus and bring recommended decisions to the full community meeting for whole group consensus. This process is grounded in a strong sense of egalitarianism and seeks to reach the best decisions for the community as a whole based on the combined insights of all of its members, often by drawing out and resolving tension among divergent but converging viewpoints.

While many community consensus processes can be quite time-consuming, Celo has, over the decades, cultivated a strong culture around this process (a culture that potential members must become familiar with during their trial membership) and a commitment to a strict, two-hour time limit on monthly community meetings. While this ensures that the immediate costs to participants in terms of time are low, thus accommodating regular participation, it also means that it may take some months to hash out difficult decisions or rule changes, thus ensuring that any big changes are slow to come and are preceded by significant deliberation. It also often means that much of this deliberation takes place outside the official monthly community meetings, either in formal committee meetings or in more ad hoc discussions and back-and-forth among community members. Thus, while participating in the main forum for community governance does not require a large amount of time and energy, those who wish to be deeply involved in sometimes contentious decisions often have large additional burdens placed on their time and energy. On the balance, this process seems to work for Celo as community membership has, for some decades now, remained stable with relatively few departures and a slow trickle of new members joining in processes of community governance.

As alluded to earlier, the formation of the institutions Celo uses to govern its commons was strongly influenced by the presence of committed Quakers in the community's early days. While not all community members today are Quakers, there is still a strong Quaker presence in the community and the rudiments of the Quaker approach to decision-making pervades the community's governance process in both explicit and implicit ways. It is worth quoting from both Quaker scholarship and Celo Community documents to get a feel for the nature of this Quaker influence on community governance.

Quaker theologian Rex Ambler describes how, in trying to reach decisions in their business meetings, Quakers seek unity. According to Ambler, Quakers "have to let go our active and fretful minds in order to do this. We go quiet and let a deeper, more sensitive awareness arise. We let go of our habitual self-concern as well, because this can distort our perception of what is going on" (2013: 67). Further on, Ambler emphasizes how Quakers, having attempted to achieve a less ego-centric state, ideally seek wisdom and input from all in the group: "When we are big enough to really hear one another, a space is created in which new understandings can emerge. A view might arise that no one had thought of before, and perhaps would not have been able to think of. Mixing all these different bits of life together we create the possibility of something quite *new* arising. It is a creative process, and to experience it is often quite awesome and amazing" (2013: 75, emphasis in original).

Sheeran, a Jesuit priest who studied Quaker decision-making in depth, describes a similar process:

> The attitude with which Friends approach a decision is different from that which prevails in the context of majority rule. In Quaker decision-making, it generally is presumed that each participant seeks the best solution; it is also generally presumed that the group, by searching together, can reach such a correct solution. . . . Behavior which evidences attitudes contrary to this searching together suffers subtle but sharp sanctions. As a result, the common search for the best solution which is dismissed as pious rhetoric in the context of majority rule becomes an effective norm in the voteless Quaker world. (1983: 55)

Celo Community's "Consensus Decision-Making Process" document describes, in very similar terms, a method for uniting the minds of Celo's members to reach the best decisions regarding governance of their commons:

> Consensus decision-making stresses cooperative development of a plan or idea with group members working together rather than competing against each other. Members strive to listen and learn from each other, thereby coming up with a decision resulting from group input rather than one or two individuals. The way you listen to each other and the way you contribute ideas can enrich and extend or limit the original idea. It is a more creative approach to reaching a decision because it can include input from everyone in the group. Group wisdom is usually a more creative solution than individual knowledge. . . . This method is more than a procedure; it is an expression of an attitude. It stems from the belief that we should come to decisions in a spirit of unity since we all have access to the light of truth. . . . Consensus decision-making can be a powerful tool for

building group unity and making creative decisions if there is an understanding of the process. Without a good understanding of the process or techniques, it can result in confusion, frustration, disruption or unrest in the group. The way we listen to each other and the way we contribute ideas can help facilitate a good decision. . . . When consensus is fully cooperated and well facilitated, group members will feel they personally contributed to the decision. The reward is that group members will have a greater ownership in the outcome, greater feelings of group unity, and a higher commitment to carrying out the decision. (Celo Community 2011)

This document, which is part of a collection of documents given to trial community members to help them become familiar with the community, goes on to describe in great detail the methods for bringing out the collective wisdom of the group including things such as the seating arrangement; the roles of the meeting facilitator; the responsibilities of members as equal participants in the meeting; appropriate ways to frame proposals, questions, or objections; and the kinds of things that can impede consensus. The point here is that Celo Community members have gone to great lengths to establish a structure of governance that allows for egalitarian participation of all members in using creativity and achieving unity regarding community governance and group decisions.

This structure of governance and the guidelines for effectively implementing it are worth delving into through further exploration of Celo's documents. As stated in the community's Membership Agreement, "each resident member has an equal voice in determining [community] policies and decisions" (Celo Community 2013a). Any member of the community or any group of members may present a proposal for a new policy, an alteration of an existing policy or specific decision. The vignette at the beginning of this chapter included a few examples of policy proposals such as the decision to move the community's reserve funds into a socially and environmentally responsible hedge fund and the proposal to designate liaisons to work with the local electric company and arranging for the community to take charge of clearing power line rights of way within community boundaries. However, conceivable proposals, policies, and decisions are numerous; they could include anything from a proposal to allow a member to build a small garden shed on their holding to the probably much more contentious proposal to draw down community reserve funds to purchase additional land.

In order to allow for small group discussion and refinement of the proposed policy prior to presenting it to the whole group for approval, such proposals are generally introduced and discussed in a meeting of the relevant committee rather than in a general, monthly community meeting. The community's procedures and rules are clear on this process:

Preferably, an issue will be discussed first at a committee meeting. The committee could make a recommendation or report [to the general meeting] that no agreement has been reached. If, after discussion at a general meeting, a proposal does not have consensus, it shall be referred to a special meeting before the next general meeting. (Celo Community 2019)

All major committees in the community—including most prominently, membership, property, and finance, although there are several others—have regularly scheduled meetings throughout the month prior to each general community meeting which are always held on the first Wednesday evening of each month. While each committee has a designated chair, cochair, and secretary, any community member may attend and propose new business at any of these committee meetings. For all but the most routine decisions, committees make recommendations about policies or decisions at the general meeting where those recommendations are then submitted to discussion and potential approval.

Once the proposal reaches the general community meeting (see figure 6.1), a relatively elaborate process of consensus decision-making is initiated. During this process, the nature of the proposal is clarified and different perspectives on the proposal are solicited and aired in an attempt to reach unanimous consent. The term *unanimous consent* does not necessarily mean universal agreement, but rather a "sense of the meeting" derived from thorough consideration and blending of all principled and considered perspectives among the group's membership. In struggling to accurately describe the meaning of Quaker-based consensus, Sheeran concludes that "the sort of agreement found in Quaker decisions is not an identity of view such that every participant ends up on the same note. Instead, they remain on different notes but blend them as the pianist blends complementary notes into a chord" (1983: 63–64). As suggested above, in Celo, the consensus process operates in such a way that it draws out and resolves tension among divergent perspectives on an issue such that they ultimately converge on common ground.

The clerk, or chair, of Celo's general meeting plays a significant role in helping the group to strike such a convergent chord. The chair plays the key role in facilitating the decision-making process at the community's monthly meeting which is the main policy-making forum in the community. Since effective clerkship of the community's general meeting, along with principled participation on the part of community members, is such an important part of the decision-making process in Celo Community, it is worth describing the role of the chair in greater detail. The meeting chair is tasked not only with providing structure and maintaining order, but with ushering the whole group through a disciplined process of diplomatic dialogue that combines the perspectives of all participants into one concordant "sense of the meeting." A chair can facilitate this process by doing technical things such as providing a

Figure 6.1   Celo Community General Meeting October 2019. *Source:* Photo by the author.

clear, well-ordered agenda, referring to previous minutes and existing policies (often with the help of the community's designated codifier), and polling
the participants to get an initial sense of the level of agreement.

However, the methods for ushering the community toward decisions of
unanimous consent also involve more subtle and nuanced directives and
capabilities. For example, the chair is charged with ensuring that all participants are on an egalitarian plane where each can see every other by arranging
the seating in a big circle. A chair also has a duty of encouraging participants
who are less quick to speak to contribute to the discussion. This is done most
prominently by keeping a "stack" of people who have raised their hands and
ensuring that each speaks in turn. It may also be done by subtly disciplining
those who have a tendency to speak more or more quickly than others and
by allowing time to pause and rest in silence while people who may be less
quick to speak gather their thoughts. The chair is charged with preventing differences in opinions or perspectives from blowing up into conflict by ensuring that participants are directing their remarks not at each other but rather
through the chair to the general issue at hand.

While the chair is in charge of facilitating the process of group decision-making by gently shepherding the group along the complex path, the responsibilities
of members themselves largely mirror the structure the chair tries to facilitate
and maintain. Again, it is worth quoting community documents at some length:

1. Address chairperson with remarks; do not dialogue with others.
2. All members are equal and each member has a responsibility to treat all others equally and honestly.

3. Members are responsible to participate and to encourage and validate each other's participation. Say "I agree," when you do. Silence may not be taken as agreement. You need to say so.

4. Try not to own an idea, but realize an idea is a seed to be planted. The group nourishes its growth.

5. Assume equal power among group members including yourself. A premise of consensus is that minority opinions may be the best choice for the group.

6. Value feelings and conflict; if you don't [they] will appear later.

7. Do not repeat what someone else has said. Say only that you agree with what another said.

8. Acknowledge that you hear each other. Chairperson can sometimes repeat what you said to make sure what you said is understood.

9. Try to limit the times you speak until someone else who wishes has spoken. Some need some silence to speak out of. Do not jump in, give others time. Chairperson can also make sure this is done.

10. Recognize that patience is required by those who have reached clarity while waiting for others to reach it. "Early clearness" is not necessarily "correct clearness" (Celo Community 2011).

Finally, the chair, working with the community members, is charged with gauging the sense of the meeting; is there a common ground that discussion is converging toward? Perhaps this was stated best by one person or perhaps no one has fully articulated it yet? If the latter, the chair may try to articulate this herself. Or, if the multiplicity of perspectives are not yet converging on common ground, the chair may decide that the issue needs to be sent back to committee for further discussion so that all participants, and especially those who feel most strongly about or have minority views on the issue, may take time to gather their thoughts and engage in smaller group dialogue outside the official decision-making forum. If the chair senses agreement, she may clarify by asking the group if they also sense this and, absent any further perspectives or differences, may try to articulate a final decision or policy that reflects the will of the group to be recorded in the minutes by the secretary.

Ultimately, the sense of the meeting may take a number of different paths. One may be consensus on a policy or decision in which case the decision is articulated, recorded in the meeting minutes ("minuted"), and takes effect when the official minutes are read at the next community meeting. Another likely path is that the chair perceives that a sense of the meeting is absent and the issue may be sent back to its originating committee for further discussion. In this case, the parties with divergent perspectives are encouraged to engage in dialogue outside the general meeting. In this case, the committee may be empowered by the group to reach a decision on its own if the divergent parties agree to dialogue in the committee. Or, the committee may be asked to bring a new recommendation to the next monthly general meeting. Finally, a chairperson may also decide that there is not really enough interest in making the decision at this time; someone or some subgroup may have felt strongly about an issue, but after group discussion it is clear that no one is any longer championing any action on the issue in which case the chair may table or drop the issue altogether or until further action by a committee. In the rare occurrence when ongoing discussion across multiple community meetings has not revealed common ground regarding an issue or proposed policy change and where the committee in charge of the discussions feels that a decision should be made, community policies allow for decisions to be reached based on an 85 percent supermajority vote. However, my review of community meeting minutes and my discussions with community members reveals that this last option of supermajority is, outside of occasional votes on new members, almost never used.

I have spent many hours observing these community meetings and, while the process does not work without fail, I have been present for its successful functioning on many occasions. However, the process is imperfect and, especially in the absence of an effective clerk or meeting chair, one or more community members can take control of a meeting by acting in ways that don't conform with the principles of consensus decision-making. Indeed, longtime community members have described how the community's decision-making process has, at various times in its history, been hijacked by one or two community members who "talked loudest" in order that their viewpoint would prevail or "blocked consensus" when they didn't agree with a decision others were willing to make. Other community members have occasionally expressed frustration with a process that, while egalitarian in theory, ends up sometimes being hierarchical in nature. These community members have described to me how those who have been community members longer or those who are more articulate will be listened to more than others who may be slower to articulate their thoughts or who may be less familiar with established community precedents. These situations have caused the community to convene task forces and organize workshops to revisit and retrain themselves on the consensus process multiple times over the decades. They also led the community to adopt the above-referenced policy of resorting to a supermajority vote for issues on which consensus cannot be achieved after three general community meetings.

Chapter 7

Keeping Each Other Honest

People shake the water off their umbrellas and hang their rain coats as they enter the Celo Community Center for tonight's property committee meeting. The looks on some of their faces betray the fact that they are weary from what has already been a long day and are not particularly happy about trudging through the cold and rain to attend a late night meeting. As people remove their galoshes and settle into an irregular circle in the center of the room, one community member offers cups of steaming tea from the kitchen in the next room.

Indicating a desire to address the items on tonight's agenda without further delay, the chair of the committee asks everyone to take their seats. She reminds those present that this is the official forum where they hold each other accountable to the agreements they've made and signed on to regarding how they use their common land. As such, they have some business to discuss regarding member requests for exceptions to community rules.

The first item up for discussion is a proposal by the members who run a children's summer camp on community land to use pesticides banned by the community to help keep down poison ivy in areas used by children at the camp. The chair notes that the community chose to ban these chemicals due to concerns about their toxic effects on people and wildlife. She also notes that the members are following community process by coming to the property committee to ask for an exception to the policy. The member who runs the children's summer camp indicates that they have dealt with an upsurge of poison ivy exposure at the camp and have struggled to find other ways of eliminating the plant and the risks it poses for children at the camp. They ask the community's gracious consideration to allow them to use a banned spray in this limited instance.

Another community member expresses her strong desire to not allow any use of ANY toxic herbicides or pesticides on community land noting that her father, a long time farmer, died from cancer that they believe was caused by exposure

157

to herbicides. While she strongly desires that no toxic pesticides be used on community land, she believes that the camp operators will use them responsibly and is willing to make an exception in this case.

Another member who serves as chair of the land use planning committee, asks about how close the areas to be sprayed are to perennial streams; he is particularly concerned about the potential for the chemicals to spread beyond their application zone via community waterways. The camp operator indicates that none of the application zones are within fifty feet of a community stream and the land use chair indicates that this satisfies his concern.

The property chair asks for other concerns and, when none are expressed, notes that community policy states that "any time restricted chemicals are applied, the area must be posted for 6 months." Is the member committed to ensuring that the areas of application are clearly marked for all to see? Once agreement is reached on this point, the property chair asks if the committee is agreed to recommend this exception to community policies on chemical sprays to the general meeting provided that the areas of application are clearly marked. All present indicate agreement and the next item of business comes up for discussion.

Jared is a long time community member whose contributions and commitment to the community are highly respected and valued by his fellow members. However, he has been at the center of controversy recently after he started felling trees on his holding in a manner that some believe was not in keeping with community policy on tree cutting. The chair reminds community members that this policy states that "members may cut any dead trees and trees under 6 diameter at breast height on their own holdings and for their own personal use." Jared knew that he wanted to cut a number of much larger trees to clear a sunshed for his new greenhouse and had, following community process, sought approval for this tree cutting from the property chair. However, he had not waited for the general community meeting to approve the cutting of a dozen large, old pines and hardwoods before he started the project. About halfway through the project a neighboring community member walking by on a community trail had become outraged at Jared's perceived tree massacre and the accompanying negative effects on the trail's viewshed. How are they to proceed with this issue?

As relatively autonomous groups, commoners must hold each other to the cooperative commitments and rules they've made regarding the resources they share. Point of orientation for commoning four states, in part, that "We monitor the respect of these commitments ourselves and sometimes we mandate others whom we trust to help reach this goal. We continually reassess whether our commitments still serve their purpose" (Bollier and Helfrich 2015b: 49). As the vignettes above illustrate, the members of Celo Community monitor the status of their common resources and the use of the resources by members in a somewhat ad hoc, case-by-case basis. Since they do not employ outside monitors, monitoring activities could place significant demands for time and energy on community members. Reflecting the trust they place in each other, the community has only a few well-defined monitoring systems and roles in place, especially with regard to the community's most tangible property such as buildings that serve as community member homes. With regard to their various commons, Celo Community has struck a tenuous balance between mutual trust and good will on the one hand and some level of necessary bureaucracy on the other. One further vignette illustrates this.

The finance committee meeting begins with a presentation from the community bookkeeper providing an overview of the balances and flows in community's various funds. The picture is one of overall good financial health with balances in most accounts growing or outgoing and incoming funds being approximately equal. There is one notable exception. The account that provides loans for community member home renovation or construction is down significantly over the past year. This is due in part to the unique circumstances whereby three new members have joined the community this past year (one via the new "fast track" option), with two of them taking out loans for new home construction. Added to that are two recent loans to existing members for significant (and in one case, much needed) home renovation projects. As a result, the balance of this fund is significantly down. The bookkeeper and the finance chair remind those present that these loans represent investments in common community property that will pay off in the long run and that they fully anticipate these loans being paid back in a timely manner. However, the finance committee should be cautious about making further significant loans from this fund until the grace period expires and members start repaying some of the principle from these loans.

The next item on the agenda concerns a community member who is significantly behind on her annual dues to the community. In fact, Allison has not paid any portion of her annual dues in each of the last three years with this year's annual assessment only a month away. The finance committee chair reminds everyone that annual dues cover county property taxes on an individual's holding along with their per head portion of property tax on community land that is not allocated to individual holdings. It also includes a small component that goes into the community's annual operating budget. It is important that we not set a precedent of allowing community members to fall behind on these dues. The last two years, Allison has not even requested a temporary moratorium on dues and, despite the property chair sending a somewhat urgent invitation to come to the meeting tonight to discuss this, she is not present.

Greta, one of Allison's closest neighbors and longtime friend, stands to offer an update on Allison's situation based on several conversations they've had over recent weeks. As everyone knows, Allison has been going through a nasty separation from her non-community member husband that has drawn out over recent years. His departure has left her household significantly down on income over the last year or so. Even though he wasn't a community member, as a full time resident on community land, some of these overdue assessments are his responsibility. Allison's remaining living parent has also been in poor health and she has had to take time off from work to help her mom move into an elder care facility. Greta indicates that Allison is quite emotionally distraught about the state of her life and, she thinks, combined with Allison's embarrassment over her failure to honor her commitments to the community, this has led to a kind of paralysis that is preventing her from even engaging. Greta asks the finance committee and bookkeeper to take these issues into account as they discuss ways to deal with Allison's arrears.

Later that night, I reflect on the finance committee meeting. In many ways, the group business of this unique intentional community is much like the financial dealings that characterize any household or community; there are budgets to maintain, loans to be paid back, interest to be collected, and dues to pay. In a world where state oversight is inescapable and market operations nearly so, no group or individual can fully dispense with monetary exchange. On the other hand, the small scale, relative autonomy, and power of group cooperation and pooling of resources make possible a set of more personal, relational, and sit-uationally-grounded considerations than might otherwise be the case. That the community has been incorporating these considerations into their operations for so many decades while very rarely having to impose significant sanctions on individual members suggests that this form of commoning is sustainable.

A Holding Agreement is not only a legal agreement but a personal moral obliga-tion (Celo Community 2019).

The Holder shall at all times seek to engage in practices that include, but are not limited to practices that represent good conservation, agricultural, and civic stan-dards, maintain his Holding and the improvements thereon in a clean and health-ful condition, keep the buildings and structures in good repair, keep the land free from noxious weeds and plants, prevent and control erosion of the soil, and spray, fumigate, or otherwise treat trees, shrubs, and other plants on the land as necessary and reasonably feasible to prevent the growth and spread of agricultural pests.

The Holder shall not make significant modifications or changes on this Holding without written consent of the Community. This includes construction, any changes to water flow or the water table, major driveway adjustments such as rerouting, and substantial earth movement. (Celo Community 2018b)

I accept the privilege and duty of participating in the Community meetings, of actively serving on committees for the management of Community affairs, and of sharing with the other members the responsibility for maintenance, growth, and

preservation of all Community land and other property and interests. I also agree
to assume my share of the yearly Community budget. (Celo Community 2013a)

The above excerpts from Celo Community's governing documents indicate the relative lack of emphasis that the community places on monitoring
of common resources and commoners' use of those resources. As one digs
into the deeper recesses of these documents, it is possible to identify some
very specific monitoring roles and mechanisms that the community has put
into official policy. These will be discussed below, but the main point I wish
to make here, a point illustrated by the above quotes, is that good, honest use
of resources in conformity with community norms and policies is considered
to be a fundamental moral obligation of community members. This moral
obligation calls on community members to engage in practices of good
conservation, maintain the land in good health, not make significant, lasting
changes to the land without seeking official permission from the community
first, and accepting the duty of actively maintaining, preserving, and contributing to the upkeep of community common property and finances. As such,
Celo Community's approach to monitoring is more prescriptive and preven-
tative than it is grounded in official bureaucratic procedures and roles.

Ostrom's commons design principle 4 is, like principles one and two, split
into two constituent parts concerning monitoring of commons resources and
commons users. Principle 4A states that "individuals who are accountable to
or are the users monitor the appropriation and provision levels of the users"
and principle 4B states that "individuals who are accountable to or are the
users monitor the condition of the resource" (Ostrom 2010: 653). Along with
principle five discussed in the following chapter, this is one area where Celo's
policies and rules are least explicit about formal procedures and institutional
roles. As a result, monitoring of commons resources and commons users in
Celo often occurs in a relatively informal, ad hoc fashion. In the following,
I will first elucidate a few instances where Celo's documents offer clarity on
this topic. Then, I will provide a discussion of more de facto procedures and
examples of monitoring in the community.

While discussions in previous chapters have centered around well-defined
processes for defining boundaries, making rules, and making decisions as laid
out in the community's main institutional documents, formal procedures for
monitoring resources and users are often, with a few exceptions, not explicitly delineated in those documents. Specific roles, systems, and processes for
monitoring the status of commons resources are most clearly defined in the
community's Job Descriptions document. Perhaps the most well-defined role
for monitoring the commons is that held by the chair of the community's
property committee. This document describes the property committee chair's

duties in terms of monitoring buildings and holdings not currently occupied by a member as follows. The Property chair should

- keep track of community-owned property including rental houses, and the furnishings and equipment of the rental houses, repair and maintenance of the [Celo Community Center]. Recommend a caretaker for each building managed by the community. Oversee whatever action is needed when a building or furnishings need repair or replacement.
- When a holding is taken up or returned to the Community, go (or delegate building caretaker to go) with the holder and Finance Chairperson to inspect the corners and boundaries and the state of the building and ground, and report to property committee. Follow-up on return of a holding promptly after a member resigns from Community. See that community files on structures and holdings are kept up to date. Make sure each member files a map/plat/sketch showing (1) water supply, (2) septic system, (3) drainfield, (4) telephone, (5) electric, (6) gas lines, and (7) any other pertinent information about his/her holding for future reference (Celo Community 2019).

This document also indicates that the property committee chair is "empowered to give permission for a Holder to cut up to six trees on a holding in a calendar year" and states that the chair should summarize the activities and decisions of the property committee in a report that is presented to the board and the community at their annual meeting every fall (Celo Community 2019).

The designated caretakers appointed by the property committee chair also have a well-elaborated list of monitoring duties. Caretakers are

- Appointed by Property Committee for each CCI-owned building to coordinate physical maintenance and keep building in good repair. Report any needed repairs to Property Committee and either do them or oversee that they are done.
- If unable to do the maintenance item and no one volunteers, the caretaker will hire someone, giving first option to community members. Unskilled labor will be put on the workday list. Refer greater needs or problems to Property Chair.
- Check monthly on vacant buildings. Have keys in possession and available.
- At beginning of rental, see to cleanliness, readiness for rental, and repairs as needed. At end of rental, see that building is clean, closed and weatherproofed. Make written reports on the condition of the house at beginning and end of rental period. This report will be kept on file with Bookkeeper's financial record on that house; it will be used to assess need for repairs and as basis for any return of rental deposit.
- Serve as liaison between renter and CCI. Respond to tenant requests and concerns. Make sure renters have a copy of "Abridged P&R" [a shorter version

of the community's Procedures and Rules document that is given to people renting holdings from the community so that they are informed about and can abide by relevant community policies]. Supervise projects that the renter has gotten Property approval to complete.

- Schedule routine chimney cleaning.
- Members who are renting will normally be caretakers for their own buildings(s). Any problems will be brought directly to Property Chair (Celo Community 2019).

Other community jobs have less detailed duties with regard to monitoring community property and physical infrastructure and reporting back to the community during official community meetings. For example, there is a designated Celo Community Center Building Manager whose duties include working with the property committee to oversee and complete maintenance, repairs, and improvements to the building and grounds and scheduling the use of the building by different individuals and groups including orienting them to the building and associated equipment, explaining their responsibilities and expectations, and sending bills to renters where applicable. Celo Community offers their community center to the wider, surrounding community as a space for events and also rents several rooms to community members and nonmembers for use as office space, so the building manager plays an important role in monitoring the activities of both official community members as well as nonmembers.

The workday chair is in charge of coordinating the clean-up and maintenance of public roads in the community and the annual clearing along the boundaries of community land. The chair of the fields committee is charged with monitoring the state of open spaces and agricultural fields that are rented (sometimes by noncommunity members) or held by community members. This includes ensuring that the field holders or renters are completing the required biannual tests to monitor soil health and the occasional mowing mandated by the community to ensure that fields do not lapse into successional forest. There is a Trail Maintenance position that is charged with monitoring community trails and footpaths for damage or obstruction (for example, from washouts or fallen trees after a storm) and coordinating their repair and maintenance. There is a "Sign Czar" that coordinates the posting and maintenance of approved signage on Celo Community property and a Cemetery and Prearrangement Committee that sees to maintenance and policy enforcement regarding the community cemetery.

The Job Descriptions document also identifies committees and individual positions that are charged with ensuring that community members and trial community members are informed about and consistently following community policies, including those regarding the use of commons resources. For example, the membership committee chair sees that all trial community members are fully informed about community policies and legal agreements (with aid from individual community members serving as Trial Member Sponsors in this case), addresses community members' failure to follow community obligations in cases that are not specifically within the remit of other committees, and helps to address conflicts among community members that require mediation or arbitration (theoretically including conflicts regarding the use of community resources; more on this in the following chapter). The membership committee chair also monitors and keeps the community up-to-date regarding any changes in community membership such as deaths or resignations of members and resultant changes in overall community population and the number of holdings available to potential new members.

Finally, there are a number of official community positions charged with monitoring the status and health of the community's financial commons, positions for which accurate knowledge of community population and status of holdings is essential. For example, stated duties the chair of the community's finance committee include drawing up annual budgets, working on annual tax bills, negotiating and overseeing financial arrangements between the community and its members, working with others such as the property committee chair to deal with financial arrangements when an individual holding is taken by an individual member or returned to the community by a departing member, and reporting annually to the community regarding the status of its financial health. Often working closely with the finance committee chair, the bookkeeper's duties include keeping "accurate, current books on CCI income, disbursements, investments, and bank accounts" as well as billing and monitoring members who have outstanding balances to the community for holding payments, loans, or annual head taxes (Celo Community 2019).

In contrast with the ways in which Celo Community monitors the status and use of its individual holdings, associated infrastructure, and financial commons, systems and processes by which Celo's members monitor their collectively held 1,200 acres of land, including the large portions of it that are not part of an individual member's holding, are not particularly well-defined or formalized. There is no one position designated to ensure that members are conforming to policies regarding the extraction of resources such as lumber, either from individual holdings or from common land. While there are policies in place that state what may or may not happen, what processes should be gone through and what approvals sought, and how such resource extraction should proceed, these policies are prescriptive and violations of such rules would likely only be identified should a community member happen to witness the process of unsanctioned resource extraction or its aftermath.

The lack of emphasis placed on monitoring common land and forests by the community is a reflection of the fact that very few community members, with a few exceptions whose main income is obtained from farming community land, derive their income directly from extracting resources from the community's land base on a daily basis. Arthur Morgan's original vision for the community included a much larger percentage of community members making a livelihood for themselves from farming and other forms of resource use. As such, and given his awareness of the degraded status of forests and soils in the region at the time he founded the community, he was careful to designate land stewardship as an important part of the community's endeavor. However, given the experimental nature of the community Morgan envisioned, he did not describe or put in place specific processes for monitoring resource use, other than the duties of the community manager, a position that did not last past the first decade of the community's existence. Thus, whereas other commons defined by direct individual or group use of physical resources place a high importance on monitoring mechanisms, such mechanisms are less important for Celo.

However, resource use and extraction by noncommunity members, including especially those that the community has no prior or direct contact with, is still an issue that the community has to address. Celo's commonly held land is adjacent to parcels of land owned and managed by both public and private entities including United States Forest Service lands designated for mixed use that run along a significant portion of the community's eastern boundary. Community land is also traversed by several public transportation routes including a state highway, a county road, and a number of trails and footpaths, many of which existed before the community was founded and which extend beyond the community's boundaries. Some of these transportation routes provide direct access to the South Toe River, a waterway that is popular for angling, floating, and swimming that also traverses, and extends beyond, Celo's land. As such, a wide variety of noncommunity members have direct access to Celo's common land and use it regularly for recreation and, sometimes, illicit resource extraction. The ways in which these noncommoners use the land may or may not accord with the rules and norms that govern the manners in which Celo's members interact with the land and, outside of consistent vigilance by community members, the community has few options for informing these users of or enforcing community rules and norms.

The community's official stance on nonmembers accessing community land is that they welcome it as long as they are using the land in a way that does not subtract from the various things that the land provides to its common stewards, things that range from lumber and clean water to the spiritual nourishment that community members obtain from interaction with intact ecosystems. This policy is reflected in the verbiage of signs the community has

posted at various intervals where public transportation routes cross the boundaries of their land (see figure 7.1). These signs read: "Wildlife Safety Zone. No
Hunting, Fishing, Trapping, or Motorized Vehicles. Hiking, Photography, and
Nature Study Permitted. Do Not Remove Forest Products. Celo Community
Inc." The posting of these signs represents the community's most recent
attempt to strike a balance between excluding outsiders entirely from their
commons and allowing some minimal, non-subtractive use of their commons
by people who are not bound by the community's official agreements, contracts, and policies.

Two examples illustrate some of the ways in which non-commoners interact with Celo's commons. The first example directly involves my old family
friend Bruce whom I referenced in the preface to the book. Bruce owns and
lives on a small parcel of land approximately a mile away from the nearest
boundary of Celo's land and he frequently drives to and parks on community
land to spend time walking the various trails that traverse it. These trails, or
at least the portions of them within community boundaries, are maintained by
a small number of community members who volunteer their time to maintain
the trails by doing things like cutting and removing downed trees and repair-
ing and replacing creek bridges that have been damaged or washed away.
During a recent visit to Celo, I joined Bruce for a hike on Celo's trail system.
During our hike he said, "This is a great benefit I get from living in such close

Figure 7.1   Celo Community Non-Extractive Use Signage. *Source:* Photo by the author.

proximity to Celo Community; I have access to miles of trails that cross this beautiful, peaceful piece of Appalachian forest but I don't have to do anything to participate in or support the maintenance of these trails." Bruce was clearly acknowledging his gratefulness that this is the kind of public good that the members of Celo are happy to provide on their common land as long as people don't exploit the land in disrespectful ways.

Many others who are less familiar with Celo Community's unique nature use their land in similar manners. The valley is known as a hiking and horseback riding destination and people engaged in these activities frequently traverse community land without damaging the land and without even knowing they are crossing a collectively owned piece of private property. Similarly, on any given day, one will often find anglers and swimmers parked along the main county road through the community, using it as an access point for the South Toe River. Other than placing a sign discouraging the presence of dogs at the main swimming area used by community members and their children, the community has had little occasion to take issue with the presence of these outside users. In cases such as this, there is little need for Celo's members to monitor outsiders' use of their commons.

On the other hand, another example illustrates the ways in which outsiders sometimes use community land by exploiting resources in illicit and subtractive manners. A couple of days after my hike with Bruce, I joined two Celo Community members for an extensive hike through some of the more remote stretches of community land. During the hike, I asked about the issue of outsiders using Celo's land for extractive, profit-seeking purposes. Parts of the land, especially those that have more fully recovered from periods of extensive logging that preceded Celo's existence, contain a number of floral species that are valued in various industries. One of the members I was with, an individual who is part of the volunteer trail maintenance crew and who thus frequently hikes community trails, described a recent instance in which he and his partner encountered two people camped out deep in the community's forests harvesting large bags full of a particular species that is valued by florists. Celo's members are well aware of overharvesting of such species in southern Appalachian forests in general and of the ways in which such extraction disrupts the functioning of the intact ecosystems that they try to steward and upon which they place other, nonmonetary values. The two community members informed the couple that they were on private property and escorted them off the property minus their illegal harvests.

This is not an isolated occurrence and it was only partially thwarted by the happenstance of a community member being in the right place at the right time. On multiple other occasions, the community has encountered only the aftermath of such resource extraction. In addition to the harvesting of flora, other examples include hunting and destructive off-road vehicle use.

That Celo does not have a procedure in place for systematically monitoring exploitative, subtractive use of their commons by outsiders has not proven particularly problematic thus far and is offset by the de facto vigilance of community members who frequently walk the community land, largely for their own enjoyment. However, as regional population grows and pressure on natural resources increases, a need may arise for the community to put a more formal monitoring system in place.

Chapter 8

When One of Us Is Not Honest

I sense heavy hearts as people assemble for tonight's community meeting. The normal level of upbeat banter and exchange that usually precedes a community meeting is absent and many members sit silently waiting for the meeting to start. There is a sense of tension in the room. For the first time in its history, the community is considering invoking the process for dismissing one or more community members. Promptly at 8 o'clock, the meeting chair notes the particularly full and potentially contentious agenda and suggests they get started.

The usual announcement period provides some respite from the tension, as good news is shared and positive contributions from community members are recognized. One community member announces the birth of a grandson to a round of heartfelt applause. She intends to go to Michigan for two months to help her daughter and son-in-law care for the new baby. Two community members' children have been accepted into prestigious graduate programs. Their areas of focus, in biology and geology, reflect the influence of growing up in the community where they lived close to the land and developed a sense of wonder and curiosity about the natural world. Finally, the newly refurbished first floor of the community center, complete with a certified industrial kitchen and adjacent dining area, hosted its first event. A four course meal, prepared by community members and several neighbors who will also benefit from having use of the community center, was well attended and raised over $500 dollars to help with further remodeling of the upstairs rooms. Jared who, despite his ongoing work developing his own holding, has spearheaded the improvements to the community center and kept the work under budget receives a standing ovation from all present.

The tone in the room quickly changes as the membership committee chair reviews the notes from their last committee meeting. Their agenda included discussion of two community members whose ongoing violation of or misalignment with community policies, rules, and procedures need to be resolved. This is not the first time these two cases have been discussed in the community's committees or general meeting. In each case, the community has exercised extreme patience and flexibility, repeatedly appointing mediators to work with the members and granting significant extensions to previously set deadlines for resolving the issues. The membership committee believes that allowing the cases to continue in an unresolved state has the potential to set a bad precedent. On the other hand, they recognize that both cases have significant extenuating circumstances and that flexibility in the application of the rules has been an important and acknowledged factor in the community's stability and relative lack of acrimony over the years.

The first case is perhaps most easily resolved. Stephanie, who has been a member of the community for just two and a half years, has not been living on community land for the last two years and has not sought a leave of absence from the community, as is policy for any community member who intends to be away or live off of community land for six months or more. Further, Stephanie has not responded to multiple attempts by representatives of the community to communicate with her about the situation. The committee chair states what most people in the room already know—Stephanie separated from her husband, the son of two longtime community members, the day after they were both admitted to the community as new members just over two and a half years ago. While clearly recognizing how challenging a divorce can be, especially when three children are involved, the membership committee believes that, given the situation with her husband which was unbeknownst to almost all community members at the time they were accepted into the community, Stephanie should have asked for an extension of her trial membership. Her lack of response to the community's overtures in the time since then suggests that she joined the community in bad faith and the committee recommends invoking the process for terminating her membership.

The ensuing discussion focuses on the community's commitment to treating each other with care and on their basic obligation to do all they can to ensure that Stephanie and her family are healthy and their needs are being met. Those who have been tasked with communicating with her emphasize their repeated and ongoing attempts to reach out to her, all of which have ultimately been frustrated. They also note that her husband, still a community member and still pursuing the establishment of his holding, is not present tonight to express his views. His mother, a longtime community member, indicates that he believes that their relationship problems are irreconcilable and that she has not had much success reaching out to Stephanie either. After a moment or two of silence, the meeting chair suggests that they return to the committee's proposal to invoke the process for dismissing Stephanie from membership. Are there any further comments or concerns? Can we test for consensus on the issue? Almost all in the room indicate agreement through silent hand gestures and no one objects. The meeting chair asks the committee chair to communicate this decision to Stephanie and ask her to consider resigning instead. He also indicates that, to his knowledge, this is the first time they have sought to revoke someone's membership. He suggests they take a moment of silence to absorb the significance of this moment.

"Now that we've had time to consider the gravity of this situation, let's turn to the second item on the agenda which may involve a quite similar decision," states the meeting chair, leading in to a discussion of how to deal with a community member who has been absent for over ten years. The chair of the membership committee provides a brief overview of how the situation developed. *"Francis and Shelly joined the community about fifteen years ago and almost all of us were thrilled with their strong commitments to simple living, environmental values, and social justice."* When they joined, they took an existing holding that was vacated by previously departed members and did some significant repairs on a house that had stood empty for some time. Five years after they joined the community, they made a fairly sudden decision to move their family to Ecuador where they planned to join some members from a commune in Virginia to build an ecovillage on the Peruvian border. Since they were uncertain about how this would work out and they wished to retain community membership, the community granted them a leave of absence.

Two years later, they were back in the U.S., but were living as trial members at the commune in Virginia rather than returning to Celo. The next year when Francis and Shelly got divorced, Shelly resigned from community membership and turned her interest in their holding over to Francis. In the ensuing six or seven years, Francis has requested and been granted multiple leaves of absence, always promising to return to the community, if not permanently, at least to meet with members and make a clear plan for stewardship of his holding until he could return. In recent years, his ability to return to the community has been complicated by an injury requiring spinal surgery, lost functioning of his only vehicle, and a lack of available funds. "During the last three or four years, we have reached out to Francis multiple times in attempts to explain how his long term absence is out of alignment with community policies and how the disrepair to his house and holding, in which the community has an equity stake due to our unique membership and landholding agreements, are causing significant consternation in the community." Following this, the committee chair reads relevant portions of several letters that have been sent to Francis:*

Concerns have repeatedly been raised about the deteriorating condition of absentee members' holdings that are being rented out, with the owner too far away to properly oversee maintenance. . . . CCI has an equity stake in the house. . . . We feel that you are not looking out for the community's interests. (Celo Community 2005)

We have not heard from you about your leave of absence. Since a leave has not been granted you must come in person to meet with folks and work it out. . . . If you are not able and willing to come in March or mid-April, the next step will be for the community to begin the process of terminating your holding agreement. Enclosed are copies of previous letters and copies of some policy information about leaves and termination of the holding agreement. (Celo Community 2006a)

The question of your leave of absence was addressed again at the November general meeting. Several folks spoke up on your behalf but there was not consensus to grant you a leave. Part of the problem is that you still have not addressed the requirement for a definite plan to return to the community. Our policy guidelines for a leave of absence states: "If members want an exception, they must come in person to answer questions. There are no open-ended leaves of absence You MUST HAVE A PLAN & PURPOSE WITH DETAILS AND VERY SPECIFIC PLANS FOR RETURN. Leaves will not be for more than 7 years unless an exception is made." . . . The community does not want you to tie up that holding for another 3-4 years and then decide to go elsewhere. . . . We are still requesting that you come to a meeting so that we can talk this through face to face. It would be helpful for you to let us know in advance when you are coming so that time can be allotted to spend with you. (Celo Community 2006b)

"I could go on. We addressed Francis again a little over two years ago. During that meeting we noted that we have been extra generous with Francis according to our own policies, contained in our Membership Agreement, on dismissal from membership." There is an audible sigh in the room, followed by a moment of silence. It is clear that no one in the community really wants to terminate Francis's membership (or Stephanie's for that matter). Indeed, they have bent over backwards to accommodate him. However, his ongoing failure over the last ten years to respond to their overtures and come into alignment with community policies has forced their hand. *"The membership committee recommends that we notify Francis that we are initiating procedures for his dismissal from community membership."* There are some pained looks on people's faces when the meeting chair asks for consensus on the recommendation, but no one objects.

Follow up note: Stephanie's membership termination was completed six months later. Francis voluntarily resigned from membership and returned his holding to the community six months after he was informed of the community's decision.

For the commons to function successfully, the commoners must abide by the rules that they themselves have set through processes of collective decision-making. One of the greatest threats to sustainable functioning of the commons is free riding whereby one commoner takes more than his or her share of benefits from the commons without contributing to the upkeep of the commons. It can be equally disruptive when one or more commoners decide to act against established rules even when their actions do not have a subtractive effect on the common resource in questions or when individuals are otherwise derelict in their duties to the group. In such cases, it is important that a set of clearly defined, consistent, and fair consequences be in place for dealing with rule violators. Point of orientation for commoning five states that "We work out appropriate rules for dealing with violations of our commitments. We determine whether and what kinds of sanctions shall be used, depending on the context and severity of a violation" (Bollier and Helfrich 2015b: 49). In Celo Community, where there is an absence of a defined set of sanctions, context and flexibility have been the most important considerations regarding how rule violators are dealt with. The only clearly defined sanction in place in Celo is dismissal from community membership, but the community has, over its history, worked through cases of rule violations on a case-by-case basis such that this ultimate sanction has rarely been invoked.

> A member is expected to abide by all duly enacted decisions of the regular Community meeting and to accept arbitration according to Community rules in case of disagreement with the Community or another member. (Celo Community 2013a)

> CCI by action in a regular meeting with the concurrence of the Directors of CCI may dismiss from membership any member who in its opinion has not acted in accordance with the purpose and objectives of CCI or who has acted against the best interest of CCI. (Celo Community 2013a)

Ostrom's Commons design principle 5 is very clear in expressing that rules violations in commons situations will be dealt with through a set of "graduated sanctions": "Sanctions for rule violations start very low but become stronger if a user repeatedly violates a rule" (Ostrom 2010: 653). This principle recognizes that individuals who may inadvertently violate a rule or do so intentionally but not out of habit need not be cast out of the community. It also recognizes that habitual rule violations must be met with increasingly consequential actions in order to steer people away from regular free riding. While each of the conditions described in Ostrom's first four commons design principles have been largely matched in Celo, this is one area where Celo is largely out of congruence with the design principles. While rule violators have historically caused disruption for the community, Celo's case-by-case process has worked effectively enough that the ultimate sanction of dismissal from membership has been invoked extremely rarely.

Celo Community's official governing documents contain very little reference to a specific set of sanctions, much less graduated sanctions, for rule violations. In fact, the only direct reference to sanctions in these documents refers to the process for "dismissal" of a community member. In language mirrored in the community's Membership Agreement, Celo's Procedures and Rules state:

> The Community, by action in a regular meeting, may, if not more than 15% of the members in residence and of the directors dissent, dismiss from membership any member who, in its opinion, has not acted in accordance with the purposes and objectives of the Community or who has acted against the best interest of the Community. (Celo Community 2019)

On the surface, this policy appears open to broad interpretation and gives the community-wide latitude for almost immediate dismissal of community members. Actions that are not in accordance with the purposes and objectives of the community or that are against the best interest of the community could be taken to include a wide variety of things. However, the policy goes on to identify more specific grounds for dismissal:

Grounds for dismissal from membership include but are not limited to:

1. Absence from CCI for more than 180 days in any 12 month period without having obtained a leave of absence.
2. Failure to honor after notice any written agreement with CCI or any of its members.
3. Failure to abide by duly enacted CCI decisions.
4. Conviction of a felony or being legally declared insane or incompetent (Celo Community 2019).

These enumerated grounds for dismissal are more specific in their reference to conditions and general community policies or decisions. They also begin to hint at a larger process that characterizes how conflict resolution and the application of sanctions actually take place in the community. The phrase "after notice" in (2) above indicates a multistep process that would be initiated should the potential dismissal of any community member come up for discussion. This process involves both de jure and de facto actions on the part of the community and its members.

The language of the de jure procedure for dismissing a member indicates that there is a quite elaborate process, if not set of sanctions, involved. The community's Membership Agreement goes on to outline the "procedure for dismissal from membership" as follows:

1. A decision is made by the general monthly meeting that adequate grounds for considering dismissal exist.

2. A special committee is appointed to meet with the member within two weeks to attempt reconciliation.
3. If this attempt to reconcile fails, the member shall be given the grounds for dismissal in writing and allowed one month to reply.
4. Following a full hearing of this reply, the meeting will vote, and the decision to dismiss becomes final if not more than 15% of the members present and voting dissent and if not more than 15% of the Directors present and voting dissent in the dismissal decision.
5. The dismissed member must leave CCI within six months after the final decision, or at the end of the next crop season if engaged in agriculture. Settlement of the holding will be made as in the case of voluntary departure (Celo Community 2013a).

While this policy does not articulate a set of graduated sanctions per se, it is clear that there is an official, multistep process in place manifested in the form of a back-and-forth conversation and negotiation between the community and the individual community member who has been accused of wrongdoing. On a de facto level, and as illustrated in the vignette at the beginning of this chapter, this process starts in a much more informal way long before the official procedure for dismissal is invoked. In practice, the community goes to great lengths to find mutually agreeable solutions to policy violations or actions by members that some other members may find inappropriate or contrary to the norms and interests of the community. In practice, the long process involved in integrating trial community members into the community and ensuring they are familiar with community procedures and rules is an effort to prevent there ever being a need to invoke the procedure for dismissing a community member.

While this process of dispute resolution is the subject of the next chapter, suffice it to say here that in the sixty plus years since the community's governing institutions took the basic form in which they exist today, only one community member has ever been dismissed from membership, and several other community members chose to resign from membership when community members made it clear that their ongoing failure to follow community rules and procedures had brought the community to a point of irreconcilability with them. In fact, my examination of community records and my conversations with community members suggest that the procedure for dismissal of a member has only been initiated three times, including the two times described in the vignette at the beginning of this chapter. This is a remarkable fact given the unique nature of the community's structure and the many people that have joined the community over the years. It is also a testament to relative effectiveness of the community's trial membership process and governance institutions which appear to serve their intended purposes of ensuring potential community members understand and agree to abide by community policies and by creating unity in terms of how community policies are created and implemented. Nonetheless, the ability to dismiss a nonconforming or disruptive member is an essential option given the potential of their actions to have an impact not only on other co-owning and cooperating community members, but on the basic institutions that are the foundation of the community itself.

Chapter 9

Dealing with Disputes
on the Commons

"It's the third time this has happened this year!" Suzy almost shouts as she enters the membership committee meeting, emotionally pointing to the scrapes and bruises on her leg. Beginning to sob lightly, she recounts running in terror across her holding from her neighbors' dog Brutus. Just as she crashed over the low rock wall that outlines the border of her garden, Stan called the dog off. It's lucky he was home to do so; Suzy is not sure what would have happened had she had to fend off the dog from the ground.

Stan's not in attendance at the meeting tonight but he has, via the committee chair, sent a note of apology. For all in the room it is clear that something more than this will have to happen to make the situation right. Suzy is not the only community member who has had a run-in with Stan and Marcie's dogs over recent years; just last month, two children in the community found themselves confronted by Brutus who had strayed far from his owners' holding. Luckily, one of the children was old enough and experienced enough to stand up to the dog. "But what if it had been younger children without the experience or judgment to do so? What if Brutus or another dog really causes serious injury one day?" says the committee chair. Clearly, this needs to be addressed. Two steps need to be taken.

"First, a mediator needs to be appointed to facilitate a discussion between Stan and Marcie on the one hand and Suzy and any other community members concerned with Brutus's (and Stan and Marcie's) behavior on the other. Is anyone here willing to take this on?" Janice, a good friend and neighbor of both Suzy and Stan and Marcie, steps forward to indicate that she has already started this process. After helping Suzy clean her wounds, she stopped by Stan and Marcie's to discuss what had happened. She has arranged a meeting between the parties at the community center on Friday afternoon this week and will do her best to facilitate discussion.

Second, and based on reported incidents with at least one other community dog, it is probably time to start formulating a specific policy that will define dog owner responsibilities in the community. It will be important to have both dog owners and those who have been challenged by community dogs on the sub-committee that will deal with this so that solutions acceptable to all can be negotiated. "Please spread the word that we are seeking volunteers. Informal discussions are encouraged; please bring specific policy ideas to the next membership committee meeting four weeks from today." Speaking with emotion, Suzy says she'll volunteer, but only if she's able to have a productive conversation with Stan and Marcie that will help cool her jets.

Noting that in the midst of their dog problems it can seem like they aren't so different from any other neighborhood in America, the committee chair moves on to the next item on the agenda. "The residents of Brookwood Estates are probably not discussing a proposal such as the one we have before us now" states the leader of the consensus decision-making working group tasked with developing workshops designed to bring community meetings and their consensus decision-making process back to a more productive state. Noting that since the 1940s, the community governance process has operated on Quaker-inspired principles of consensus decision-making whereby all are supposed to have equal input into discussions and decisions, Susan points out the reasons for the formation of the working group, a situation that everyone is already quite familiar with: recently, some have the perception that one longtime community member has been abusing the consensus process by adopting a position early in the decision-making process and refusing to budge or, according to the perceptions of many, even listen to other points of view. The consensus process is supposed to draw out the tension between different points of view and find creative common ground among them. Fred, however, has been making up his mind on his own and "blocking consensus."

This has prevented the community from productively resolving a number of issues over recent years. In fact, Fred's perceived stubbornness has led other community members to take hard line stances of their own on particular issues. The result has been a phenomenon whereby community members are "taking sides" on issues the community is considering rather than opening themselves up to the exchange of ideas and alternative perspectives. A number of issues have been particularly sticky. Among them have been the acceptance of one particular trial member, the process of reaching decisions on accepting or rejecting trial members in general, and the process of identifying potential new holding sites on community land for new members that are accepted into the community. As sides have been taken, the community's governance process has bogged down and a sense of acrimony is beginning to pervade the community. Rather than creative solutions being reached, hurt feelings and extended arguments among members are beginning to predominate. The withdrawal of one trial member from the application process due to ongoing conflict about her membership and the stalling of the community's land use plan have cast a per-ceived pall over the community.

In response to this situation, several community members suggested that a task force on consensus decision-making should be convened in the community. *Since multiple parties seemed intent on circumventing the process and preventing decisions from being made even before all points of view had been aired, it was felt that the community needed to remind itself of the fundamental principles of consensus decision-making. It was hoped that this process would allow everyone to take a deep breath and step away from the emotional and personal feelings that had come to dominate what is supposed to be a purely principled process. After consulting Quaker publications describing the consensus decision-making pro-cess and inviting an outside consensus decision-making expert to speak with them, the task force came up with the following recommendation to the community:*

We want the outcome of the consensus process in CCI meetings to be decisions that reflect the general agreement of the group. We don't want to ignore minor-ity concerns, even if they are being expressed by just one individual, but we also don't want one or a few persons to have a veto power that can be used to control the community. This is a difficult balance to achieve.

There is a significant feeling in CCI that our consensus decision-making process is not achieving a good balance—that the group will is too frequently blocked or extinguished by threats of blockage [one person not aligning with the rest and thus preventing a decision from being made or a policy implemented], and that this imbalance has created a conservative and negative spirit that discourages participation.

Our task force is responding to this situation by recommending three pro-posals for adoption by the community. Two of them aim at making consensus seeking in our meetings more effective and efficient. The third offers a way for us to proceed to find the most universally acceptable decision when a minority is not willing to unite with the group. (Celo Community 1984)

The proposals focus on the ways in which community meetings are prepared for, structured, and conducted. They aim to provide opportunity for dialogue in small groups prior to the full monthly meetings, bring more clarity and structure to the way topics are discussed in the general meetings, and provide a clearer process for the discussions, guided by a trained meeting chair, to proceed with a goal of reaching consensus based on finding creative common ground among all viewpoints. The final recommendation seeks to circumvent situations where a small minority cannot find common ground with others by providing a fallback option of supermajority voting when consensus has not been reached after a number of meetings. The hope is to avoid the type of conflict that is currently causing significant rifts and emotional trauma in the community.

Follow up note: After many long discussions over many meetings, the community added a fairly lengthy dog policy to its Procedures & Rules document. In addition to acknowledging both the desires of dog owners and the legitimate concerns of those impacted by dogs as well as spelling out the responsibilities of dog owners, the policy includes specific processes of conflict resolution for dog issues that may arise in the future. Among these is the following statement: "CCI will appoint several persons as needed to act as mediators in cases where resolution of dog related issues cannot be obtained through direct negotiation between affected parties" (Celo Community 2019). Regarding the troublesome consensus decision-making process, the recommendations of the task force were largely adopted and most in the community feel that the process has been more productive since then. However, a small number of community members largely withdrew from the decision-making process after the recommendations of the task force were discussed. Most of them returned to the process after allowing time for their personal hard feelings to subside, but at least two of the members have not returned to the meetings ten years later. The community has, since then, conducted at least one more consensus decision-making workshop for community members. Achieving unanimous consent through consensus decision-making is clearly a challenging process, especially for people raised in a particularly individualistic culture.

Sharing and cooperation almost inevitably lead to disagreement and conflict. This is especially true in the West where a culture of individualism has prevailed for some time and where those with forceful personalities are used to getting their way. It is thus important for every group of commoners to have mechanisms for addressing disagreement and resolving conflicts when they arise. The sixth point of orientation for commoning states that "Every commoner can make use of a space and means for conflict resolution. We seek to resolve conflicts among us in an easily accessible and straightforward way" (Bollier and Helfrich 2015b: 49). In Celo, the consensus decision-making process at the heart of the community's governance procedures is the primary arena in which disagreements are fleshed out and conflicts resolved. Operating through the consensus process described above, Celo's general meetings aim to preempt conflict by establishing policies that are the result of slow, deliberate, and creative collaboration and deliberation among all interested community members. This results in rules and norms that, in theory, everyone feels ownership of and is more inclined to abide by. Where conflict arises outside of this process, Celo has practices of mediation in place to help address interpersonal conflicts among individual community members. Finally, there is a seldom-used arbitration process in place for resolving conflicts over property values between departing members and the community itself.

Blocking consensus is a very controversial aspect of consensus decision-making. It is OK to disagree but a decision by an individual to block consensus is a <u>momentous one</u>.

It is important to express feelings honestly and feel you are being heard. If it seems there is an agreed-upon decision after full group participation but you are unable to unite with that decision, then ask to have the decision delayed for more time to consider.

It is never appropriate to begin a discussion with "I will block consensus on this issue." This means that the individual is not participating in the group process by listening to others in the group. (Celo Community 2011, emphasis in original)

Section 2. If after at least two meetings on a particular item of business a member requests a decision by vote, this method is approved with not more than 15% of the members present and voting in dissent. When a vote is taken, there is approval if not more than 15% of members present and voting dissent for all decisions. (Celo Community 2009)

In order to avoid festering of unresolved problems, it is expected that members who have concerns about dogs or who are involved in a dog incident will approach the dog owner to discuss the concern or incident, or will contact a mediator for assistance. It is expected that dog owners who are aware of an incident or problem will contact the affected person or persons to discuss and resolve the problem. It is expected that concerns will be resolved with mutual consideration, respect and compassion. (Celo Community 2019)

Commons design principle 6 states that "Rapid, low cost, local arenas exist for resolving conflicts among users or with officials" (Ostrom 2010: 653). Conflicts and disagreements are part of everyday life in any cooperative community. As suggested above, Celo Community takes a preemptive approach to dealing with such conflicts by establishing a rule-making procedure that is designed to draw out conflicts and establish creative, collaborative solutions to them. Nonetheless conflict—sometimes quite disruptive conflict—has arisen within the community. When such conflicts arise, they need to be dealt with quickly and in a relatively autonomous fashion that does not impose undue burden on the parties involved. While Celo does have some minimally defined conflict resolution mechanisms in place, the process of resolution also often plays out in quite quotidian ways. While these conflicts in Celo have almost always been handled locally and without recourse to outside authorities, the processes involved are arguably not rapid nor low cost in terms of the time, energy, and emotional processing required of community members.

Celo's official governing documents such as the Membership Agreement, the Landholding Agreement, and the Procedures and Rules, make very little mention of any official process of conflict resolution. This is surprising not only in light of Ostrom's identification of conflict resolution mechanisms as a key commons design principle, but also considering the importance assigned to it by both scholars and practitioners of intentional community. For example, Christian, in her widely cited book on practical tools for creating intentional communities (2003), includes an entire chapter on "communication, process, and dealing with conflict." Gibson and Koontz (1998), in their comparative study of two intentional communities in Indiana, point to lack of effective conflict resolution mechanisms as one of the key factors underlying the failure of one of the two communities to create sustainable institutions for land stewardship.

However, the lack of specific language and policies about conflict resolution in Celo's main governing documents does not mean that the community does not devote significant energy to it. In fact, as with the ways in which some of the other design principles are manifest in Celo, conflict resolution is integrated into community institutions in an implicit, preemptive manner. The community's consensus decision-making process is, to a significant degree, a mechanism by which the tension among conflicting opinions and perspectives is drawn out and, through deliberate effort, turned into a creative process of finding common ground among divergent positions. In this way, monthly committee and community meetings serve as de facto, preemptive conflict resolution forums.

There are a small number of places where official community policy documents mention formal policy resolution mechanisms. One example is the community's Job Descriptions document which includes a position of "Mediator" whose full job description is to be "available when conflicts arise between two or more parties in the community. When requested, convene and facilitate a meeting between the parties in conflict. As a neutral facilitator, seek to have both parties listen to each other and find a resolution to the conflict" (Celo Community 2019). As in the vignette above, a mediator might be deployed to deal with a dispute arising over the behavior of a community member household and their dogs. In this case, a process of mediation led to a more formal process of policy-making within the community's official governance process.

Another example of official conflict resolution policy comes from the community's Membership Agreement which, in Article 5, includes the statement that "a member is expected to abide by all duly enacted decisions of the regular Community meeting and to accept arbitration according to Community rules in case of disagreement with the Community or another member" (Celo Community 2013a). A final example comes from the Celo Community

Holding Agreement, Article 10 which states that "in the event of any controversy arising under the terms of this Agreement between the Holder and the Community, the controversy shall be submitted to the Board of Arbitration for decision. The Board of Arbitration shall consist of one person chosen by the Holder, one by the Community, and a third chosen by the first two arbitrators" (Celo Community 2018b). Interestingly, my observations, my examination of community records and archives, and my conversations with community members indicate that, with the exception of the vaguely defined "mediator" position, these formal conflict resolution procedures are very seldom if ever used; most conflict resolution occurs in less explicit, more ad hoc, and somewhat preemptive manners.

As alluded to above, the main official forums for conflict resolution in Celo Community are committee and community meetings where decisions are made on the basis of consensus. The community's "Consensus Decision-Making Process" document refers mostly to processes of developing ideas and policy proposals. However, this decision-making forum often does bring out conflicting points of view that must be reconciled in the process of reaching consensus on a decision or proposed policy and, in addition, sometimes a policy is proposed as a way of addressing a conflict that has arisen among community members. Not only that, but the process of consensus decision-making can itself be the source of conflict, especially if it is poorly understood by the participants and facilitators. Even where the process is clearly understood, it can lead to conflict due to misunderstandings of participants' statements or diametrically opposed and strongly held views among the participants.

The consensus document makes very few direct, explicit references to conflict resolution. However, much of the document is a description of the ways in which consensus decision-making processes are themselves designed to draw together diverse, sometimes divergent, points of view in such a way that creative solutions can be reached while avoiding destructive conflict. The nature of this process is elusive and can be hard to grasp, not only for those of us who are familiar with standard parliamentary procedures characteristic of Western-style deliberative democracy, but even for longtime participants in consensus decision-making. As such, it is useful to review descriptions of the consensus decision-making process at some length.

The beginning of Celo's "Consensus Decision-Making Process" document emphasizes how the consensus process is about *working together* in unity of purpose and with collective understanding of the process in order to *avoid* competition and conflict:

> Consensus decision-making stresses cooperative development of a plan or idea with group members working together rather than competing against one

another. Members strive to listen and learn from each other, thereby coming up with a decision resulting from group input rather than one or two individuals. The way you listen to each other and the way you contribute ideas can enrich and extend or limit the original idea. It is a more creative approach to reaching a decision because it can include input from everyone in the group. Group wisdom is usually a more creative solution than individual knowledge. . .

Consensus decision-making can be a powerful tool for building group unity and making creative decisions if there is an understanding of the process. Without a good understanding of the process or techniques, it can result in confusion, frustration, disruption or unrest in the group. (Celo Community 2011)

The document goes on to describe things that the facilitator of the meeting and the participants in the meeting can do to prevent the process from leading to confusion, frustration, disruption, unrest, or conflict. For example, the chairperson should encourage meeting participants to sit in a circle so everyone is on an equal playing field, have a clearly laid out agenda for the meeting, frame questions or proposals in a neutral, unbiased manner, elicit clarifying questions so that all participants understand the issue, idea or proposal, elicit comments from all participants in the meeting, especially participants who are slower to speak and who might otherwise feel left out, and encourage those who are repeating themselves or talking significantly more than others to allow time for others to speak. A few expectations of the facilitator speak more directly to the theme of avoiding conflict and deserve full enumeration here:

Diplomacy: Chairperson is responsible for dealing with chronic objectors. Deal with this person considerately. This might be the time to say that we are aware of your disagreement, but it seems that the "sense of the meeting" is to accept the proposal. Be gracious but firm. This might also be done outside the meeting in order for that person to feel heard.

Dialogue: Request and monitor that members direct remarks through the chairperson and not dialogue with each other: Raise hand to speak.

Silence: Call for silence if [there is a perceived] need to pause when there is conflict over an issue. This gives members a chance to think of a way to rephrase a statement or cool off if angry.

Conflict: The chairperson or an individual group might ask for individuals to meet outside the meeting to resolve conflict or misunderstanding or to reach clearness. (Celo Community 2011)

Expectations for participants in a consensus-based meeting largely reflect the roles of the chairperson or facilitator. These include things such as treating other participants as equals, listening and being patient while others speak, speaking your views in turn, and directing your views at the chair rather than at other individual participants. Of particular note here is the statement that members have a responsibility to "value feelings and conflict; if you don't [they] will appear later" (Celo Community 2011). This particular statement refers not to the encouragement of conflict between two individuals or viewpoints, but rather to the idea that there is productive tension in the space between two points of view that needs to be drawn out to reach a sound decision or policy that all participants can unite around and support. It also suggests that if this productive tension is not articulated during the decision-making process, it may emerge in a more disruptive way after the decision has been made or the policy has been implemented.

A final set of considerations here with regard to conflict resolution in Celo's process of consensus governance regards the ways that individual participants may state their stance on a proposed policy or decision and the way in which the chairperson or facilitator states the resultant overall "sense of the meeting." The options available to meeting participants reflect the fact that conflict and unity are not simple binaries of agreement or disagreement. It also reflects the recognition that sometimes a disagreement with a policy or decision may not be important enough for someone to stand in the way of a decision being made or a policy being implemented as long as their reservations are heard by the group and duly noted. The range of possible ways to frame the sense of the meeting with regard to a proposed policy include:

1. Agreement: Agreement without reservation, consensus is reached and proposal accepted.
2. Agreement with Reservation: Proposal is generally supported, but there are some reservations. Proposal is altered after reservations are considered or proposal is accepted as is.
3. Agreement with Reservation Recorded: Disagreement or reservation are considered. Proposal is altered or accepted, and reservations are recorded. Can be stated by the chairperson as, "*the sense of the meeting is that ..., and it will be noted in the minutes that John Smith has reservations.*" (Reservations should be minuted)
4. Stand Aside and do not need to be recorded. [In this case, an individual may have reservations about a proposed policy, but does not feel strongly enough about the policy or reservations to voice them and is willing to let the group go ahead with a decision without vocally supporting it or objecting to it].
5. Unable to Unite. If one individual is unable to unite with a proposal and is unwilling to stand aside, then the chairperson must decide whether to delay action on a proposal or to ask the individual if he or she would be willing to be minuted as opposed. At the next meeting, very often,

agreement is possible after more time to reflect on the proposal (Celo Community 2011).

Depending on what the "sense of the meeting" is in terms of the options described above and the expressed views of individual meeting participants, there are multiple options for what potential action may be taken on the proposed policy or decision. Most of these options entail adjustments to the policy or decision via further deliberation by community members:

1. Accepted: Consensus with full agreement reached. The proposal is accepted with full agreement reached.
2. Committee Discussion: More information is needed before a decision can be reached. Those with strong opinions should attend the discussion. Sometimes a committee can be empowered to act. Usually, it will then bring the proposal back to the whole group.
3. Delay Decision: Group not ready to make this decision now. Discussion tabled to later time.
4. Dropped: Not enough interest at this time by the group to discuss this issue.
5. Difficult Decision: It might be that most of the proposal has agreement. Pull out the parts that are agreed on and accept. At next meeting, focus on the difficult part. Do not have to discuss entire proposal again, just the unresolved difficult part. (Celo Community 2011)

Working productively through conflict to achieve unified decisions means that Celo's decision-making process is often long and drawn out. This is one reason why Celo has a lengthy trial membership period; it allows potential community members to become familiar with the community's processes of decision-making and conflict resolution and to adjust expectations they may have based on common experience in other contexts where individual autonomy or majority voting allow for decisions to be made more quickly.

The above descriptions of the consensus decision-making process are ideal versions that are rarely fully reflected in practice in any given meeting. My conversations with community members who have served as chair of the community meeting indicate that they rarely have the full range of consensus guidelines in mind during any given meeting and that any individual meeting proceeds in a somewhat ad hoc manner. It is clear that ideals of egalitarianism and whole group input are rarely fully realized. In fact, community members tell me that sometimes it is important for one or a few individuals to have more voice than others because they simply have more wisdom or a clearer understanding of community rules and procedures as they relate the specific discussion at hand. It is also clear that some community members feel marginalized in individual deliberations or, sometimes, in the whole decision-making process; those who are less able to articulate their thoughts on the fly or in front of a large audience of opinionated neighbors easily get frustrated with the process. Nonetheless, the community seems to have cultivated a culture of consensus decision-making that, in general, works. Where many other intentional communities have had to move away from consensus decision-making due to dysfunction in groups much smaller than Celo Community, Celo has, with some exceptions, made consensus work for over seventy years.

In anticipation of cases where consensus cannot be reached, but it is important for the community to make a decision, the community has implemented a fall back option of super-majority voting. This "voting procedure" is described in the community's Procedures and Rules document III, C, d & e, page 15:

d. Voting procedure: Preferably, an issue will be discussed first at a committee meeting. The committee could make a recommendation or report that no agreement has been reached. If, after full discussion at a general meeting, a proposal does not have consensus, it shall be referred to a special meeting before the next general meeting. The special meeting should try for creative solutions that meet concerns as much as possible. This committee can offer a new solution, report that no new solution has been found or that more time is needed for additional information. The recommendation of the special meeting will be presented at the next general meeting and again there will be an attempt to reach consensus. If consensus cannot be reached, a vote will be taken. The proposal passes if not more than 15 percent of the members present and voting dissent.

e. Special Decision procedure: On controversial issues the chairperson may use the following guidelines for reaching a decision about a proposal:

- Initial discussion is limited to clarifying questions about the proposal and directed to the committee chairperson.
- When there are no more questions, discussion can turn to the pros and cons. First, the committee chairperson should summarize the pros and cons raised at the committee meeting. Next, members are asked to raise additional pros and cons, especially concerns. The CCI chairperson will call on people in the order of hands raised to discourage debate between individuals.
- When all concerns have been expressed, the chairperson asks for creative amendments that will satisfy concerns in a way acceptable to everyone.
- If any concerns cannot be satisfied by amendments within the time allocated to the issue, the CCI chairperson should seek to postpone

the decision until the next meeting and schedule a time for a specially appointed committee to lead further discussion among the members. The special committee is charged with formulating an amended proposal which satisfies as many as possible of the concerns raised regarding the issue. The committee will present this new "consensus" proposal in writing to the general meeting.

- At the next general meeting the amended proposal will be placed first on the agenda and up to half an hour allotted for discussion. If there is consensus for further amendments, they may be added to the proposal. At the end of the discussion, the chairperson will ask if there is consensus for the proposal. If not, the *Voting Procedure* will be used. (Celo Community 2019)

There are, of course, conflicts between community members in Celo that arise outside the consensus decision-making process. Sometimes those individual conflicts need to be resolved in the immediate term among the individuals involved, often with the help of an appointed mediator. However, they also often lead to a proposal in a community meeting. So, personal conversations among community members outside of any formal setting such as a committee or community meeting are part of the process of conflict resolution in Celo. When community members are unable to resolve their differences on a one-on-one basis, official community forums have, for decades provided effective mechanisms for bringing disputes to resolution. As suggested in the vignette(s) above, the community has had multiple long running or divisive conflicts. Some of these have even contributed to the decisions of individual members to voluntarily depart from the community. Given how frequently unresolved conflicts contribute directly to the dissolution of intentional communities and given that such communities often find it difficult to live up to the ideals of consensus decision-making, it is remarkable that Celo Community has made consensus work as their central governing principle over many decades.

I would like to end this chapter with a brief discussion of a unique instance in which a conflict was not sufficiently resolved, resulting in some disruptions to the fabric of the community's membership. This example involves an ongoing conflict that remains unresolved at the time of this writing. With regard to the policy of allowing the anonymous submission of rationales for votes on the rejection of some trial members, one community member in particular has been unable to accept this policy. Her issue is not only that trial members may be rejected based on a supermajority vote, a process which is not in keeping with the ideal of consensus as she understands it. Rather, her point of contention is that the inability to know from whence and whom opposition to a trial member comes causes hurt feelings not only for the potentially rejected trial members themselves but also for existing community members who have served as their sponsors and for other members who have grown close to them during their trial membership and wish to accept them into the community. As a result of her dissatisfaction with this policy and in protest of it, this particular community member stopped participating in the community's consensus decision-making process over a decade ago. That this individual is a Quaker and the primary author of the community's "Consensus Decision-Making Process" document suggests that she has particularly strong feelings that the community's process is imperfect.

Chapter 10

Gaining Official Recognition

In the intermission between Celo Community's 2019 annual membership meeting and its annual board of directors meeting, people cluster around a table on one side of the room where members of the community's history committee have set out old community documents along with old photos of land, buildings, and community members from the community's early days. As community members laugh and share remembrances, I note how important it is for current community members to recognize the collective past out of which they have come, the struggles that the founders and early community members engaged in to establish a truly unique community.

One thing that the founders and early community members had to negotiate was how to set the community on sound legal footing given its aims of fostering cooperative self-governance and land tenure that were quite different from the arrangements that predominated in the United States at the time. The solution to this problem that Arthur Morgan and the other founders settled on was to incorporate the community as a nonprofit corporation under the laws of the state of North Carolina. As a result of their efforts, a 99 year corporate charter was awarded to Celo Community, Inc. in 1938, one year after the community's founding.

In recent years, some community members recognized that this corporate charter will expire in the not-too-distant future. As the CCI Board of Directors meeting convenes, with many community members remaining in attendance from the earlier membership meeting, the President of the Board convenes the meeting by turning to this issue. The good news, he states, is that current practice in North Carolina is that nonprofits receive a perpetual charter rather than a 99 year charter. "So, we won't have to remember to go through this process of renewing the charter in another 100 years," he states in his characteristic dry humor to a hearty round of laughs and sarcastic applause. "But, in all seriousness, there are some issues we need to attend to in order to ensure that the renewal goes smoothly." After a short discussion, the board passes a resolution making necessary changes to the stipulated terms for members of the Board of Directors in the corporation's by-laws.

One of the community members raises the question of whether they might consider changing the language of the community's corporate charter; after all, it is quite technical and does not very well reflect the actual nature of the communal enterprise that led to them all being in this room together. "For example, might we actually say something about cooperative governance, co-ownership, and land stewardship in the charter?" asks one community member. The board chair, familiar with state bureaucracy from his years spent working in Washington DC, expresses a note of caution. "The charter is an enabling document, not a defining document. Having it in place has allowed us to flourish for the past 81 years doing just what we want to do. We have our forms of cooperative governance, ownership, and stewardship in place even if they aren't directly referenced in the charter. We are not doing anything that goes against what the charter says and our activities have not drawn any unwanted attention from government officials. I would be very cautious about making unnecessary changes to this document as we work with the government towards its renewal."

A few more members express mild desires to bring the community's idealism in line with its actual legal foundation, but no one feels strongly enough about this to push the issue any further. The president of the board is given the go-ahead to contact attorneys who may help with the renewal of the community's corporate charter and the board moves on to its next item of business. I'm not sure if others feel the same way, but a vague sense of unease seems to hang in the room. Might the community's unique, intertwined institutions of landholding and community membership be in danger of forced dissolution if they are not well articulated in legal documents and someone challenges those institutions in court?

Every group of commoners needs a reasonable degree of autonomy to function sustainably. As Scott makes clear in Seeing Like a State (1998), the imposition of major rules and stipulations from powerful state agencies unfamiliar with local history and social and environmental conditions could easily throw off the delicate balance that commoners have constructed during the life of their commons. Reflecting the importance of autonomy to the commons, point of orientation for commoning seven states that "we regulate our own affairs, and external authorities respect that" (Bollier and Helfrich 2015b: 49). Due to the significant foresight of community founders and early members who wrangled with the unique nature of the community endeavor and sought advice from legal scholars and lawyers before incorporating the community, Celo has, to some degree, been able to take this autonomy for granted.

The day after the Board of Directors meeting, I'm sitting in the community's archives digging through early correspondence among the community's founders and early members trying to gain insight into the issues they wrangled with when they set the community up and established its corporate charter. It is clear that they struggled to accurately describe and find legal precedence or grounding for the unique institutions they wished to create. Excerpts from some of these community documents make this clear. The first excerpt is from a 1940 letter that Arthur Morgan sent to legal scholars and lawyers, accompanied by an early draft copy of the community's holding agreement.

The ownership and the renting of land is in a very unsatisfactory condition in America. Either a man owns the land outright, and may abuse it and destroy it by neglect without regard to the harm he may do the community as a whole; or he is a tenant with very little protection for his interests, and with very little incentive to have pride in his land or to build up the soil and buildings. There is a growing feeling over the country that principles of land holding should be worked out which will give security and protection to the holder, so that he can take pride in his property and be assured that if he improves the soil and buildings and improves the property generally he will get the benefit of that improvement; while on the other hand he should not be allowed to abuse and destroy his land or to treat it so that the community as whole will be less valuable and less desirable, and he should not use it for illegal or immoral purposes to the harm of the community. The community as a whole should protect the interests of the individual holders, and the individual holders should respect the reasonable interests of the community.

If the community should find any holder or his family to be destructive or bad citizens and neighbors, the community should be able to require that the holder leave, but in that case the holder should not lose any value he has added to his property by his work. He should be paid for his property at its real value. On the other hand, if a holder does not like the community and wants to leave, the community should have a right to buy his property in its real value, to make sure that it shall not be sold for some undesirable purpose.

Since most people have no experience with land holding except for outright ownership or renting, they may not at first see what we are arriving at. While we have given a great deal of thought to the most desirable arrangements for land holding, and are continuing to study the matter with specialists in that field, the land holders may have suggestions that will be helpful. They can go ahead in the development of their properties knowing that any value they add by their work is an investment which they will not lose if they should leave for any reason. We have tried to work out arrangements that will make the interest of the individual holder be the same as the interest of the community as a whole. If we do a good job in this we may set a standard that can be used over the country. We should like to have your opinion on this form of agreement, of which a copy is inclosed [sic]. (Morgan 1940)

By the 1950s, community members had largely taken charge of the affairs of the community and Arthur Morgan and the other founders were not nearly as involved in the daily operations of the community as they had once been. By this time, new community members were signing early versions of the community's holding agreement when they joined the community. However, departures of two member households in the 1940s and 1950s were accompanied by the granting of deeds to their individual holdings either because the terms of the contracts that those families signed were unclear or because the contracts were contested by departing community members. By 1955, when the following exchange between a community member and Arthur Morgan took place, there was clearly still some uncertainty and concern about legal recognition for the community's agreements.

Dear Arthur Morgan,
    We have found and plugged up several loopholes in the Holding Agreement, and several others have appeared. Lawyers seem not to like it because it does not fit into any of their categories. They say it would go hard with us in court, if litigation arose with respect to one, regardless of the merits of the case.
    The Community is wondering whether we should devise a new form, more conventional, rather than continue plugging up the old. Operation of land by the productive user and control by the conscientious community—the world over—is one of the principles of my religion. I regard our Holding Agreement as an expression of that principle, but wonder why a lease would not do just as well or better. (Thomas, Wendell, letter to Arthur Morgan, September 6, 1955, courtesy Antiochiana Archives)

Dear Wendell Thomas,
    . . . Our trouble is that lawyers and courts do not like to think new. They are like the postmaster distributing mail. He has a number of boxes, each with a name on it. The only question in his mind is in which of the existing boxes he will put any letters. The lawyer or judge may try to find the most appropriate pigeon hole, and put your case in that. It was for that reason I specifically provided that this is not a lease. I wanted to make it necessary for the courts to look at the arrangement on its merits, and not throw it into the nearest legal pigeon hole. You had better look up the implications of the word "lease" and then proceed according to your advice and judgement. (Morgan, Arthur, letter to Wendell Thomas, September 13, 1955a)

I marvel at the largeness of the implications of the issues community members were dealing with and at the legal frontier they were venturing onto. Whatever actions came out of this particular exchange, the community never did change the wording of the Holding Agreement to describe it as a lease. In fact, the first line of the

Holding Agreement still states: "The Holding Agreement is neither a deed nor a lease but a legal contract defining the legal relationship between Celo Community, Inc., and the Holders in regard to the use of real property within the Community when taken as a Holding" (Celo Community 2018b). The courts have still not had the opportunity to weigh in on the status of this agreement. Celo Community, Inc. is, as of this writing, still working on renewing their corporate charter.

"This is to certify that we, the undersigned, do hereby associate themselves into a corporation, under and by virtue of the laws of the State of North Carolina as contained in Chapter 22 of the Consolidated Statutes of North Carolina, entitled "Corporations," and the several Amendments thereto, and to that end do hereby set forth:

1. The name of this corporation is CELO COMMUNITY, INC.
2. The location of the principal office of the corporation in this State is at Celo, Yancey County, North Carolina.

This corporation shall have a right to do all and everything necessary, suitable, convenient or proper for the encouragement of any of the purposes or the attainment of any one or more of the objects herein enumerated, or consistent with the powers herein named, or which shall at any time appear conducive or expedient for the protection or benefit of the corporation, either as holders of or interests in any property or otherwise; with all the powers now or hereafter conferred by the laws of North Carolina, under the law as hereinbefore referred to, including the right to make any and all such by-laws as said corporation may deem wise and not inconsistent with the laws of the State of North Carolina. (Celo Community 1938)

Commons design principle 7 indicates that successful commons arrangements are dependent on the state for "minimal recognition of rights" to exist and operate, stating that "the rights of local users to make their own rules are recognized by the government" (Ostrom 2010: 653). Whereas for millennia, many commons functioned of their own accord as a means by which local peoples cooperatively used resources to meet their needs, in today's world where state-based forms of political-economic organization claim sovereignty over nearly every square inch of land on the planet, the existence of commons arrangements are inevitably subject to state power. In a world in which states typically design policies to facilitate the privatization and commodification of resources, many states fail to provide legal recognition to commons arrangements that have long existed or that are newly emergent. In these cases, as in the case of Celo, commoners often have to find existing policies and legal vessels that can be used to provide the appropriate recognition and rights.

Celo Community, Inc. is legally organized as a corporation in the state of North Carolina and, at the federal level, has status as a tax exempt 501(c)4 social welfare organization. State recognition for Celo Community's existence is, in some ways, clear-cut but, at a deeper level, it is also ambiguous. This reflects a broader challenge faced by intentional communities and other commoning endeavors working in the context of states largely oriented around the commodification of land and other resources whether under private ownership or state management. While the state may provide legal forms that can technically serve as vessels for what such groups do or intend to do, those legal forms rarely fully capture or even effectively conceptualize the nature of commoning itself. As such, commons communities such as Celo are on potentially tenuous legal ground and could find themselves facing significant legal challenges should their conflict resolution processes fail resulting in one or more members seeking arbitration through the courts. Before discussing this potential eventuality—one that has not arisen in the eighty plus years of the community's existence—let us review the ways in which the community does have official standing in the eyes of the state.

Upon its founding, Celo was originally organized as a nonprofit corporation under the laws of the state of North Carolina. The language of Celo's Certificate of Incorporation is quite general legalese and contrasts significantly with the ways in which Arthur Morgan and other early community members spoke of the community in terms of human fellowship and ethical, community-based living. For example, the language below from the community's original constitution contrasts with the clauses from the community's original charter which follow:

> The aim of Celo Community is to provide an opportunity for its members to enjoy a life that includes personal expression, neighborly friendship and cooperation, and appreciative care of the natural environment. . . . In the relation of the Community to its members the legal is an instrument of the moral. The relation is not an external one between a soulless corporation and independent individuals. It is the internal relation between one person of a friendly neighborhood group and all other persons including himself. (Celo Community 2018a)

In contrast, the community's original Certificate of Incorporation or corporate charter, which is still in effect, states in part:

> The objects for which this corporation is formed are as follows:
>
> (c) To acquire and undertake the whole or any part of the business, property, assets and liabilities of any person, firm o[r] corporation.
>
> (d) To acquire any good will, rights, property and assets of all kinds and to undertake the whole or any part of the liabilities of any person, firm or

corporation or association and pay for the same in cash, bonds, debentures, or other securities of the corporation or otherwise. (Celo Community 1938)

Thus, on official grounds, Celo is a corporation organized to acquire property, assets, and liabilities from persons, firms, and corporations using cash, bonds, or other securities. On the other hand, the internal conceptualization is of a community where "the legal is the instrument of the moral" and it is organized in direct contrast to a situation in which legal instruments are used to mediate the relationship between a "soulless corporation" and a group of independent individuals joined in cooperative endeavor. Celo's early members clearly recognized this tension and articulated it as they constructed the documents and institutions that govern the community. The result, in terms of state recognition, is that the community is left in an ambiguous position because the ways in which the community handles business decisions, property transactions, and associative relationships among its members do not conform to the technical, legalistic mechanisms that the state expects will govern such matters.

On the other hand, while the "objects for which this corporation are formed" as recognized in the community's corporate charter, do not accurately reflect the way the community operates, the corporate charter does, in broad and vague language, grant the corporate entity significant "rights":

This corporation shall have a right to do all and everything necessary, suitable, convenient or proper for the encouragement of any of the purposes or the attainment of any one or more of the objects herein enumerated, or consistent with the powers herein named, or which shall appear conducive or expedient for the protection or benefit of the corporation, either as holders of or interests in any property or otherwise; with all the powers now or hereafter conferred by the laws of North Carolina, under the law as hereinbefore referred to, including the right to make any and all such by-laws as said corporation may deem wise and not inconsistent with the laws of the State of North Carolina. (Celo Community 1938)

This broad and vague set of rights can be used by any existing corporation for any number of specified ends or "objects." What distinguishes Celo Community, Inc. from many other corporations formed under similar charters is that the objects it has chosen to pursue are primarily situated around cooperative, communal forms of political and economic organization that generally fall beyond the normal objects pursued by other nonprofit or, especially, for-profit corporations. Nonetheless, this charter can be interpreted as granting the community the right to draw up and enter into contracts such as their Membership and Holding Agreements described in an earlier chapter.

Shortly after incorporating at the state level, Celo Community was granted status by the Internal Revenue Service as a 501(c)4 social welfare organization. While the main reason for applying for this status was to gain an exemption from federal income tax requirements, the 501(c)4 classification comes closer to providing recognition for Celo's nature than does North Carolina's corporate charter, perhaps because what precisely counts as a social welfare organization is not well defined. According to the Internal Revenue Service, social welfare organizations include:

> Civic leagues or organizations not organized for profit but operated exclusively for the promotion of social welfare. (Internal Revenue Service 2019a)

Some nonprofit organizations that qualify as social welfare organizations include:

- An organization operating an airport that serves the general public in an area with no other airport and that is on land owned by a local government, which supervises the airport's operation,
- A community association that works to improve public services, housing and residential parking; publishes a free community newspaper; sponsors a community sports league, holiday programs and meetings; and contracts with a private security service to patrol the community,
- A community association devoted to preserving the community's traditions, architecture and appearance by representing it before the local legislature and administrative agencies in zoning, traffic and parking matters,
- An organization that tries to encourage industrial development and relieve unemployment in an area by making loans to businesses so they will relocate to the area, and
- An organization that holds an annual festival of regional customs and traditions (Internal Revenue Service 2019b).

While none of these examples captures the forms of economic and political sharing and cooperation that are the fundamental foundation of Celo Community (in particular, common ownership of land), the 501(c)4 category does at least provide a broad set of meanings that begin to encapsulate Celo's characteristics and, thus, provide a legal means by which the state may recognize Celo's right to exist.

The problem stems from the lack of specific recognition for Celo's conjoined forms of land tenure and community membership and the resultant possibility that, should a departing or dismissed community member dispute the terms of the community's membership agreement, holding agreement, or other governing documents, these contracts may or may not be recognized by the state. How would the courts respond to a petition by a disgruntled, departing member who wished to retain title to their holding if Celo's forms of membership and collective landholding are without precedence in official jurisprudence?

Recall from a previous chapter that, in some of its documents, the community refers to itself as a "land trust community." One document entitled "Land Reform as Practiced at Celo Community" that is typically provided to people outside the community who express interest in learning more about Celo's landholding arrangements includes the following statement:

> Celo Community . . . developed an arrangement similar to a land trust whereby the land is owned by the corporation, and individual families purchase "holdings". This avoids the exploitation and abuse of land while carrying most of the benefits of actual ownership. Members of the community are able to obtain land in most cases at costs far below the costs in the surrounding areas—but they can't profiteer by it. (Celo Community, no date)

In reality, the community does not have any legal standing as a land trust, although the ways in which the corporate body is organized do incorporate land trust principles. Their land tenure arrangement is, in its details, truly unique, falling somewhere between a land trust, a legal form which generally focuses on land conservation, and a community land trust, which generally focuses on provision of affordable housing and access to land. Celo's land tenure arrangement aims to accomplish both of these goals simultaneously in a relatively autonomous communal context. This arrangement links back to the second commons design principle above regarding fitting rules to the local context; it reflects the importance of both of these goals to community members. The fact that this arrangement has not been fully tested under state or federal jurisprudence is a testament to the effectiveness of the community's procedures for membership, governance, and dispute resolution; despite the potentially significant loss of equity, no departing members have ever felt compelled to challenge the terms of the community's holding agreement by seeking redress with the state. This also illustrates the levels of mutual trust and goodwill that the community has cultivated very deliberately over the years.

While the lack of official status regarding community membership and landholding agreements may seem like a metaphorical legal albatross hanging around the community's collective, metaphorical neck, in reality the community is not, legally, any different from any other incorporated organization or legal individual who engages in legal transactions and contracts. Any corporate entity or individual may be taken to court by any other corporate entity or individual who wishes to challenge the terms of a contract they have entered into. While Celo's contracts may be more unique than an average legal agreement, the community and its benefactors did extensive consulting work with lawyers and legal scholars both within North Carolina and across the country in the 1940s and 1950s when community members were figuring out how the community should structure the relationships both among members and between members and the corporate community. It is hoped that this legal advice was sound. However, if the experience of the last fifty or sixty years holds, the community will not find itself in the situation of facing such a test thanks to the deliberateness with which they have cultivated mutual trust, caring, goodwill, and understanding among their members (including trial members) and between their members and the community itself as a legal entity.

The functioning of principles underlying the idea of a land trust is also evident in the way Celo has developed cooperative agreements with government agencies regarding the management of their common land. In the mid-1980s, Celo worked in conjunction with the state of North Carolina's Department of Natural Resources and Community Development to identify portions of their land that are significant for their ecological characteristics and to develop an agreement whereby those pieces of land are set aside as a Natural Heritage Area that is recognized by the state but administered by the community. This process was set in motion by one of Celo's members who was trained as an ecologist. As part of his broader research on southern Appalachia, he undertook a survey of the floral and faunal communities that exist within the boundaries of Celo's commonly owned land and shared this knowledge with other community members. One ecological community that he identified was an acre of Southern Appalachian Bog, a critically endangered natural habitat type. The significance of this micro-ecosystem was recognized quite early in the community's existence. A 1946 letter from Arthur Morgan to William Regnery indicates Morgan's inclination to practices of natural conservation on Celo's land:

> Two naturalists . . . in exploring at Celo have located a small woodland marsh and pool which they say has an unusually fine collection of mountain plant and water animals, some of them known only in one or two other locations. They would like to have this made into a ten acre preserve, they to build a small stone field station, and spend part of the year there in study of the life of the area. I should be inclined to set aside the tract of 9 or 10 acres they request as a natural life preserve, and to give them the privilege of looking after it and studying there. . . . [W]e might call them "associate members," without voting rights or financial interests, but with a recognized social interest in the community. (Morgan 1946)

It is unclear whether this particular arrangement ever came to pass, but four decades later the "bog" as it is now known in the community was still intact and the community, now inhabited by significant contingent of back-to-the-landers who arrived in the 1970s was ready to take action to give it special protection.

Rather than setting aside only the bog which the community wished to protect, Celo Community, acting on their understanding of the interconnected nature of ecosystems, chose to include broad buffers for the bog and other ecologically significant areas such as riparian corridors in their land use plan. They designated approximately 300 of their collectively held 1,200 acres as wilderness to be protected from further development or extractive use. The significance of this in terms of Ostrom's principles is demonstrated in materials produced by the Natural Heritage Program, Division of Parks and Recreation, North Carolina Department of Natural Resources in support of the establishment of Celo's Natural Heritage Area: "The presence in excellent condition of a critically endangered natural community type, the Southern Appalachian Bog, makes the Celo Community Natural Area of considerable importance. The Natural Area protects not only the bog itself, but also much of the surrounding watershed, a valuable insurance for the long-term viability of the wetland" (Weakley and Mansberg 1985: 1). The report goes on to note that the natural area contains "four Special Status plant species as well as a good representation of the forested communities of slopes and floodplains at lower and middle elevations of the Southern Appalachians. Although some parts of the area do not have exceptionally old timber, the protection (provided by the charter of Celo Community) from any future timbering greatly augments the natural significance of the area. Nearly all forest lands in the mountains are destined for timber cutting" (Weakley and Mansberg 1985: 1).

Celo's voluntary designation of this "wilderness" area includes the provision that no timbering will take place on this portion of their land. With the help of representatives from the North Carolina Department of Natural Resources, they were able to convince the U.S. Forest Service to forego plans for logging on lands upslope from the Celo Natural Heritage Area that are part of a much larger national forest area. While these plans are subject to change as the U.S. Forest Service rewrites its management plans every five years, this situation has remained stable partly due to the rough topography of the area, partly to the forest service's recognition that intact forests generate tourist revenue in this part of Southern Appalachia especially, and partly due to the ongoing efforts and vigilance of some members of Celo Community who remain actively engaged in providing public feedback on the forest service's proposed plans. Further, in consultation with the Department of Natural Resources, Celo Community developed an active management plan for the bog habitat that involves, in the absence of natural fire regimes, the manual removal of woody species encroaching on the bog.

These collaborative arrangements resulted in the community being granted an exemption on their property taxes for the 300 of their collectively held acres that are set aside as wilderness. The point to make here is that, in the process of forming and managing their commons, the community appears to have carved out a unique niche for their commons arrangements in relation to state policies and the state agencies that administer them. In so doing, the community has not only nested their commons system in larger political and economic structures, they also appear to have, in a small way, enabled larger state agencies to see and acknowledge the value of their commons arrangements and even to, perhaps, play on the words of James Scott (1998), "see like a commons," even if only for a moment.

With regard to state recognition of Celo Community, Inc.'s right to exist, there is one final point of interest. As indicated above, the community is already anticipating the need to renew their original, ninety-nine-year corporate charter in the near future. The president of the corporate community's board of directors, himself a community member, indicates that he does not anticipate any significant legal wrangling to secure the renewal of their charter. However, the political and economic circumstances in the second and third decades of the twenty-first century are significantly different than those that prevailed in the fourth decade of the twentieth century when the community was granted its original charter. It will be interesting to see how the state interprets Celo Community, Inc.'s application for a new charter. Will this bode well for other efforts to establish cooperative communities on sound legal footing? It remains to be seen.

Chapter 11

The Commons and Larger
Democratic Systems

Today is the day for the big meeting on the community's draft land use plan. This meeting is a partial culmination of almost ten years of slow and arduous discussion and group land walks aimed at developing a comprehensive plan for how the community will use and inhabit their 1,200 acres into the future. The plan represents the community's principle of allowing decision-making to operate at the most local level possible and involved significant tacking back and forth between whole-community discussion and individual neighborhood planning. The land use planning committee chair reminds everyone that a community self-study identified the following broad priorities that individual neighborhoods should try to focus on: 1. Preserve wilderness, 2. Encourage local food production, 3. Maintain the ability for people of less economic means to obtain a holding, 4. Provide some business sites for retail sales that can be accessed easily on paved roads, 5. Come up with a list of accepted holding sites that can be shown to prospective community members, 6. Identify areas for possible retirement cluster housing, 7. Encourage alternative energy production, 8. Identify trails that skirt houses, 9. Keep a natural park like look to the community, and 10. Create a plan that is somewhat flexible and open to review and revision at designated intervals.

Through a series of land walks and meetings over several years, community members in individual neighborhoods worked together to develop a plan that addressed these priorities in their local area of the community. In the ensuing years, the land use committee, working in conjunction with the property committee, collated individual neighborhood plans into an overall draft plan, sometimes asking individual neighborhoods to revise their recommendations where they, for example, encroached on wilderness areas that the community as whole had set aside some time ago. Tonight is the first general community meeting at which the plan will be discussed.

Championed especially by a number of community members who are concerned to maintain portions of community land in a wild state, the land use plan is an attempt to implement a balance between community growth and development and environmental conservation. Even after years of discussions, tension remains between those who experience social relationships as a primary benefit of community membership and those who experience intact natural landscapes as a primary benefit of the community. As discussion proceeds back and forth among the community members present, it is clear that this dichotomous characterization is an overgeneralization; all present value the community for both things, it is just a question of how they are prioritized and brought into balance. The land use committee chair summarizes this quandary with a succinct question that hangs before the group: "How much of our collective land do we make available for development of new holding sites and how much do we choose to set aside as intact natural habitat for nonhuman inhabitants of our community?"

The committee chair passes out a document that accompanies a large colored map on display at the front of the room. The document, entitled "CCI Land Use Categories" delineates the different purposes for which community held land may be used and identifies some of the common resources that community members might obtain from the land. Land use categories include: wilderness areas, greenways, wildlife corridors, communal use parks, wood lots, community orchards, fields, rejected house sites, new holding sites, business holding sites, non-retail business sites, trails, driveways and power lines, co-housing or eldercare housing, and designation undecided. Embedded within the description of each of these categories are identifications of types of resources that community members may obtain from the land. These include: land in its natural state, wildlife habitat, firewood, recreation spaces, fruit from the orchard, agricultural soils, home sites, business sites, and travel routes.

Balancing these different ways of using land and accessing resources is challenging not only because current community members place different weight on different uses and resources. Some in the community, including some in the room tonight, feel that it is unfair for people who have already joined the community to reserve common resources for themselves and exclude others from their use. They say: "Wasn't the intent of the community to allow people to have affordable access to land and participate in this experiment in cooperation?" Others in the community, including the land use chair, suggest that environmentally sound land stewardship was also an important aim of the community. The say: "Doesn't allowing more and more people into the community detract from our ability to do this?" Although the plan under discussion includes very few sites designated for future holding development, those in the room agree, some of them grudgingly, to go along with recommending the plan for approval at the general community meeting in two weeks. The proviso that made this acceptable is that the land use plan will be up for review and revision; every three years, community members will be invited to participate in land use planning commit-tee discussions from which will emerge proposed changes to the plan that will be up for deliberation at the community's general meeting.

After the meeting, back at the community member's home I'm staying in while I do my field research, I try to analyze the complex sets of viewpoints and the processes the community uses to construct a delicate balance and find creative common ground and convergence among them. Reviewing the minutes of land use committee meetings over the last ten years and comparing them against the outcome of tonight's meeting, it is apparent that this is destined to be an ongoing process rather than a finished product. As the community intends, small group discussions among neighbors will evolve into recommendations by the land use planning committee which, through great deliberation, will be translated into policy through the community's general meeting. This is a group of people trying to develop a set of rules for how they relate to each other and to their common land and resources in a context characterized by constantly shifting social characteristics. This will become even more complicated not only as new members join the community, but also as climate change introduces new environmental variables into the equation. One indication of this is the current die off of hemlock trees throughout the region, including on community land, due to the spread of the exotic invasive hemlock wooly adelgid. I marvel at people's willingness to dedicate so much time, energy, and emotions to these ongoing discussions and wonder what it would be like if more people would make this commitment.

The next year, I'm back in Celo for a brief visit. I've asked John, one of the principle champions for the development of the community's land use plan, to sit down and discuss some of the history of the community's relationship with land use; I want to put the land use plan in broader context. We're sitting on the deck of his house overlooking the Celo bog and a good portion of Celo's biggest desig-nated wilderness area. John built this quirky little house with his wife in the early 1970s, raised two kids in it, and used it as a home base for developing his passion as a naturalist painter into a full-fledged career. He's happy that the land use plan passed; after all, he put a lot of energy into it. However, he's still concerned that the community, especially the newer members are moving away from a com-mitment to ecologically sensitive land stewardship. He's also concerned that the community has not been able to agree on any sites that might be suitable for clus-ter housing which he thinks is a potential solution to two problems: slowing the community's expanding footprint on the land even as its membership continues to grow and providing accessible housing for the community's aging members.

I ask John to tell me about the history of his involvement with land use strug-gles in the community and the broader area. John tells me that as a back-to-the-lander he always recognized that there were legitimate and appropriate ways to use land to meet one's needs. On the other hand, as a naturalist painter, he needed open spaces to serve as inspiration for his landscape paintings and habitats for the individual species he sought to capture in great detail in those paintings. He, along with the community's resident member ecologist, was involved in the community's early efforts to set aside the acreage surrounding the bog as a designated wilderness area. He shows me the letter he received from the North Carolina Natural Heritage Program recognizing the Celo Natural Heritage Area. In addition to working with the state on this designation, he also joined another community member who worked in the county tax assessor's office to develop an agreement with county, still in effect, whereby the community would not have to pay property taxes on its 300 acre natural heritage wilderness area.

"Wow! So your work on this took you far beyond the bounds of the community then?" I ask. "Oh sure." He responds. "I was pretty heavily involved in broad-based campaigns in the region to help stop clear cutting on our mountains as well." It turns out John was a board member for an activist organization called the Western North Carolina Alliance that opposed policies of designating public lands in the area as wilderness on the one hand and, on the other, the U.S. Forest Service's policy of allowing the land to be clear cut. Recognizing the value of sensitive, mixed use of land and seeking allies in his stance against clear cutting especially, John joined this group of local activists, many of whom come from families whose history in the area stretches back to the days when much of the land in the region was used as one big commons that provided food and foraged materials for people's needs. Those in the group were united by the sentiment that both wilderness designation and clear cutting reserved the value of the land for quite small groups.

"We did a number of direct actions aimed at affecting Forest Service policy back in the 1970s and 1980s," says John. "But we also worked through the system. I sat in on many public meetings with the Forest Service. By making our arguments as clear as possible and stating them over and over again, we finally got the Forest Service to see past the short term interests of logging companies and think about the longer term health of the forests and the multiple interests locals had in using those forests. This also gave me the knowledge and personal connections to work with the Forest Service to get them to leave logging on the section adjacent to Celo's eastern boundary out of multiple five year plans. Did you know the USFS is the largest landowner adjacent to Celo?" John goes on to talk about how he recently hosted a group from a nearby university who studied the creek that flows near his house, identifying it as one of the most ecologically healthy creeks in the region. John says this would not be possible without the community's designated wilderness area and the U.S. Forest Service's moratorium on logging upstream from the community. Working across scales, from conversations with his most immediate neighbors in the community, to serving as past chair of the community's land use planning committee and acting as

President of the community's Board of Directors, on up through his work with the county, state, and federal government, John, along with other community members, have committed countless hours to shaping land use approaches in the community and the surrounding region.

Commons involve multiple individuals with different interests and perspectives. They are also always situated in larger ecological, sociocultural, and political-economic contexts. As such commoners must find ways to work through the differences among the members of their group and also to build bridges to larger social groups that use or make policy affecting the broader regions and ecosystems within which the commoners work. Point of orientation for commoning eight states that "we realize that every commons is part of a larger whole. Therefore, different institutions working at different scales are needed to coordinate stewardship and to cooperate with each other" (Bollier and Helfrich 2015b: 49). As the vignettes above illustrate, Celo has managed to work across multiple, nested scales of activity and decision-making both within and beyond the community. This work is ongoing and is a fundamental part of the ethical commitment that Celo's members make when they join in cooperative endeavor. A continuation of such work is an embodiment of the community's core principle, expressed in its constitution, that the relation among community members "is not an external one between a soulless corporation and independent individuals. It is the internal relation between one person of a friendly neighborhood group and all other persons including himself" (Celo Community 2018a).

> Legally, authority is vested in a self-perpetuating Board of Directors. By formal action of the Board, the Community is autonomous, and the members of the Board are elected after nomination by the members. Community decisions are reached at the General Meetings (first Wednesday of each month) and at occasional special meetings of the Community. New business is first discussed by the appropriate committee. All meetings, both general and committee, are open to all who wish to attend. Members and trial members are expected to attend as regularly as possible, but attendance is not compulsory. . . . All matters of Community concern should be discussed first by the appropriate committee. In case of routine items, the committee will bring its recommendation to the general meeting, with details of execution. In case of controversial items, the committee will search out the pertinent facts and present these with the essentials of conflicting opinions to the general meeting. Unless specifically authorized, the committees take no action until approved by the general meeting. (Celo Community 2019)

Commons design principle 8 states that "when a common-pool resource is closely connected to a larger social-ecological system, governance activities are organized in multiple nested layers" (Ostrom 2010: 653). This means that effective commons institutions are characterized by systems of polycentric governance whereby governance activities are devolved, wherever possible to smaller-scale governance entities that are themselves under the umbrella of larger-scale governance entities. In terms of its internal governance structures and processes, Celo has clearly put this principle into practice; it recognizes and empowers a variety of entities at various scales from the household to the neighborhood to the committee to the entire community working across a variety of scales. The smaller-scale entities are nested within and make recommendations to larger-scale entities regarding decisions and policies that have a significant effect on the larger commons community, but decision-making is devolved to the smallest-scale entity wherever possible and practical. As has been alluded to above, the community, as with most any corporate entity in the contemporary, state-based world, also operates under the umbrella of various larger, mostly state-based, entities that do things such as levy taxes and institute legislation and policies that apply to all individuals and entities under their authority.

As clearly stated in community documents, individual community members and their households are free to make most decisions about how to run their household and how to use their individual landholding on a daily basis. Much like the broader society in which Celo exists, individual households— often composed of nuclear families or couples, but sometimes of single individuals or other arrangements—are the basic economic and decision-making unit in the community. As an incorporated entity, Celo Community, Inc. is not interested in dictating how its individual constituent households derive their income, manage their budgets, divide household labor, or go about their daily lives. Membership in the community is not in any way officially restricted by what type of career one pursues, how much money one makes, or with whom one is in domestic partnership. On the other hand, individual households who exhibit clear outward expressions of a keep-up-with-the-Joneses attitude of conspicuous consumption would likely be viewed skeptically as potential trial members (and they likely would not be interested in community membership anyway).

However, because the community is the collective owner of all land including individual holdings and because all buildings built on individual landholdings revert to community ownership before they are taken by another member (unless that other member is already on the current holding agreement), some decisions by individual households about land use and buildings on individual holdings must be discussed, debated, and approved by larger governance entities in the community. As discussed in earlier chapters, a family who joins the community and takes a new landholding must have their building design and placement approved through a community process that can be, but is not always, quite cumbersome. The household would first be encouraged to at least informally consult about their plans with other member households who would be their immediate neighbors. Then the proposed designs would be brought formally before the property committee which would, in a forum open to any community member, review, debate, and recommend adjustments to the proposed designs. Once the property committee was comfortable recommending approval for the designs, the household, with assistance from the property committee, would also seek approval from the general community meeting.

A household seeking a loan from the community's financial commons would go through a very similar process of governance and oversight. The community's finance committee, in considering their loan application may make requests that may force the household to make significant changes to their plans for their home in order for the community to feel comfortable with the financial risk entailed in making such a loan and in guaranteeing a portion of the household's equity in its home. In addition to having the loan approved at the community's general meeting, the household would also only receive the loan in installments following community inspection of each stage of their land clearing and home construction.

The next level above the household that functions as an informal governance unit in the community is the neighborhood. As suggested above, immediate neighbors are often the initial level of consultation and, due to their interest in their future neighbors, often have the most to say about the proposed design for new homes and landholdings. In recent decades, the neighborhood has also become a de facto governance unit during the community's process of developing and occasionally revising their comprehensive land use plan. After initially encountering significant difficulties in trying to engage a whole-community process for designing their land use plan, the community made a decision to devolve some aspects of land use planning to designated neighborhood areas for initial discussion and recommendations to the land use committee. For example, groups of households that were clustered together geographically met informally and identified possible new holding sites as well as areas they thought should be set aside for other uses such as green space. Once all the households in a designated neighborhood agreed on this, they brought their recommendations to the land use planning committee which, working with the property committee, agglomerated these recommendations into a more complex and comprehensive draft plan for the entire 1,200-acre commons. This plan and accompanying recommendations were brought to the general community meeting for further discussion as part of the community's consensus decision-making process.

As has been indicated in the paragraphs above, individual committees are designated to be the first level of official governance for issues regarding the various common resources stewarded by the community. For example, the land use planning and property committees deal directly with issues regarding land and infrastructure. The finance committee deals with issues of dues, loans, community reserve funds, and holding transfers. And the membership committee has the first level of oversight regarding new and departing members as well as conflicts among members or rules violations by members. Each of these committees meets at least once a month at regularly scheduled times and, while there are designated leaders of and spokespersons for each committee, any community member may participate in processes of deliberation undertaken by an individual committee. Each individual committee is permitted to make decisions on some issues that are deemed to be of relatively minor import. However, any significant decisions or actions such as those involving the admittance and dismissal of a member, the establishment or transfer of a holding, the disbursement of large sums of money, or the creation of a new, community-wide policy must be brought first as recommendations to the monthly general community meeting. While the average community member will not likely attend every committee meeting, they will at least hear about if not be able to officially express their concordance with or reservations about community decisions when the committee chairs report to the monthly community meeting.

The monthly general community meeting is the main, central arena of community governance. As discussed elsewhere, all community members are expected and strongly encouraged to regularly participate in this meeting and in the processes of deliberation and consensus decision-making that define it. While individual households, neighborhoods, and especially committees have some decision-making power, all major issues that will have an impact on the entire community must be brought before the monthly general community meeting for consideration, discussion, and attempted consensus. While these processes of deliberation were discussed at length in preceding chapters, it is worth reiterating some of the basic outlines here and adding some additional details.

Each monthly general community meeting begins promptly at 8 pm on the first Wednesday of each month in a large room in the Celo Community Center and is almost always attended by a strong majority of community members. This forum serves not only as the main decision-making body for the community, but also as a method of distributing information among community members. The person serving as chair of any given monthly meeting begins by asking that minutes from the previous general meeting be read by the recording secretary and corrections made if necessary. Next, noncommunity member guests in attendance briefly introduce themselves. Oftentimes, guests include trial members, people considering trial membership, and others who are, in one way or another, guests on community land, so this is an opportunity for community members to stay informed about new persons in their midst. Introductions are followed by announcements which often include things like upcoming events such as weddings, business openings or fundraisers; announcements of personal milestones; and statements about local developments such as proposed new forest service policies or information about reported crimes in the area.

After introductions and announcements, the meeting chair asks individual committee chairs to inform the meeting about discussions had, decisions made, and recommendations offered by that committee during the last month. There is no formal agenda distributed prior to each general meeting; however, the minutes from the committee meetings during the prior month are distributed prior to the general meeting. Thus, either through attendance at committee meetings or through reading their minutes, each community member is informed about topics that will come up at the general meeting. If there is a major issue that a committee did not have the authority to make a decision on and thus needs to make a recommendation to the general meeting, the committee chair will read the recommendation and provide context for it including details from the discussion that took place in the committee meeting. The general meeting chair will then ask community members if there are questions aimed at clarifying the nature of the recommendation. Once those questions are answered, the chair will ask for concerns or reservations. As these are offered, discussion may lead to the concern being withdrawn or to a modification of the committee's recommendation. Once the concerns have been addressed, the meeting chair will test for consensus by stating what she perceives to be the sense of the meeting. If there are no objections, the recording secretary will minute the recommendation as a decision and it becomes policy at the next general meeting when the previous month's meeting minutes are read. If there are still concerns, there may be further discussion or, depending on how full the rest of the agenda is or how intractable the differences seem to be, the issue may be sent back to the relevant committee for further deliberation at their next meeting.

The highest, largest-scale level in the community's internal governance system is the corporate board of directors. As described in a previous chapter, during the early years of the community, the board was composed entirely of noncommunity members—initially, Arthur Morgan, William H. Regnery, and Clarence Pickett—and exercised a high level of authority over community policies and decisions. However, as was the founders' intent, as the community's institutions became more clearly defined and as the community developed the ability to more effectively govern themselves, both the composition and the power of the board underwent significant shifts. Technically, the board still has approval or veto power over all community decisions and policies. In practice, the board, now composed of a majority community members with the remaining noncommunity board members selected by community members serves mostly as a rubber stamp for decisions made and policies implemented by committees and the community's general meeting. However, the community may seek advice from the board, especially from outside board members who may have been chosen because of their particular area of expertise, if there is an especially challenging issue that the community is dealing with.

Celo Community's board of directors acts at a fulcrum point between the community's internal governance processes and governance authorities whose source of power lies outside the community. The existence of the board of directors is a stipulation of the legal vessel—the corporate charter—through which the state recognizes the community's existence and right to act. Thus, as with all corporations and other legal entities operating in a state-based world, the community itself is nested within higher authoritative bodies that exercise some power over community actions.

For example, while the community, as a 501(c)4 social welfare organization, is exempt from federal income taxes, it is required to pay county property taxes based on periodic assessment of the value of its collective property. All houses, land, and infrastructure in the community, including those held by individual community members and those held in common by the community, are assessed individually but included in one corporate tax bill which the community pays as a whole. The community assesses each individual community member (and each individual, noncommunity member living on the land for more than six months out of the year) for their individual holding taxes and their per-head share of taxes for the remainder of the property held in common.

As the region around the South Toe Valley has developed, the community has found itself under the power of a growing number of county and state agencies charged with ensuring public safety and accountability. For example, while there were no zoning or building codes in the area at the time the community was founded, the community now has to ensure that new individual homes and publicly accessible buildings within the community conform to a growing number of building codes designed to do things such as ensure fire safety and accessibility and to prevent the pollution of waterways. The county also maintains the main unpaved road that runs through the heart of the community and, should the county decide to significantly alter the road by widening or paving it, the county's actions could have a significant effect on the community by increasing accessibility, traffic volume, and speed. When there is a significant action or policy change pending before the county, the community sometimes designates a community member to act as an official liaison with these entities and represent the community's interests and stance.

Beyond the county level, the community's autonomy is also affected by regional and state level governmental and nongovernmental organizations. For example, the cooperative company that provides electric power to the region, the French Broad Electric Membership Corporation (FBEMC), has legal rights of way to maintain its power line routes wherever they cross public or private property. Since the community disagrees with some of the methods the corporation uses to maintain these rights of way (herbicide spraying and wholesale vegetation clearing among them), and since the staff of the corporation and the make-up of their right of way crews is constantly changing, the community is in ongoing negotiations with the FBEMC to allow the community to maintain the rights of way in more environmentally sensitive manners where they cross community land (see the description of this in an earlier chapter).

As stated in the preceding chapter, the community's existence and its ability to enact contracts such as the Membership and Holding Agreements that define its existence is dependent on the corporate charter granted to the community by the State of North Carolina. Since the original charter was granted in 1938, there has been little official interaction with the state, but it is conceivable that the state could, especially if someone challenged community practices in court, interfere and force the community to change the way it conducts its business. This seems unlikely given the relatively small nature of the community and the many thousands of other corporations whose charters are granted by the state. However, as stated above, the process of renewing the community's corporate charter before it expires in 2037 could raise some unforeseen issues.

As with every citizen and corporate entity in the United States, the community is theoretically nested within the authority of the nation-state. The two main ways in which federal authority directly affects the community are through the granting of their tax exempt status and via the actions of the U.S. Forest Service, both of which have, to this point, served the community in a positive manner. As stated before, soon after receiving its corporate charter in 1938, the community petitioned for and received federal tax exempt status from the Internal Revenue Service. The federal government thus recognizes North Carolina's designation of the community as a nonprofit corporation and does not impose federal income tax requirements on Celo Community, Inc. The U.S. Forest Service is the largest land manager in the southern Appalachian region (see Newfont 2012), including significant portions of land abutting the community's boundaries. In part through deliberate efforts of community members, the U.S. Forest Service was convinced to not designate lands adjacent to the community for timber harvesting and this has remained the case since the 1980s. However, should the U.S. Forest Service change the designation of said plans in any one of their five-year management plans, this could have a significant impact on the community and on the lands that the community has designated as wilderness, especially where those lands lie downstream from Forest Service lands.

On the whole, and moving from the individual household level all the way up through the federal government, the community clearly manifests the fully functioning "nested enterprises" identified by commons design principle eight. Internally, the community devolves power wherever possible to the lowest possible level. Households are free to operate as they choose as long as their actions don't have an adverse impact on their neighbors or on community common property. Neighborhoods act in advisory capacity both in terms of having input on household land use within the neighborhood and in terms of recommending policies that will specifically impact their local area within the larger commons. Individual committees within the community, with input from individual community members and households, make decisions and take actions on relatively inconsequential issues within their area of remit and, where the issue is of greater concern and may affect the community as a whole, make recommendations to the community's general meeting. The monthly general meeting, involving all community members and households who choose to participate, is the main decision-making arena in the community. Sometimes with advice from, and almost always with the rubber stamp of, Celo Community, Inc.'s board of directors, the general meeting makes and amends final policies pertaining to internal community matters.

As with almost all commons today, the community finds itself both empowered and potentially constrained by agencies and institutions that embody the power of the state. The county enforces codes and collects property taxes but also provides services such as road maintenance and grants the community a property tax exemption on their designated wilderness area. The regional electric cooperative provides power to the community but also alters the community's landscape. The state of North Carolina provides the community's corporate charter, maintains highway 80 which bisects the community, and recognizes the significance of the community's designated wilderness area. The federal government grants the community tax exempt status and, as the owner and manager of the largest piece of land abutting the community (via the U.S. Forest Service) makes land use policies that can significantly affect the community's land that lies downstream. While none of these government agencies or institutions have a primary directive of enabling or working with commons institutions, they have had the effect of doing so.

Chapter 12

Beyond the Design Principles

Other Factors That Make Celo Work

> The original intent was that the Community be an evolving experiment whose people, free from the pressures of urban society, might explore the possibilities of rural living, social change and social cooperation. (Celo Community 2012)

As we have seen, Ostrom's commons design principles are, for the most part, embodied in the governance institutions and processes that characterize Celo Community. That Celo has sustained itself for so long lends further support to the idea that these design principles characterize Celo's successful commoning endeavors. It also suggests the utility of the principles to those who may wish to construct lasting intentional communities and other sorts of commons, especially where commonly owned land and other resources are to be a foundation for the commoning endeavor. However, based on my research on Celo Community over the last two plus decades, it is also clear that Celo's longevity and stability are not reducible solely to the factors encapsulated by Ostrom's design principles. What other factors are in play here?

One major factor in Celo's success is that the community started with a significant nest egg. Celo's founders financed the purchase of 1,200 acres of land and gifted that acreage to the community along with periodic influxes of operating funds during the community's early years. While the community has been financially self-sufficient for some time now, it is quite likely that the community would not have coalesced in the way it did—that they would not have been able to focus as much energy and attention on creating smoothly functioning governance institutions or on environmentally sensitive land stewardship—if community members themselves had to finance the purchase of their common land. This touches on broader themes of the inequitable distribution of wealth in society and poses significant issues for the utility of Celo as a model for commons communities elsewhere, not least of all in Appalachia, a region characterized by extreme inequality. I will return to this theme in the concluding chapter.

Freed from the need to finance the purchase of their common property, Celo's members were able to engage in ongoing group and individual endeavors of community building and place-making (Nabhan 1997, Northcott 2015). Absent an immediate need to extract monetary value from the land to finance its purchase or even to immediately use the land to support community members' livelihoods, Celo's members were free to derive and assign different kinds of meanings and significance to the land. Especially with the arrival of back-to-the-landers in the 1970s, Arthur Morgan's original emphasis on land stewardship for sustainable economic use (for example, through forestry and agricultural methods that did not decimate forest and soil) was translated into an appreciation for and identification with ecologically intact landscapes and ecosystems. The land provided community members with a spiritual respite from the onslaught of a rapidly expanding industrial, consumer society. Beyond that, many in the community recognized an inherent value in the land and its other-than-human inhabitants.

In my conversations with community members, many spoke of their personal affinity with the land and of a relationship with the land that embodies mutual care and nourishment. Celo's members do, in many ways, conceptualize their land as a form of property whose utility to humans is expressed in political and economic terms. They occasionally assign dollar values to it, mark group and individual property boundaries on it, map it and designate it for different uses, extract usable resources from it, and make rules about the human use of it. However, for most community members, the personal significance of the land goes beyond these strictly utilitarian terms. A quotation from one of my interviews embodies this attitude: "To me the land is of primary importance. Managing it in a caring, thoughtful, environmentally sensitive way. It is the base on which all other activities exist. . . . It nurtures the spiritual and aesthetic qualities that lead to a fulfilling life" (Interview with author in Celo Community on October 4, 2019). In their proscriptions on subdividing or making speculative profit on the land, in their group efforts to recognize and attempts to maintain the ecological health of unique habitats, in their identification of places of power and spiritual sustenance on the land, community members express a form of communion with the land and a willingness to forego utilitarian economic considerations in favor of a relationship with the land that recognizes it as equal to or even greater than them. In some senses, and for some community members more than others, the land is a living place and they are but a part of it.

In community members' interactions with each other within this shared place—and, manifested within the governance institutions and processes that embody the design principles—are significant degrees of trust, mutual respect, goodwill, and tolerance among community members. One expression of this goodwill is that community members have been able to continue to cooperatively govern themselves and their land despite significant differences in the emphasis individual members place on making the community accessible to more people on the one hand or preserving intact land on the other. The relative lack of formal mechanisms by which the use of land by individual community members is monitored is another direct manifestation of this. Due in part to the long trial membership process and to the relative stability of community membership, community members are known to each other and, despite any differences in perspective and values among them, they do not generally perceive each other as adversaries. This does not mean that trust, mutual respect, and goodwill are extended by all members to all members in equal degrees at all times. In my research, a small minority of community members expressed concern that their views, opinions, and perspectives sometimes did not receive the same level of respect as did those of others. A few members perceived an adversarial relationship between those who wanted the community's membership to expand and "the no-growthers" who wanted to focus on land stewardship. Some felt that the opinions of longer-term members carried more weight and others felt that as aging community members, they were not listened to as much. But in general, community members, especially through the consensus governance process over the last three or four decades, have cultivated a strong attitude of mutual trust, respect, and goodwill that goes a long way toward preventing personal agendas or vendettas from getting in the way of group commitments to cooperation and common endeavor.

These interpersonal attitudes of trust, mutual respect, goodwill, and tolerance seem also to translate into the governance institutions and processes of the community in the form of a significant degree of flexibility in the application of rules. In other words, community members have struck a balance between record keeping, policy-making, and rule enforcement on the one hand and situational interpretation and loose application of the rules and policies on the other. This is an important point that I have tried to draw out in the examples and discussions of the design principles in the preceding chapters. In my view, it is significant enough that I considered proposing "flexibility" as a ninth design principle.

The community, as a relatively small group of people who are known to each other and share an attitude of mutual respect, are able to consider the application of the rules on a case-by-case basis within the general outline of existing policies and rules. In doing so, they avoid an approach of bureaucratic indifference to unique personal circumstances and situational context. The community also regularly exercises the power to change or adjust their

policies and rules to meet the changing needs and circumstances of the community in general. This approach is expressed in the "Celo Community Self-
Evaluation Questionnaire" that they send out to people who express interest
in community membership: "There is a great deal of *flexibility* in Community
structure and policies. Rulings and decisions made by the Community are
subject to revision and change. Would you feel comfortable with the vague-
ness this often produces?" (Celo Community 2012, emphasis added). Celo's
previous ethnographer remarked on this flexibility in the application of community rules and policies with disdain, as if the community was a failure
because they couldn't find rules they could all agree on and stick to. In the
concluding chapter, I will return to my disagreement with Hicks's analysis of
the community and the ways in which our differing conclusions are dependent on different understandings and analyses of the concept of utopia. For
now, I just wish to point out that flexibility seems an essential part of what
makes Celo work.

This flexibility is dependent on a certain scale of community operations
that tends to be characteristic of functioning commons and which is very
difficult to achieve at the scale of the state. The commons literature supports
the assertion that scale and flexibility are important to successful commons
functioning (Harvey 2011, Wall 2017) and Scott (1998) identifies flexibility
and adaptability as things that get swept aside when state-based approaches
to development and conservation are imposed on local commons and communities. I will return to these issues in the conclusion. For now, suffice it to
say that, almost twenty years after Celo's founding, Arthur Morgan reflected
back on the community's history and identified flexibility as an important
factor in Celo's endurance:

> Is it not possible that the absence of a specific ideology, and in fact a dislike
> for ideologies, and the normal discriminating development of individual and
> community life, have been advantageous rather than harmful? Is it not possible
> that rigidity of pattern and limitation of responsible, free expression of personal-
> ity have been among the more important reasons for the usual short life of an
> ideological cooperative community? Life persistently breaks over ideologies.
> (Morgan 1955b: 31)

Another factor that has contributed to Celo's longevity is the degree to
which the community has managed to cultivate positive relations with local
residents in the area surrounding the community. Other scholars (Miller 1999,
Sargisson 2007) have noted how, in the absence of such positive relations,
suspicion and misunderstanding of the nature of intentional communities
have led to significant antagonism between local residents and the newer
intentional communities in their midst, sometimes resulting in the dissolution

of the communities. While such suspicions and misunderstandings did exist during the early years of Celo, community members deliberately built bridges of understanding to local people and prevented any antagonism from defining their relationships with local residents.

Two avenues for building positive relationships with local people came through community members' involvement in local churches and through their employment in local public agencies. Both provided local residents with opportunities to interact with members of Celo Community on a daily basis and to develop understandings of them as individuals that complicated vague conceptions of "the community people." Throughout the life of the community, a number of community members have been regularly attendees at worship services or participants in volunteer activities sponsored by one or another of the various small, local churches in the area. Some community members did this even while also being regular participants in the Friends Meeting in Celo Community. One manifestation of the positive relationships thus developed is that, in the fall of 2019, a memorial service was held at a local church for Arthur Morgan's recently deceased granddaughter who had been a member of the community for many decades but who was also a member of a local congregation made up almost entirely of non-Celo Community members.

Starting in the 1950s, one of the Quaker conscientious objectors to World War II who provided some of the first real stability for community membership began working as a teacher in local public schools. While he soon moved on to running a youth summer camp in the community for mostly nonlocal youth, he was remembered fondly by many local residents who had him as a teacher. One local resident spoke at this community member's funeral indicating that, while they clearly had different positions on political issues, that community member taught him important lessons about how to be a good person, lessons that stuck with him throughout the rest of his life. At least two community members worked in the local volunteer fire department, with one of them helping to establish it and both of them rising to the rank of captain. Working with local residents to save property and lives in the face of potential tragedy clearly served to break down barriers of misunderstanding that might have existed between community members and locals.

Another factor that helped to put a positive shine on the community for local residents was the establishment of the Celo Health Center on community land in the 1940s. Especially prior to the 1960s, the South Toe Valley was quite rural and local people did not have easy access to doctors or healthcare facilities. Recognizing this need in the local community and seizing on addressing it as a way to build positive relationships with local people, Arthur Morgan and other community founders raised funds to build a health center on community land and recruited a doctor to join the community's membership and staff the health center. They immediately began offering low-cost, basic medical services to local residents and continue to do so to this day. In the early 2000s, a new, larger health center building was constructed on community land to house expanded health services for local residents. That the community has provided space for local residents to access affordable health services on community land for seventy years has almost certainly served to break down at least some barriers of suspicion about the community.

One of the most distressing things about the community for local residents was that powerful outsiders came in from other parts of the country and expended significant finances to purchase what was widely perceived to be some of the best land in the valley. Even though the land was sold to Celo's founders by local residents (and absentee landowners) who were simply exercising their rights as private property owners, it should be remembered that when the land was purchased during the 1930s, the old system of treating undeveloped land, even when privately owned, as a de facto commons for hunting and gathering was still somewhat intact. That early community members went to some lengths to stop local residents from accessing their 1,200-acre tract in such manners was a point of consternation. At the same time, as local patterns of commons use were being displaced by more individually oriented, profit-seeking uses of the land, the fact that community members did not conform to these patterns and instead owned the land communally and sought to protect it from development and extractive use was also a point of contention.

However, over the decades, as more and more outsiders have bought up real estate in the area, cleared forests for homes, and put up fences and no trespassing signs to protect their property, the community began shifting its approach to excluding locals from hunting on community land. In the early 2000s, the community made a deliberate decision to post no hunting signs around the interior of their land close to where individual holdings and homes were located and not around the perimeter of their collective property. This had the effect of allowing use of their undeveloped land as a hunting commons in the traditional sense. In more recent years, the community has cautiously developed a more explicit process for approving local residents who are known to them to occasionally use their land—including land located in greater proximity to their holdings—for hiking, hunting, and fishing. That the community's relationship with at least some of the locals has changed from one of suspicion to one of appreciation for helping to preserve at least some of the rural character of the area was brought home via a letter from a member of long time local family that was read at the community's 2019 annual meeting:

> I want to thank . . . all the folks at Celo Community for letting me fish in your little stream and hike on your trails. It is the most beautiful and peaceful and nice place that I know. Thank you so much. May God Bless. Your Friend . . .

There is also an intangible, almost indescribable, factor that underlies Celo's success and longevity. Multiple members of the community expressed to me that serendipitous circumstances surrounded their discovery of or decision to join the community. For example, multiple long-term community members' descriptions of their decisions to join the community included accounts of just happening to stumble across some small snippet of writing about Arthur Morgan and his work in developing a small intentional community in southern Appalachia. For a number of community members, this happened just at a point in their life when they were faced with uncertainty or were looking to make a significant change in location or lifestyle. Others spoke about taking a job at the Arthur Morgan School or the Camp Celo summer camp, both operating on community land for many decades, and simply "knowing" that the place where they belong had found them.

This kind of serendipity has even affected the decisions of people who grew up in Celo. On one of my most recent visits to the community, I made an effort to speak with some of the second and third generation members who have joined the community especially during the last decade. One of them, now a third generation member, described how he had moved away from the community to go to college. He and his wife, having finished college, wanted to operate a youth summer camp similar to the one that their parents and grandparents had operated in Celo before them. They were pretty sure they didn't want to come back to Celo to do so, but after visiting several other summer camps with openings, they were unimpressed with the prospects. Upon returning to Celo to visit family, this community member described to me a moment of "magical" clarity when he recognized the special nature of what existed in the community and at Camp Celo. That same visit, his parents expressed their desire to retire from operating the camp and asked if he and his wife were interested. While it is difficult to empirically assess the effects of these serendipitous circumstances, anecdotally it does seem that they have occurred with some frequency, often bringing people into the community who have made long lasting, positive contributions to its functioning and stability.

Finally, it is worth considering other factors that scholars have identified as essential to the "success" of intentional communities and the degrees to which they played a role in Celo. The issue of how to define success in intentional communities has been the subject of significant debate in the communal studies literature, but one criterion that has been used is longevity (Kanter 1972, Wagner 1985). Perhaps the most influential study along these lines is Kanter's 1972 book *Commitment and Community: Communes and Utopias in Sociological Perspective*. Defining a successful community as one that has lasted at least twenty-five years, Kanter surveyed ninety-one communal projects that existed from 1780 to 1860 in the United States, seeking common factors that characterized these communities and enabled their success. Among the factors that Kanter identified were defined membership boundaries, rituals, and "commitment mechanisms" of various sorts including sacrifice, investment, renunciation, communion, mortification, and transcendence.

This study of Celo Community generally supports Kanter's conclusions albeit only by interpreting them in a slightly different manner. The importance of defined membership boundaries is among the first of Ostrom's design principles and was fully elaborated in an earlier chapter where I identified it as key to Celo's longevity. I find less clear support for the role of rituals as a contributing factor to Celo's longevity, although an argument can be made in their favor. Outside Celo Friends Meeting, the local Quaker worship group, rituals of a specifically religious character are largely absent in Celo. Even in the Quaker meeting, the ritual is one of gathering for silent worship preceded by group singing and succeeded by collective greetings and a potluck. However, there is no requirement for community members to participate in the Friends meeting and, today, most participants in the group are not community members. On the other hand, there are regular, repetitive group events in Celo that have been practiced across the decades. One may describe the community's monthly general meetings and workdays as ritualistic in nature in that they entail repeated, patterned behavior. The same can be said of the community's annual meeting which always entails significant nods to the community's history and development. While these rituals, if we can identify them as such, are largely devoid of significant ceremonial aspects that we would normally associate with religious rituals, they do serve to bring most community members together, allow them to acknowledge their collective endeavor and the values it embodies, and participate in group activity, decision-making, and group identity building. These rituals generally serve to reinforce the commitment mechanism that Kanter identifies as communion, although I would characterize it as a fairly light form of communion, especially compared with deeply religious groups such as the Shakers that Kanter used to exemplify what she meant by communion.

Some of the other commitment mechanisms that Kanter identified— renunciation, mortification, and transcendence, in particular—are generally understood to be of a religious character and these are largely absent in Celo. Mortification involves the reduction of the separate, individual ego and its replacement with a new group identity and is clearly not emphasized in Celo; in fact, community documents explicitly identify the cultivation of individuality within the context of group cooperation as a primary goal. Similarly, transcendence, characterized by attachment to an overarching ideological belief system, often embodied in the form of a charismatic leader, is clearly not in evidence at Celo. Renunciation, as a commitment mechanism, generally means requiring members to forego something—sex or alcohol, for example—that might otherwise be a part of daily life outside the group. Other than renouncing the ability to speculatively profit on buying and selling property, clearly not a daily activity unless one is a real estate investor, renunciation is not something Celo asks of its members. Indeed, the community states quite clearly that they are not interested in regulating or monitoring the daily behavior patterns of members where they don't involve subtractive use of common resources.

On the other hand, a strong argument can be made for the existence of commitment mechanisms that involve sacrifice and investment. As described in the chapters above, clear commitments that one makes when one joins the community, commitments that the community goes to some lengths to make clear, involve the sacrifice of predominant patterns of owning and using private property as a source of personal profit or of building personal financial equity. Instead, one makes a commitment to cooperative group ownership and governance of land and other common resources. This commitment, along with the costs and benefits associated with it (as described above), has the effect of limiting one's mobility, resulting in a significant commitment to stay in a place and be part of a group. In other words, joining Celo Community entails some sacrifice of economic individualism in favor of an investment in people and place.

In *Alienation and Charisma: A Study of Contemporary American Communes* (1980), Zablocki identified strong, charismatic leadership and limited density of "dyadic love" relationships among community members as keys to the survival of American intentional communities. This summary requires some clarification and caveats. First, Zablocki's study of community disintegration, in contrast with Kanter's analysis, focused solely on intentional communities in the first few years of their existence. As such, it is of limited relevance to my analysis of Celo Community, now in its ninth decade of existence. Second, Zablocki had trouble explaining how a greater density of love relationships among members contributed to community disintegration, at one point concluding that a "fundamental truth about all communal structures is revealed here: they tend to reduce interpersonal distances beyond the humanly tolerable" (1980: 133). Third, Zablocki concluded that the presence of charismatic leadership contributed to the stability of intentional communities only in the sense that it served to offset the negative effects of high densities of dyadic love relationships.

The factors identified by Zablocki seem of little relevance to this analysis of Celo Community. In addition to the fact that Zablocki's focus was on communities in their infancy while mine is on a quite mature community, it is clear that an overwhelming density of dyadic love relationships never existed in nor posed a threat to Celo. This is especially true during the community's first decade or so when, as described above, the lack of close relationships among community members seemed as much a threat to community stability as anything else. In the absence of the problems posed by intense interpersonal love relationships, the presence of charismatic leadership would have been less relevant according to Zablocki's analysis. Nonetheless, we might briefly consider it.

While the community's founder, Arthur Morgan, has been characterized as a strong leader with an unwillingness to compromise (see Purcell 2014), he notably never lived in nor was he a member of Celo Community. In fact, beyond the community's first decade or so, he was rarely if ever directly involved in community decision-making. He has himself described the community as an evolving experiment that he established and allowed to run its course. Over the years, at least two community members exhibited tendencies toward authoritarianism expressed through strong personalities and an unwillingness to compromise in community meetings but, as discussed in the chapters above, the history of the community reads these episodes mostly, though not without exception, as disruptive and out of line with the overall trajectory of the egalitarian exercise of power in the community. Indeed, the community's history, grounded as it is in a Quaker heritage of consensus decision-making, can be read as an ongoing effort to establish and maintain a nonhierarchical, nonauthoritarian governance system. For the last two or three decades, a time during which the community has flourished, this system seems to have functioned at its highest level (though, again, not without exceptions) and with the largest number of participants.

A more recent study of success in intentional communities conducted by Rubin, Willis, and Ludwig (2019) takes a different approach to defining success and comes to conclusions quite different from those of Zablocki and other previous scholars. Rubin, Willis, and Ludwig define success in terms to the degree to which intentional community members are invested in their communities, measured in terms of their steady and ongoing participation in community endeavors. Based on a survey of contemporary intentional communities that sought to measure multiple perceptions of community process and structure, they correlated the highest levels of success/participation with communities that have the most egalitarian governance structures. My study of Celo Community suggests that it fits this pattern to a significant degree; people come to Celo and remain there in part because they perceive and experience a real opportunity to participate in shaping the direction and policies of the community. While some community members do occasionally step away from community process and structure for some time, over the last twenty years I have grown accustomed to seeing the same familiar faces (complemented by newer faces of recently accepted community members) at the community meetings I attend. In general, Celo's members maintain a relatively steady level of participation in community processes.

This selective review of the ways in which the current study of Celo does or does not align with other studies of factors that contribute to success in intentional communities supports and adds to the thesis that commons design principles can provide important guideposts for other commoning endeavors. Specifically, those who wish to form or enter into land-based intentional communities in an effort to shape a more desirable, more just, and more sustainable world through shared endeavor may find something of value in Celo's experience. The above studies support the idea that defined membership boundaries and accessible, egalitarian, collective decision-making arenas—factors clearly identified in the design principles—are important factors that help make commoning endeavors sustainable. To those and the other factors identified in the design principles we may now add to the list a number of other factors including financial nest eggs, flexibility in the application of rule and policies, establishing meaningful relationships with place, building bridges to local communities, and some forms of investment and commitment mechanisms. With these in mind, we might now turn to the broader significance of this study and of the larger bodies of research on the commons and intentional communities to a world clearly facing a global-scale tragedy of the commons.

Conclusion

Cultivating Commons Subjects in and Beyond Intentional Community

The groundswell of efforts to (re)create ways of thinking, seeing, and being like commoners, and to preserve such ways where they have not already been foreclosed, provide an important counter-narrative to the idea that projects of authoritarian high modernism promulgated through state and capital constitute the only path to increased security and well-being. Indeed, as Scott (1998) reveals, such schemes so often fail because they ignore real, essential features of sociocultural and ecological realities, because they exclude the necessary role of local knowledge and know-how so often developed through informal processes of commoning and cultivated among unsanctioned communities of commoners.

> In each case, the necessarily thin, schematic model of social organization and production animating the planning was inadequate as a set of instructions for creating a successful social order. By themselves, the simplified rules can never generate a functioning community, city, or economy. Formal order, to be more explicit, is always and to some considerable degree parasitic on informal processes, which the formal scheme does not recognize, without which it could not exist, and which it alone cannot create or maintain. (Scott 1998: 310)

Scott's is not an argument that local knowledge and practice are free from problems, inequalities, and oppressions. It is also not an argument against the state in all forms and at all times. As he acknowledged, his critique might also best be directed at global capitalism which, while perhaps initially dependent on and certainly still intertwined with state governance, is becoming even more powerful than states as a proponent of "inadequate" sets of instructions for "creating a successful social order." Ironically, for Scott, the growing power of capital leaves the state to sometimes be a protector of local

227

knowledge and practice in the face of capitalism's unrelenting abstraction. Ostrom's second to last commons design principle, minimal recognition of rights, calls on the state to provide vessels by which the value of local commons in all their diversity may be acknowledged and by which they may be enabled to flourish. The ability of states to grant some degree of autonomy to local commons communities, as has been the case to some degree with Celo Community, is one important component of developing societies that can be more resilient in the face of increasingly rapid social and environmental change.

Scott's treatise is an argument for the value of sociocultural and natural diversity and an argument that there are limits on what the state and industrial capitalism can know about diverse, complex sociocultural and ecological systems, especially given the need of state and capital to see through filters that oversimplify the world to make it legible. While Scott does not use the language of the commons in *Seeing Like a State*, his analysis clearly leads to the conclusion that solutions to the problems he outlines are to be found, at least in part, in learning to "see like a commons." In reviewing the disasters of development, Scott makes the case for "the indispensable role of practical knowledge, informal processes, and improvisation in the face of unpredictability" in achieving social and natural stability (Scott 1998: 6). Practical, local knowledge is as accurate and efficient as it needs to be for addressing the problems at hand; it is applied in the local community, on the local landscape and it does not have higher or more abstract aspirations.

Scott uses the term *mētis*, from ancient Greek, to denote this type of knowledge that comes from practical experience. "Broadly understood, mētis represents a wide array of practical skills and acquired intelligence in responding to a constantly changing natural and human environment" (Scott 1998: 313). These skills and knowledge that constitute mētis cannot be taught in the abstract and are place- and community-specific, requiring constant attunement to constantly changing circumstances and new and changing settings. All human activity requires some degree of mētis to successfully engage with complex social and natural worlds in adaptive, sustainable ways. These activities must be constantly and repeatedly engaged in to be understood and mastered. Mētis applies equally to how humans interact with their environment and how they interact with each other. Mētis is generated among commoners acting in a constantly evolving commoning context.

My argument in this book is that the members of Celo Community have, over the last eighty plus years, cultivated a particular body of knowledge and practice that is applicable to a particular social and ecological context. This body of knowledge and practice, developed through an ongoing process of figuring out how to share and collectively manage a set of resources, has manifested in the form of quite particular and still evolving sets of rules, norms, and institutions. These rules, norms, and institutions allow for a significant degree of flexibility by which community members may respond to changing circumstances. They also enable the cultivation of particular forms of subjectivity and habitus that facilitate the constant becoming of commons community members.

The development of these forms of subjectivity and habitus represent a significant break from other forms of subjectivity and habitus that are cultivated by assumptions about individualism and short-term utilitarianism that underlay both ways of seeing like a state and the parable of the "rational" herdsmen at the heart of Hardin's conceptualization of the tragedy of the commons. Celo's members, like other neo-commoners everywhere, are developing a different worldview, a different approach to action, one that begins the process of decolonizing our minds and repopulating them with more proximate knowledge, skills, and affective experience. This worldview is cultivated in a communal context but also with a view to broader social and environmental conditions and the forces that shape them. This active reconstruction of human subjects must be intentional but it cannot be reduced to a set of design principles or best practices. "Commoning is a radical concept because it insists upon the active, knowing participation of people in shaping their own lives and meeting their own needs. A commons is not just about allocating a common-pool resource, something that a computer algorithm could arguably achieve. A commons requires active, ongoing participation with others in implementing and maintaining a shared purpose" (Bollier and Helfrich 2015a: 11).

The process of extracting ourselves from the utopian logic and totalitarian rationality of market and state, with their too often disastrous outcomes currently playing out across both local and global commons, is ongoing, affective, and simultaneously intensely personal and inherently collective.

> Just as market culture makes and shapes specific ways of being, so does commoning. Thinking in categories of commons and generating action from that thinking (and vice versa) helps to develop personal capacities and competencies that are essential to a happy, flourishing, creative life. A person's intentionality and affective, emotional labor matters. . . . Through countless acts of commoning, we develop essential capacities and competencies that self-replicate and spread through an entire collective. The resulting culture becomes a kind of emotional and cognitive "air that we breathe"—a way of perceiving and experiencing the world that flows through us and is taken for granted. (Bollier and Helfrich 2015a: 11)

Learning to see like a commons, whether in Celo, in other intentional communities, or in other kinds of commoning endeavors, will be a process of what Jared Phillips, in his account of the transformative impact of back-to-the-landers in the Ozarks (2019), refers to as "deep revolution." The desired changes in being humans in relationship with each other and with the other-than-human world will take generations to take effect and will come about only through deliberate effort, a willingness to collectively push against the grain, and an ability to constantly adjust to new and changing circumstances. Such a "deep revolution" is starting to happen in Celo, but it is important to acknowledge that it will probably never be complete.

This perspective is embodied in a quotation from one member of Celo Community that I introduced earlier. "I don't think utopia is a possibility. I don't think it's the goal. . . . We're in process and utopia implies an end. And to me, that's a pitfall, to think that we're going to get to an end. Then in it can become the 'end justifies the means.' The means are the end if you want to get really simplistic about it" (interview with author in Celo Community, November 9, 2004). That this particular take on Celo's utopian community-building endeavor was offered by Arthur Morgan's granddaughter, the third generation of her family to be part of Celo, makes it all the more powerful. This particular insight parallels, and indeed inspired, my attempt to frame the significance of the transformative potential of intentional community building. "Transformative utopianism recognizes that achieving a completely transcendent utopia is impossible, but it also recognizes the transformative potential of the ongoing process of utopian striving that plays out across generations, historical eras and the boundaries of individual intentional communities" (Lockyer 2009: 6).

The development of Celo's particular rules, norms, institutions, subjectivity, and habitus—their cultivated ability to "see like a commons"—developed through an organic process that must be characteristic of any commoning endeavor, taking place as it does in a specific sociocultural and ecological context. While I have analyzed this process using Ostrom's commons design principles as a heuristic framework, it is clear that the community's ability to see like a commons is not a direct result of implementing a specific set of best practices, as must be true for the construction of any commons community. Indeed, for Bollier and Helfrich, "[a]ll this cannot simply be designed into an organization or a procedure through legal or administrative means. In other words, commoning is a form and process that *flows through us*" (2015a: 11, emphasis in the original). Even if it cannot be reduced to a list of best practices, does the story of Celo Community, viewed through the lens of Ostrom's commons design principles, offer lessons that may be applied by other intentional communitarians or by others attempting to cultivate commons? The answer appears to be yes, but only in the vaguest outlines. If, following Sargent, there can be no blueprint for utopia, there is also no blueprint for the commons nor for intentional community.

If Scott's exploration of the disastrous outcomes of state and capital development projects was an argument against one-size-fits-all approaches to solving social and environmental problems so was Ostrom's argument about the value and viability of smaller-scale commons endeavors. Scott's utopian social engineering schemes of state and capital attempted to override mētis and install abstract knowledge and practices, ignoring social and ecological particularities of places and communities and, in the process, inviting practical failure, social disillusionment, and environmental destruction. If this is so, Ostrom recognized that it would be equally foolish to project commons arrangements, even abstract commons design principles derived from a meta-study of the commons, as a catch-all solution for solving human problems surrounding cooperative use of resources. Ostrom did not intend for her design principles or any of her analytic tools to offer a panacea (see Ostrom 2007).

Equally, Celo Community does not constitute, in the words of Hicks, "a 'master community,' a model to be emulated far and wide" (2001: 172). But neither should it be considered "an embarrassment to those who joined in the 1970s and afterward" nor can its primary enterprise be understood simply as "careful stewardship of commonly owned land" (2001: 211). The fact is that the members of Celo Community have slowly been brewing a "deep revolution" by cultivating different ways of relating to one another and to the land and other resources that they share. Indeed, in learning how to share with each other, with noncommunity members, and with other-than-human beings that inhabit their land they are cultivating a different kind of subjectivity, one that will be essential to the work of learning to share our overpopulated, over-exploited, rapidly changing common planet. As such, the members of Celo Community have been engaged in that essential work of utopianism identified by Sargent, Brown, and Marcus and Fisher—hope for the future cultivated in active epistemological critique of the present and ongoing cross-cultural juxtaposition of the present with what might be and what is already becoming.

In a context constantly shaped by the hegemonic forces of market and state and associated forms of totalitarian rationality and subjectivity, some degree of autonomous space and separation from the larger society are required to allow for experimentation with commoning and intentional community building. Without such space, there is no room to experiment with different ways of knowing, seeing, being, and doing. Bollier and Helfrich state this succinctly:

> Commoning is a process of constantly trying things out and putting them into practice. It requires the opportunity to make mistakes, to scrap ideas, to consult with others, and to start over, time and again. . . . It requires protected spaces for experimenting, for developing a sense of independence and confidence, and for acknowledging skepticism and resistance. Furthermore, people must have

psychic room and time for processing (both intellectually and emotionally) what is happening in a particular circumstance so that *something different* can emerge from the interpersonal relationships and the specific relationships between human beings and nature (or other resources). People must have space to make sense of their problems and circumstances, and be able to experiment in finding solutions, without the coercive threat of enclosure. This is an important political challenge: to retain open spaces for commoning. (2015c: 272–273)

Sargisson makes a similar point about the important utopian work of intentional community building. "In order to function as utopian spaces, and in order to begin to realise their intent, intentional communities require distance from the wider community. . . . [T]hat physical separation facilitates the development of alternative normative agendas and practices. It permits people to begin to explore their version of the good life in a relatively safe space. From this space, they view the wider world with an estranged gaze that has glimpsed a better way" (Sargisson 2007: 416–417). Celo Community has managed to develop their commoning practice, their intentional community-building endeavor, in such a safe space characterized by a certain degree of estrangement.

It is important to acknowledge that access to this safe space was only available to them because of a significant degree of exclusive privilege characteristic of Celo's members, and especially of the community's founder, Arthur Morgan, a subject I will return to below. For now, we can recognize that Celo's safe space has allowed them to develop patterns of commoning and to cultivate certain subjectivities, certain ways of seeing like a commons that have served them and their commons well and that may offer valuable lessons and perspectives to others attempting to develop their own particular commoning communities elsewhere. However, as Sargisson also points out, the "estrangement" that intentional community members need to inhabit to work on creating the social alternatives they envision can also place community members in a dangerous position of "otherness." "Otherness is part of the utopian project, and utopias encapsulate radical difference. This otherness can be empowering, exciting, and inspirational. It has a certain glamour. But the life of a perpetual outsider is a lonely one" (Sargisson 2007: 417).

This perceived otherness that Sargisson references cuts both ways. Intentional community members experience themselves as alienated from the mainstream society and, equally, individuals in the surrounding society perceive the estranged intentional communitarians on their margins as alien and incomprehensible. Without some effort to bridge the chasm of otherness, utopian estrangement can negate the potentially transformative power of the group endeavor. "Collective alienation can lead groups to become more oppositional and less utopian; they can become impelled by fear and mistrust, and no longer compelled towards an idea of a better life. Ontologically, total estrangement negates the critical utopian function of these groups. Utopias must be connected to the now to enable the critical gaze" (Sargisson 2007: 418). For Sargisson, the negative effects of estrangement experienced by intentional communities can be mediated by taking actions that build bridges to and open up lines of communication with members of surrounding communities.

As suggested in preceding chapters, part of Celo Community's relative success and resilience can be attributed in part to their deliberate attempts to mediate estrangement by building such bridges of communication and relationships to both proximate communities and to those further away. If Celo was originally viewed by residents of existing local communities as incomprehensible, that incomprehensibility began to break down as Celo's members and their neighbors came to know and trust one another. The sincere engagement of Celo's members in a variety of local institutions—schools, churches, charitable organizations, and the local volunteer fire department only a few among them—has built relationships of familiarity and trust. Recognizing that the land they now inhabit was long used by local residents as part of a broad, de facto commons, Celo's members took deliberate steps to open up portions of their land to outside users for occasional hunting, harvesting, and other, non-subtractive uses. As indicated by the recent communique sent by one member of a longtime local family and read at a Celo Community meeting, local residents have even begun to appreciate Celo's land stewardship efforts as ownership of surrounding lands in the valley has become increasingly fragmented and has fallen ever more into the hands of speculative outsiders.

Celo's members have also played active roles in broader, utopian, intentional community-building movements. In the community's early years, they were an active member of the Fellowship of Intentional Communities, sometimes submitting reports on Celo's progress for inclusion in this international organization's newsletter aimed at sharing information with broader publics looking for cooperative alternatives to the status quo (see Fellowship of Intentional Communities 1959). Although Celo has moved away from an overtly public-facing collective involvement in broader intentional community building, sustainability, and social justice movements, individual community members continue to serve quietly as nodes in a number of local and regional initiatives involving permaculture, mutual aid, conservation, justice for immigrants, and racial reconciliation. In so doing, they inevitably bring their emerging ability to see like a commons to these initiatives and thus contribute to their resilience. In the process, they are helping to construct what Haluza-Delay (2013) has called a "distributed ecovillage" in the wider South Toe Valley, a broader community that shares a commitment to developing a more cooperative, more equitable, and more ecologically oriented habitus.

Without explicit, collective intent, Celo has also served as a model for the construction of other intentional commons communities. As documented elsewhere (Lockyer 2007, 2009), Celo Community provided direct inspiration for the founding of a much newer utopian, intentional community-building endeavor on the other side of the Blue Ridge. The founders of Earthaven Ecovillage, including one woman who took a several year hiatus from her membership in Celo to help start Earthaven, used Celo's institutions as partial models for establishing this newer commoning endeavor, one that is much more radically insistent on sustainable living and self-provisioning. As Earthaven's members have developed their own particular rules, norms, institutions, subjectivity, and habitus, they have deliberately built bridges to broader publics to share their experiences and any lessons that may be learned from them. Through education and outreach organizations such as Culture's Edge and the School of Integrated Living, Earthaven invites the public to come into their community and experience their models of commoning so that Earthaveners may "inspire and empower participants to live responsible and creative lives by providing experiential education in integrated living and regenerative systems" (School of Integrated Living 2020).

My exploration of the relationship between these two utopian community-building endeavors contributed to my understanding of the transformative potential of utopianism. In conversation with the work of Donald Pitzer and George Hicks, I challenged scholars of intentional communities to shift their frame of reference and to move away from analyses that focused on the degree to which individual intentional communities have achieved completely transcendent utopian visions. "Transformative utopianism shifts the frame of analysis to broader movements and historical forces within which intentional communities and their individual utopian visions are only single components. . . . Utopian striving is seen as a manifestation of human agency that is always somewhat constrained by larger cultural, historical and material forces even as it is partially successful at creating cultural change" (Lockyer 2009: 6). This perspective, standing on the shoulders of other utopian and communal studies scholars, is part of a broader aim to draw attention to the persistent, emancipatory, and transformative potential of intentional communities, communities that have been a consistent part of and contributors to the unfolding of our broader societal story, especially in the United States of America.

It is here that scholars may have a role to play in mediating the estrangement that separates intentional communities and other neo-commoners from mainstream society. Can we break down the psycho-social, cultural barriers that have been thrown up by derogatory and dismissive deployments of terms like "utopia," "commune," and "commons" promulgated by powerful actors committed to maintaining the status quo and the powerful and profitable advantages it grants them (see Linebaugh 2008)? I believe we can do just this by working as critical allies, translating the visions and outcomes (both successes and failures), and highlighting the ways in which the hard work of commoners, utopians, and intentional communitarians has taken effect in the world. Equally, and as critical allies, we must help identify ways that the ongoing processes of utopian striving by these groups must still rise to meet further challenges and address inconsistencies between the theories and visions that inspire their endeavors and the lived enactment of those theories and visions.

Scholarship highlighting the impact, both potential and realized, of utopian communitarians is already fairly widespread. Documenting the ways in which intentional communitarians pioneered collective experiments in areas as diverse as sustainable food production and consumption, holistic healthcare, public and alternative education, and peace work and racial reconciliation among other things, Pitzer notes that "it is increasingly clear that pioneering concepts and practices from this explosion of communal social laboratories have been integrated into world culture" (2013: 38). A number of recent studies have used empirical data to demonstrate that people living in ecovillages and a variety of other ecologically focused intentional communities are consuming fewer resources and demonstrating how people in affluent societies can reduce the ecological footprints (see Boyer 2016, Daly 2017, Lockyer 2017, Sherry 2014). These and other studies explore how such communities reduce their environmental impact using a combination of deliberately reduced consumption, technological innovations, and alternative methods of social organization such as commoning. Other recent studies have also demonstrated that these types of communities maintain or even enhance the quality of life experienced by their members despite living on fewer resources and actively engaging in ongoing experiments with different forms of commons organization (Grinde et al. 2016 and Mulder, Costanza, and Erickson 2006).

While the above-cited literature on intentional communities identifies the positive transformative impact and potential of such communities, scholars have equally noted significant shortcomings and challenges faced by such communities, especially with regard to broader issues of diversity and inclusion. Hall (2017) has pointed out that even among relatively homogenous groups of communitarians, it can be extremely difficult to even agree on a set of social values to live by much less enact them in a communal living context. Other scholars have made clear that intentional communities often fall short of their professed goals of providing inclusive spaces for exploring social alternatives. Specifically, Tummers and MacGregor (2019) and Chitewere

(2010) call out intentional communities for a lack of attention to the ways in which inequitable dynamics of race, class, and gender among other differences play out in their midst and shape access to the opportunities they aim to provide. This results in an inability among intentional communitarians to address broader patterns of injustice and leaves their communities as but "niche" endeavors that will not be effective at scaling up or scaling out the solutions they propose.

Like many other intentional communities, Celo explicitly aspires to offer an inviting and inclusive environment for all who may wish to join their experiment in commoning. This intent was clearly articulated in the early years when community members formulated their community constitution. The community's vision of inclusivity was expanded in 2018 when they made what has been the sole revision to that document, indicated in brackets in the following quotation. "The aim of Celo Community is to provide an opportunity for its members to enjoy a life that includes personal expression, neighborly friendship and cooperation, and appreciative care of the natural environment. No person is excluded from membership because of national or racial origin, religious belief, [disability, sexual orientation, or gender identity]." Despite their stated aims, Celo remains a largely homogenous group, composed mostly of people from white, middle-class backgrounds. As Tummers and MacGregor (2019) note, the ability of groups of people so positioned to design alternative structures that foster reduced consumption, less social alienation, and greater care for humans and for the land and the more-than-human others it hosts can make important contributions to facilitating greater environmental sustainability and greater social and environmental justice. However, without more deliberate attention to issues of diversity and exclusion, and to histories of expropriation and enclosure, the stated vision of inclusivity too often remains only "wishful thinking."

Further highlighting this point, Nightingale emphasizes that commons communities are always political communities that are engaged in ongoing "renegotiations of who and what belong to 'the community' " (2019: 17); the creation of any non-open-access commons entails both inclusions and exclusions. These ongoing negotiations take place at the crossroads of intersectionality and require constant attention to avoid "inadvertent exclusions and harm to both human and non-human others, exclusions which can undermine long term commoning goals" (2019: 18). Some kind of exclusion also is inherent in Ostrom's design principles which call for the existence of distinctly bounded groups of users and distinctly bounded resources. In order to create a functioning commons, Celo Community necessarily excluded some who did not explicitly share their (or Arthur Morgan's) emergent understandings of community and cooperation. With a few notable exceptions, local residents and people of color were among those excluded. The construction of Celo's commons also entailed constructing a distinction between the human community and the land they joined together to steward. This distinction almost necessarily entails the exclusion of the land and its other-than-human inhabitants from participating in the power-laden institutions and decision-making processes that govern the community.

This criticism is not to fault the members of Celo nor to characterize their efforts as a failure. Indeed, the thrust of this work suggests that what they have achieved in terms of cultivating their collective ability to see like a commons is quite laudable and impactful even beyond the boundaries of their particular commons community. However, it does aim to point to the ever-incomplete nature of commoning whether in Celo Community or elsewhere. As Nightingale reminds us,

> [A] core part of the commoning project needs to be staying with the trouble, keeping in view the exclusions, others, and power over that commoning practices create. Without constant consciousness, these troubles can un-do commoning efforts and their achievements. Commoning ultimately requires normative choices about which humans, which non-humans and which socionatural relations to attend, although such attention will always be partial. It is not possible to control and direct all the outcomes of commoning. Many will be unexpected, footloose and surprising, some desirable, some less so. (2019: 31)

These kind of power-laden negotiations regarding inclusions and exclusions, and their unexpected outcomes, are characteristic of the commons everywhere and certainly of the ways in which the commons are constructed and negotiated in Appalachia. As scholars such as Boyer (2008) and Newfont (2012) reminds us, there have been several waves of commoning in Appalachia, each with its own particular ontological gaze. Each wave was characterized by particular forms of subjectivity and habitus and associated negotiations of inclusivity or exclusivity, and each was disrupted by shifts in power and the institutions that deal in it. A precolonial indigenous commons was displaced by a system of white supremacy that justified the expropriation of native lands. During the period of settler colonialism, a de facto commons spread across the region even as a regime of private property was laid across it by an emerging capitalist class working in tandem with the state. Well into the twentieth century, mountain families used "unimproved" land as a de facto subsistence commons, even when that land was owned by absentee landlords or partially developed by local residents.

During the second half of the nineteenth century, regimes of legibility and simplicity and associated projects of authoritarian high modernism took increasing hold of the region. Individual capitalist ventures extracted and exported the region's natural resources and, later, state projects of development and conservation, including Arthur Morgan's Tennessee Valley Authority, sought, not completely successfully, to impose a total vision and order on the landscape and its people. Such projects included the management of national forest lands by the federal government for "maximum sustained yield" through processes of clear-cutting and uniform forest plantations. All of these twentieth-century projects involved the displacement of preceding commoners, in part through the deliberate "racialization" of indigenous peoples and Appalachian folk, the construction of mountaineers as inferior others to justify top-down intervention in their lives and livelihoods, and the co-optation of their households' ability to collectively produce for themselves (Stoll 2017).

Yet throughout this history, networks and processes of grassroots commoning endeavors have endured and, to some degree, successfully pushed back against these totalizing projects. Newfont's account of the Western North Carolina Alliance's (WNCA) campaign of "commons-based environmentalism" shows how a diverse range of stakeholders successfully rallied against the National Forest Service's use of clear-cutting to manage the large swathes of land under their purview in southern Appalachia. Newfont reveals the intensity and hard work it took to build a coalition capable of a relatively inclusive vision of the commons on Appalachia's public lands (see Newfont 2011 and 2012). However, this campaign no doubt left exclusions in place, not least of which would be the perspectives of indigenous peoples, other-than-human inhabitants of the land, and of intact, functioning ecosystems. Indeed, the WNCA only achieved the effectiveness it did by refusing to adopt a "wilderness environmentalism" platform which was unpopular amongst so many local residents accustomed to using public commons lands for extractive, subsistence uses. This exclusion leaves intact a human-nature dualism that, at a fundamental level, will be necessary to overcome if we are to avert the ultimate tragedy of our planetary commons. And it almost certainly left intact perceived divisions that exist along racial and ethnic lines.

So still, much work remains to be done. As Stoll's recent account of "the ordeal of Applachia" makes clear, Appalachian communities and environments continue to suffer the onslaught of Scott's projects of authoritarian high modernism. Stoll offers his "Commons Communities Act," with its foundation in Ostrom's commons design principles as an imagined solution to these circumstances. It is a call for returning the land to local communities and it is a call imbued with the "wishful thinking" of so many commons activists. But it is also a call that recognizes the challenges of addressing the exclusions and exclusivity that so often attend the politically charged construction of the commons.

Optimism always requires greater effort. If our sense of the possible doesn't contain an element of the unlikely, then it's only a compromise with what is.

There can be no improvement without a viable political identity. This would require the white working class of the southern mountains to stop identifying their interests with those of the rich and powerful, a position that leaves them poorer and more powerless than they have ever been. They should also consider abandoning false and imploding racial distinctions. Instead of telling a story about themselves that separates them from African-Americans, American Indians, and all those who have been dispossessed, they could tell a story about their common predicament. They could organize for true democracy, as they once did. Nearly everything that the industrial workers of Appalachia have ever gained . . . came from collective politics. It came, in other words, from people who refused to be divided by imaginary differences. (Stoll 2017: 270–271)

Could such a collective, intersectional political identity drive the creation of new commons communities in Appalachia? If such were to happen, it would require much more than optimism and wishful thinking. As Celo's experience demonstrates, even those who start with relative privilege, positive intent, and significant homogeneity, struggle immensely to constitute an effective commons community that is somewhat inclusive and significantly democratic. And, as per Celo's experience wherein a significant block of land was granted to their experiment in commoning, the creation of new commons communities would also require a significant program of land redistribution.

Such a program of land redistribution would be an essential part of the true democratization of society by giving people an ecological base from which to act. Agrarian thinker Wendell Berry speaks directly to this proposition.

Shall the usable property of our country be democratically divided, or not? Shall the power of property be a democratic power, nor not? If many people do not own the usable property, then they must submit to the few who do own it. They cannot eat or be sheltered or clothed except in submission. They will find themselves entirely dependent on money; they will find costs always higher, and money always harder to get. To renounce the principle of democratic property, which is the only basis of democratic liberty, in exchange for specious notions of efficiency or the economics of the so-called free market is a tragic folly. (1987: 165)

As Stoll's analysis reveals, the latter is precisely what has happened as coal and timber interests, aided by enablers in the state, increasingly enclosed the commons in Appalachia.

Were a program of land redistribution to take shape in this society, it can't simply follow the path that led to Celo Community. In Celo's case, wealthy benefactors bought land that had already been expropriated from original inhabitants and turned into private property. They handed control of it over to a group of mostly middle-class white folks who moved to the Appalachian region from elsewhere in the country to experiment with cooperative living. Indeed, one irony of Celo's story is that Arthur Morgan created the community as an experiment in commoning in a region where he, as first director of the Tennessee Valley Authority, had just finished imposing an industrial-scale, state-based development program on local residents, in the process, massively displacing local populations and contributing to ongoing processes of commons enclosure and dispossession. The interventions and enclosures that have characterized Appalachia (and been experienced by "racialized" Appalachians) have been, whether implemented by state or capital, suggested by Hardin's parable of the tragedy of the commons with its false overgeneralizations about human nature. They are driven by a white supremacist colonialism that has led to social and ecological disaster in Appalachia and far beyond. For Wall, they depend on "a colonial perspective that suggests that white western experts need to be in charge. There is a rather dubious and racist history of conservation involving representatives from European colonial powers removing land from local people because they are viewed as degrading it" (2017: 111). Any successful, democratic programs of land redistribution and commons community building will have to overcome this vision.

Part of the power that emerges from Scott's story of seeing like a state is that the state cannot continue to function without acknowledging and valuing the nearly invisible work of people making a living in real places and cooperating in actual communities. Near the end of his account of the ordeal of Appalachia, Stoll points to this counternarrative to state power, a story embodied in Celo Community:

> We all live in communities. In a sense, no one really lives in the United States but in neighborhoods, towns, and counties. Strengthening those bonds within environments that allow for economic autonomy seems like a way of creating space between people and the nation-state. It might also offer a way to endure during times of climate disruption, when the United States might not be capable of compensating for any number of possible disasters. The Commons Communities Act proposes land reform and collective governance. It proposes nothing new, but rather something very old, a sense of ownership without the enclosure and the abuse of power characteristic of private property. (2017: 276–277)

Were such an initiative as Stoll's Commons Communities Act to become a viable possibility, Ostrom's commons design principles may provide a useful practical guide, but the particularities would have to be worked out amongst the diverse coalitions of people involved in each locale. And, while the state would almost inevitably have to be involved in facilitating it, it could not be achieved entirely through a top-down program. As Bollier and Helfrich remind us,

> [T]his perspective on the commons requires that we adopt a different intellectual approach and methodology than one that focuses on inventing or changing laws in existing institutional structures. . . . This very idea presumes that experts armed with sufficient authority and resources can generate, through a complex calculus, the results they wish. The struggle for a free, fair, and sustainable future must always begin with the question of how we wish to live together, and how this communal life is to be designed so that nobody feels taken advantage of. This implies asking: Who is affected? Who is responsible? Who can shape things, and for what reasons? Who can say no? Who can support or obstruct things, and why? Such questions inevitably lead to larger questions about the whole economic and social system. (2015c: 273)

This challenging work must be engaged by people on the ground, working hard to see and hear each other across real and imagined differences, and to reach some consensus on how to shape a just and sustainable commons. This is the utopian, potentially transformative, and likely emancipatory work of learning to see like a commons. It is the kind of work that the members of Celo Community have been engaged in for over eighty years and, hopefully, will be engaged in for another eighty more.

The experience of Celo Community and its members demonstrates another key point made by Bollier and Helfrich and one that I wish to reemphasize as I close.

> [C]ommons must be "seen from the inside"—through the experiences, feelings, history and cultures of every participant. This helps explain why it is not really possible to "design" a commons from the outside and import a specific set of "best practices" or "golden rules" to manage a particular commons. A commons must arise from the personal engagement of commoners themselves. It is unavoidably the product of unique personalities, geographic locations, cultural contexts, moments in time and political circumstances of that particular commons. Yet finding a workable *common* language to generalize about commons remains an important challenge. It can help commoners draw connections between their experiences and the aspirations of others, and help all to see the wider ramifications and potential for societal transformation. (Bollier and Helfrich 2015a: 9–10)

Arrangements, perspectives, and practices such as those worked out in Celo are probably not replicable at the larger scales of state or planet, but they provide some guideposts for a larger program of commons community building.

The rules, norms, institutions, and forms of subjectivity and habitus cultivated by the members of Celo Community are unique to their particular time, place, and people. It is a fundamental anthropological truism to point to the uniqueness of any human group and say that their particular experience cannot be used as a measure for any other group. But it is also an anthropological truism to recognize that we can learn something about ourselves, and about how to apply ourselves and the policies we make, to making the world a better, more equitable, and more resilient place by learning from others. It is hoped that the story of Celo Community—a story created through the hard work and dedication of so many people over so many years cultivating an ability to see like a commons—might be one small piece of this larger endeavor.

References

Ambler, Rex. 2013. *The Quaker Way: A Rediscovery*. Alresford, Hants, UK: Christian Alternative Books.

Andelson, Jonathan G. 1997. "The Community of True Inspiration from Germany to the Amana Colonies." In *America's Communal Utopias*, D.E. Pitzer (ed.), pp. 181–203. Chapel Hill, NC: The University of North Carolina Press.

Appalachian Institute for Mountain Studies. 2020. "Our Mission." https://southernseedlegacy.wordpress.com/our-mission/. Accessed on July 2, 2020.

Arthur Morgan Institute for Community Solutions. 2019. "Mission Statement." https://www.communitysolution.org/. Accessed on November 21, 2019.

Bacon, Margaret Hope. 1999. *The Quiet Rebels: The Story of the Quakers in America*. Wallingford, PA: Pendle Hill Publications.

Baden, John A. 1998. "Communitarianism and the Logic of the Commons." In *Managing the Commons*, J.A. Baden and D.S. Noonan (eds.), pp. 135–153. Bloomington, IN: Indiana University Press.

Bennett, John W. 1974. "Cultural Integrity and Personal Identity: The Communitarian Response." In *The Cultural Drama: Modern Identities and Social Ferment*, W.S. Dillon (ed.), pp. 196–235. Washington, DC: Smithsonian Institution Press.

Berry, Wendell. 1987. "A Defense of the Family Farm." In *Home Economics*, pp. 162–178. Berkeley, CA: Counterpoint.

Bestor, Arthur Eugene. 1950. *Backwoods Utopias: The Sectarian and Owenite Phases of Communitarian Socialism in America, 1663-1829*. Philadelphia, PA: University of Pennsylvania Press.

Bollier, David. 2014. *Think Like a Commoner: A Short Introduction to the Life of the Commons*. Gabriola Island, BC: New Society Publishers.

Bollier, David and Silke Helfrich. 2012. "Introduction: The Commons as a Transformative Vision." In *The Wealth of the Commons*, D. Bollier and S. Helfrich (eds.), pp. xi–xix. Amherst, MA: Levellers Press.

———. 2015a. "Overture." In *Patterns of Commoning*, D. Bollier and S. Helfrich (eds.), pp. 1–12. Amherst, MA: The Commons Strategies Group.

———. 2015b. "Eight Points of Orientation for Commoning." In *Patterns of Commoning*, D. Bollier and S. Helfrich (eds.), pp. 48–49. Amherst, MA: The Commons Strategies Group.

———. 2015c. "Intermezzo II: The Internal Dimensions of the External World: On Commons and Commoning." In *Patterns of Commoning*, D. Bollier and S. Helfrich (eds.), pp. 271–274. Amherst, MA: The Commons Strategies Group.

Boyer, Jefferson C. 2008. "Reinventing the Appalachian Commons." In *The Global Idea of the Commons*, D.M. Nonini (ed.), pp. 89–114. New York: Berghahn Books.

Boyer, Paul S. 1997. "Forward." In *America's Communal Utopias*, D.E. Pitzer (ed.), pp. ix–xiii. Chapel Hill, NC: The University of North Carolina Press.

Boyer, Robert H.W. 2016. "Achieving One-Planet Living Through Transitions in Social Practice: A Case Study of Dancing Rabbit Ecovillage." *Sustainability: Science, Practice and Policy* 12(1): 47–59.

Brewer, Priscilla J. 1997. "The Shakers of Mother Ann Lee." In *America's Communal Utopias*, D.E. Pitzer (ed.), pp. 37–56. Chapel Hill, NC: The University of North Carolina Press.

Brown, J.C. Jr. 1957. "Celo: This Little Bit of Heaven Was Planned, But There's No Standard Design for the Angels." In *The Carolina Farmer*, pp. 10–15, December 1957. Wilmington, NC: George W. Cameron.

Brown, Susan Love. 2002a. "Introduction." In *Intentional Community: An Anthropological Perspective*, S.L. Brown (ed.), pp. 1–15. Albany, NY: State University of New York Press.

———. 2002b. "Community as Cultural Critique." In *Intentional Community: An Anthropological Perspective*, S.L. Brown (ed.), pp. 153–179. Albany, NY: State University of New York Press.

Campbell, Marcia Caton and Danielle A. Salus. 2003. "Community and Conservation Land Trusts as Unlikely Partners? The Case of Troy Gardens, Madison, Wisconsin." *Land Use Policy* 20: 169–180.

Carr, Mike. 2004. *Bioregionalism and Civil Society: Democratic Challenges to Corporate Globalism*. Vancouver: UBC Press.

Celo Community. No Date. "About Celo Community." Unpublished document. Celo Community archives.

———. No Date. "Welcome to Celo Community." Unpublished document. Celo Community archives.

———. No Date. "Land Reform as Practiced at Celo Community." Unpublished document. Celo Community archives.

———. 1938. "Certificate of Incorporation (Charter) of Celo Community, Inc." Unpublished document. Celo Community archives.

———. 1946. "About Celo Community." Unpublished document. Celo Community archives.

———. 1984. "Task Force Report on CCI Decision-making." Unpublished document. Celo Community archives.

———. 2005. "CCI General Meeting Minutes, August 3, 2005." Unpublished document. Celo Community archives.

————. 2006a. "Letter to Francis 11-04-05 & Francis's Response." Unpublished Celo Community group email correspondence on March 22, 2006.

————. 2006b. "To CCI Membership." Unpublished Celo Community group email correspondence on March 22, 2006.

————. 2009. "Celo Community By-Laws." Unpublished document. Celo Community archives.

————. 2011. "Consensus Decision-Making Process." Unpublished document. Celo Community archives.

————. 2012. "Celo Community Self-Evaluation Questionnaire." Unpublished document. Celo Community archives.

————. 2013a. "Membership Agreement." Unpublished document. Celo Community archives.

————. 2013b. "CCI Fields Committee Report to Annual Meeting 2013." Unpublished document. Celo Community archives.

————. 2014. "Workday Report, October 4, 2014." Unpublished document. Celo Community archives.

————. 2015. "Codifier's Annual Report." Unpublished document. Celo Community archives.

————. 2018a. "Celo Community Constitution." Unpublished document. Celo Community archives.

————. 2018b. "Celo Community Holding Agreement." Unpublished document. Celo Community archives.

————. 2019. "CCI Procedures and Rules and Job Descriptions." Unpublished document. Celo Community archives.

Chitewere, Tendai. 2010. "Equity in Sustainable Communities: Exploring Tools from Environmental Justice and Political Ecology." *Natural Resources* 50: 315–339.

Christian, Diana Leafe. 2003. *Creating a Life Together: Practical Tools to Grow Ecovillages and Intentional Communities.* Gabriola Island, BC, Canada: New Society Publishers.

Communal Studies Association. 2020. "About." https://www.communalstudies.org/about/. Accessed on June 16, 2020.

Community Service, Inc. 2007. "About Us: We're All About Community." http://www.communitysolution.org/aboutus.html. Accessed on March 7, 2007.

Contreras, Jorge L. 2014. "Constructing the Genome Commons." In *Governing Knowledge Commons,* B.M. Frischmann, M.J. Madison, and K.J. Standburg (eds.), pp. 99–136. New York: Oxford University Press.

Cox, Michael, Gwen Arnold, and Sergio Villamayor Tomás. 2010. "A Review of Design Principles for Community-Based Natural Resource Management." *Ecology and Society* 15(4): 38.

Daly, Matthew. 2017. "Quantifying the Environmental Impact of Ecovillages and Co-housing Communities: A Systematic Literature Review." *Local Environment* 22(11): 1358–1377.

Davis, Donald Edward. 2000. *Where There Are Mountains: An Environmental History of the Southern Appalachians.* Athens, GA: The University of Georgia Press.

Dolšak, Nives and Elinor Ostrom. 2003. *The Commons in the New Millennium: Challenges and Adaptations.* Cambridge, MA: MIT Press.

Engels Frederick. 1892. *Socialism: Utopian and Scientific.* New York: Charles Scribner's Sons.

Escobar, Arturo. 1995. *Encountering Development: The Making and Unmaking of the Third World.* Princeton, NJ: Princeton University Press.

———. 2008. *Territories of Difference: Place, Movements, Life,* Redes. Durham, NC: Duke University Press.

———. 2017. *Designs for the Pluriverse: Radical Interdependence, Autonomy, and the Making of Worlds.* Durham, NC: Duke University Press.

Fellowship of Intentional Communities. 1959. "The Intentional Communities: 1959 Yearbook of the Fellowship of Intentional Communities." Yellow Springs, OH: Fellowship of Intentional Communities.

Frischmann, Brett M., Michael J. Madison, and Katherine J. Strandburg. 2014. *Governing Knowledge Commons.* New York: Oxford University Press.

Gibson, Clark C. and Tomas Koontz. 1998. "When 'Community' Is Not Enough: Institutions and Values in Community-Based Forest Management in Southern Indiana." *Human Ecology* 26(4): 621–647.

Gibson-Graham, J.K. 2006. *A Postcapitalist Politics.* Minneapolis, MN: University of Minnesota Press.

———. 2014. "Rethinking the Economy with Thick Description and Weak Theory." *Current Anthropology* 55(S9): S147–S153.

Gilman, Robert. 1990. "The Idea of Owning Land." In *Communities Directory,* Fellowship for Intentional Community (ed.), pp. 109-113. Rutledge, MO: Fellowship for Intentional Community.

Graeber, David. 2004. *Fragments of an Anarchist Anthropology.* Chicago, IL: Prickly Paradigm Press.

Greenbough, Anna. 1959. "Childhood at Winterstar." *Liberation* IV(6): 13–16.

Grinde, Bjørn, Ragnhild Bang Nes, Ian F. MacDonald, and David Sloan Wilson. 2017. "Quality of Life in Intentional Communities." *Social Indicators Research* 137(2): online only/no page numbers. DOI: 10.1007/s11205-017-1615-3

Halewood, Michael, Isabel López Noriega, and Selim Louafi. 2013. *Crop Genetic Resources as a Global Commons: Challenges in International Law and Governance.* New York: Routledge.

Hall, Amy Cox. 2017. "Neo-Monastics in North Carolina, De-growth and a Theology of Enough." *Journal of Political Ecology* 24: 425–466.

Haluza-Delay and Ron Berezan. 2013. "Permaculture in the City: Ecological Habitus and the Distributed Ecovillage." In *Environmental Anthropology Engaging Ecotopia: Bioregionalism, Permaculture, and Ecovillages,* J. Lockyer and J.R. Veteto (eds.), pp. 130–145. New York: Berghahn Books.

Hardin, Garrett. 1968. "The Tragedy of the Commons: The Population Problem has no Technical Solution; It Requires a Fundamental Extension in Morality." *Science* 162: 1243–1248.

Harvey, David. 2011. "The Future of the Commons." *Radical History Review* 109: 101–107.

Hess, Charlotte and Elinor Ostrom. 2011. *Understanding Knowledge as a Commons.* Cambridge, MA: MIT Press.

Hicks, George L. 1969. "Ideology and Change in an American Utopian Community." University of Illinois. Doctoral Dissertation.

———. 2001. *Experimental Americans: Celo and Utopian Community in the Twentieth Century.* Urbana: University of Illinois Press

Hine, Robert V. 1997. "California's Socialist Utopias." In *America's Communal Utopias,* D.E. Pitzer (ed.), pp. 419–431. Chapel Hill, NC: The University of North Carolina Press.

Hollis, Joe. 2020. "Paradise Gardening." https://www.mountaingardensherbs.com/paradise-gardening. Accessed on July 2, 2020.

Infield, Henrik F. 1955. *Utopia and Experiment: Essays in the Sociology of Cooperation.* New York: F.A. Praeger.

Institute for Community Economics. 1982. *The Community Land Trust Handbook.* Emmaus, PA: Rodale Press.

Internal Revenue Service. 2019a. "Types of Organizations Exempt Under Section 501(c)(4)." https://www.irs.gov/charities-non-profits/other-non-profits/types-of-organizations-exempt-under-section-501c4. Accessed on September 3, 2019.

Internal Revenue Service. 2019b. "Social Welfare Organizations Examples." https://www.irs.gov/charities-non-profits/other-non-profits/social-welfare-organizations-examples. Accessed on September 3, 2019.

Ioris, Antonio A.R. 2014. *The Political Ecology of the State: The Basis and Evolution of Environmental Statehood.* New York: Routledge.

Jacob, Jeffrey. 1997. *New Pioneers: The Back-to-the-Land Movement and the Search for a Sustainable Future.* University Park, PA: Pennsylvania State University Press.

Janzen, Donald E. 1981. "The Intentional Community – National Community Interface: An Approach to the Study of Communal Societies." *Communal Societies* 1: 37–42.

Kahoe, Walter. 1977. *Arthur Morgan: A Biography and Memoir.* Moylan, PA: The Whimsie Press.

Kanter, Rosabeth Moss. 1972. *Commitment and Community: Communes and Utopias in Sociological Perspective.* Cambridge, MA: Harvard University Press.

Leuba, Clarence James. 1971. *A Road to Creativity: Arthur Morgan: Engineer, Educator, Administrator.* North Quincy, MA: Christopher Publishing House.

Linebaugh, Peter. 2008. *The Magna Carta Manifesto: Liberties and Commons for All.* Berkeley, CA: University of California Press.

Litfin, Karen T. 2014. *Ecovillages: Lessons for Sustainable Community.* Malden, MA: Polity Press.

Lockyer, Joshua. 2007. "Sustainability and Utopia: An Ethnography of Cultural Critique in Contemporary Intentional Communities." Ph.D. Dissertation. University of Georgia.

———. 2009. "From Developmental Communalism to Transformative Utopianism: An Imagined Conversation with Donald Pitzer." *Communal Societies* 29(1): 1–14.

————. 2017. "Community, Commons, and Degrowth at Dancing Rabbit Ecovillage." *Journal of Political Ecology* 24: 425–466.

Lockyer, Joshua and James R. Veteto. 2013. *Environmental Anthropology Engaging Ecotopia: Bioregionalism, Permaculture, and Ecovillages.* New York: Berghahn Books.

Marcus, George E. and Michael M.J. Fischer. 1986. *Anthropology as Cultural Critique: An Experimental Moment in the Human Sciences.* Chicago, IL: University of Chicago Press.

Metcalf, Bill. 2004. *The Findhorn Book of Community Living.* Scotland, UK: Findhorn Press.

Miller, Timothy. 1990. *American Communes, 1860-1960: A Bibliography.* New York: Garland Publications.

————. 1999. *The 60s Communes: Hippies and Beyond.* Syracuse, NY: Syracuse University Press.

————. 2010. "A Matter of Definition: Just What Is an Intentional Community?" *Communal Societies* 30(1): 1–15.

————. 2015. *The Encyclopedic Guide to American Intentional Communities.* Clinton, NY: Richard W. Couper Press.

————. 2019. *Communes in America, 1975-2000.* Syracuse, NY: Syracuse University Press.

Moody, Ruby and Louise Toness. 1950. "About Celo Community." *The Interpreter,* July 15, 1950.

Moore, Tom and Kim McKee. 2012. "Empowering Local Communities? An International Review of Community Land Trusts." *Housing Studies* 27(2): 280–290.

Morgan, Arthur E. 1937. Letter to Henry Regnery dated November 1, 1937. Yellow Springs, OH: Antiochiana Archives.

————. 1939. "The Celo Community Project." Unpublished document. Celo Community archives.

————. 1940. "Some Notes About the Plan for Celo." Unpublished document. Yellow Springs, OH: Antiochiana Archives.

————. 1942. *The Small Community: Foundation of Democratic Life.* Yellow Springs, OH: Community Service, Inc.

————. 1946. Letter to William Regnery. Unpublished document. Yellow Springs, OH: Antiochiana Archives.

————. 1955a. Letter to Wendell Thomas. Unpublished document. Yellow Springs, OH: Antiochiana Archives.

————. 1955b. "The Prospects for Communal Societies." *Community Service News* XIII(1): 24–32.

————. 1957a. *The Community of the Future and the Future of Community.* Yellow Springs, OH: Community Service, Inc.

————. 1957b. "Notes from Memory by Arthur E. Morgan and Griscom Morgan on the Beginnings of Celo Community in North Carolina." Unpublished document. Celo Community archives.

Morgan, Ernest. 1959. "1959 Yearbook of the Fellowship of Intentional Communities." Yellow Springs, Ohio: Fellowship of Intentional Communities.

Mulder, Kenneth, Robert Costanza, and Jon Erickson. 2006. "The Contribution of Built, Human, Social and Natural Capital to Quality of Life in Intentional and Unintentional Communities." *Ecological Economics* 59: 13–23.

Murdock, George Peter. 1949. *Social Structure.* New York: Macmillan Company.

Nabhan, Gary Paul. 1997. *Cultures of Habitat: On Nature, Culture, and Story.* Washington, DC: Counterpoint.

Naurekas, Jim. 1990. "Land Trusts Offer American Land Reform." In *Communities Directory,* Fellowship for Intentional Community (ed.), pp. 114–115. Rutledge, MO: Fellowship for Intentional Community.

Newfont, Kathryn. 2011. "Commons Environmentalism Mobilized: The Western North Carolina Alliance and the Cut the Clearcutting! Campaign." In *Mountains of Injustice: Social and Environmental Justice in Appalachia,* M. Morrone and G.L. Buckley (eds.), pp. 99–125. Athens, OH: Ohio University Press.

———. 2012. *Blue Ridge Commons: Environmental Activism and Forest History in Western North Carolina.* Athens, GA: The University of Georgia Press.

Nightingale, Andrea J. 2019. "Commoning for Inclusion? Political Communities, Commons, Exclusion, Property and Socio-natural Becomings." *International Journal of the Commons* 13(1): 16–35.

Northcott. Michael S. 2015. *Place, Ecology and the Sacred: The Moral Geography of Sustainable Communities.* London: Bloomsbury.

Ohle, Epenor. 1957. "Notes on the History of Celo Community." pp. 98. Unpublished document. Celo Community Archives.

Ostrom, Elinor. 1990. *Governing the Commons: The Evolution of Institutions for Collective Action.* Cambridge: Cambridge University Press.

———. 2007. "A Diagnostic Approach for Going Beyond Panaceas." *Proceedings of the National Academy of Sciences* 104(39): 15181–15187.

———. 2010. "Beyond Markets and States: Polycentric Governance of Complex Economic Systems." *The American Economic Review* 100(3): 641–672.

———. 2012. "The Future of the Commons: Beyond Market Failure and Government Regulation." In *The Future of the Commons,* E. Ostrom (ed.), pp. 68–83. London: The Institute of Economic Affairs.

Ostrom Elinor, Roy Gardner, and James Walker. 1994. *Rules, Games, and Common Pool Resources.* Ann Arbor, MI: University of Michigan Press.

Ostrom, Elinor, Thomas Dietz, Nives Dolsak, Paul C. Stern, Susan Stonich, and Elke U. Weber (eds.). 2002. *The Drama of the Commons.* Washington, DC: National Academy Press.

Ostrom Elinor and Vincent Ostrom. 2014. *Choice, Rules, and Collective Action.* Essex: ECPR Press.

Phillips, Jared M. 2019. *Hipbillies: Deep Revolution in the Arkansas Ozarks.* Fayetteville, AR: The University of Arkansas Press.

Pitzer, Donald E. 1989. "Developmental Communalism: An Alternative Approach to Communal Studies." In *Utopian Thought and Communal Experience,* D. Hardy and L. Davidson (eds.), pp. 68–76. Enfield, England: School of Geography and Planning, Middlesex Polytechnic.

————. (ed.) 1997a. *America's Communal Utopias.* Chapel Hill, NC: The University of North Carolina Press.

————. 1997b. "The New Moral World of Robert Owen and New Harmony." In *America's Communal Utopias,* D.E. Pitzer (ed.), pp. 88–134. Chapel Hill, NC: The University of North Carolina Press.

————. 1997c. "Introduction." In *America's Communal Utopias,* D.E. Pitzer (ed.), pp. 3–13. Chapel Hill, NC: The University of North Carolina Press.

————. 2008. "Response to Lockyer's 'From Developmental Communalism to Transformative Utopianism'." *Communal Societies* 29(1): 15–21.

————. 2013. "Developmental Communalism into the Twenty-First Century." In *The Communal Idea in the 21st Century,* E. Ben-Rafael, Y. Oved, and M. Tipel (eds.), pp. 33–52. Leiden: Brill.

Purcell, Aaron D. 1997. "The Engineering of Forever: Arthur E. Morgan, the Seneca Indians, and the Kinzua Dam." *New York History* LXXVIII(3): 309–336.

————. 2000. "Pursuing Peace: Arthur Morgan and Ohio's League to Enforce Peace, 1915-1920." *Ohio History* 109: 24–46.

————. 2001. "Plumb Lines, Politics, and Projections: The Florida Everglades and the Wright Report Controversy." *The Florida Historical Quarterly* 80(2): 161–197.

————. 2002. "Reclaiming Lost Ground: Arthur Morgan and the Miami Conservancy District Labor Camps." *The Historian* 64: 367–390.

————. 2003. "Collaboration and the Small Community: Arthur Morgan and the Mitraniketan Project in Kerala." *The Historian* 65(3): 643–664.

————. 2014. *Arthur Morgan: A Progressive Vision for American Reform.* Knoxville, TN: The University of Tennessee Press.

Questenberry, Dan. 1990. "Residential Land Trust Organizing: The School of Living; Community Service, Inc.; and the Land Trust Movement." In *Communities Directory,* Fellowship for Intentional Community (ed.), pp. 116–121. Rutledge, MO: Fellowship for Intentional Community.

Rubin, Zach, Don Willis, and Mayana Ludwig. 2019. "Measuring Success in Intentional Communities: A Critical Evaluation of Commitment and Longevity Theories." *Sociological Spectrum.* DOI: 10.1080/02732173.2019.1645063

Sale, Kirkpatrick. 2000. *Dwellers in the Land: The Bioreginal Vision.* Athens, GA: The University of Georgia Press.

Sanford, A. Whitney. 2017. *Living Sustainably: What Intentional Communities Can Teach Us about Democracy, Simplicity, and Nonviolence.* Lexington, KY: The University Press of Kentucky.

Sargent, Lyman Tower. 1994. "The Three Faces of Utopianism Revisited." *Utopian Studies* 5(1): 1–37.

————. 2006. "In Defense of Utopia." *Diogenes* 209: 11–17.

————. 2010. *Utopianism: A Very Short Introduction.* New York: Oxford University Press.

Sargisson, Lucy. 2007. "Strange Places: Estrangement, Utopianism, and Intentional Communities." *Utopian Studies* 18(3): 393–424.

————. 2012. "Second-Wave Cohousing: A Modern Utopia?" *Utopian Studies* 23(1): 28–56.

Sargisson, Lucy and Lyman Tower Sargent. 2004. *Living in Utopia: New Zealand's Intentional Communities.* Burlington, VT: Ashgate Publishing Company.

Schehr, Robert C. 1997. *Dynamic Utopia: Establishing Intentional Communities as a New Social Movement.* Westport, CT: Bergin & Garvey.

School of Integrated Living. 2020. "Mission." https://www.schoolofintegratedliving.org/about/mission/. Accessed on June 25, 2020.

Scott, James C. 1998. *Seeing Like a State: How Certain Schemes to Improve the Human Condition Have Failed.* New Haven, CT: Yale University Press.

———. 2006. "High Modernist Social Engineering: The Case of The Tennessee Valley Authority." In *Experiencing the State*, L.I. Rudolph and J.K. Jacobsen (eds.), pp. 3–52. New York: Oxford University Press.

———. 2009. *The Art of Not Being Governed: An Anarchist History of Upland Southeast Asia.* New Haven, CT: Yale University Press.

———. 2017. *Against the Grain: A Deep History of the Earliest States.* New Haven, CT: Yale University Press.

Sheeran, Michael J. 1983. *Beyond Majority Rule: Voteless Decisions in the Religious Society of Friends.* Philadelphia, PA: Philadelphia Yearly Meeting of the Religious Society of Friends.

Sherry, Jesse. 2014. "Community Supported Sustainability: How Ecovillages Model More Sustainable Community." Ph.D. Dissertation. Rutgers: The State University of New Jersey.

Silver, Timothy. 2003. *Mount Mitchell & the Black Mountains: An Environmental History of the Highest Peaks in Eastern America.* Chapel Hill, NC: The University of North Carolina Press.

Solnit, Rebecca. 2009. *A Paradise Built in Hell: The Extraordinary Communities that Arise in Disaster.* New York: Penguin Books.

Stoll, Steven. 2017. *Ramp Hollow: The Ordeal of Appalachia.* New York: Hill and Wang.

Stucki, Jubal and Artie Yeatman. 1990. "Community Land Trusts." In *Communities Directory*, Fellowship for Intentional Community (ed.), pp. 104–108. Rutledge, MO: Fellowship for Intentional Community.

Talbert, Roy 1987. *FDR's Utopian: Arthur Morgan of the TVA.* Jackson, MI: University Press of Mississippi.

Thomas, Wendell. 1955. Letter to Arthur E. Morgan. Unpublished document. Yellow Springs, OH: Antiochiana Archives.

Tummers, Lidewij and Sherilyn MacGregor. 2019. "Beyond Wishful Thinking: A FPE Perspective on Commoning, Care, and the Promise of Co-housing." *International Journal of the Commons* 13(1): 62–83.

Vaccaro, Ismael and Oriol Beltran. 2019. "What Do We Mean by 'the Commons?' An Examination of Conceptual Blurring Over Time." *Human Ecology* 47: 331–340.

Vogler, John. 2012. "Global Commons Revisited." *Global Policy* 3(1): 61–71.

Wagner, Jon. 1985. "Success in Intentional Communities: The Problem of Evaluation." *Communal Societies* 5: 89–100.

Wall, Derek. 2017. *Elinor Ostrom's Rules for Radicals: Cooperative Alternative Beyond Markets and States.* London: Pluto Press.

Weakley, Alan and Laura Mansberg. 1985. "Celo Community Natural Area." North Carolina Department of Natural Resources and Community Development, North Carolina Natural Heritage Program. Unpublished government document. Celo Community archives.

Zablocki, Benjamin. 1980. *Alienation and Charisma: A Study of Contemporary American Communes*. New York: The Free Press.

Index

About the Author

Joshua Lockyer, PhD, is an Associate Professor of Anthropology at Arkansas Tech University. He has been studying intentional communities for over twenty years and currently serves on the boards of directors for a number of relevant organizations including the Communal Studies Association and the Center for Communal Studies at the University of Southern Indiana. With James R. Veteto, he is coeditor of the volume *Environmental Anthropology Engaging Ecotopia: Bioregionalism, Permaculture, and Ecovillages.*